The
Economics
of
Slavery

The
Economics
of
Slavery

The *Economics* *of* *Slavery*

and Other Studies in Econometric History

Alfred H. Conrad & John R. Meyer

Routledge
Taylor & Francis Group

LONDON AND NEW YORK

First published 1964 by Transaction Publishers

Published 2017 by Routledge
2 Park Square, Milton Park, Abingdon, Oxon OX14 4RN
711 Third Avenue, New York, NY 10017, USA

Routledge is an imprint of the Taylor & Francis Group, an informa business

Library of Congress Catalog Number: 2006048042

Library of Congress Cataloging-in-Publication Data

Conrad, Alfred H.
  The economics of slavery : and other studies in econometric history /
    Alfred H. Conrad and John R. Meyer.
        p. cm.
  Originally published: Chicago : Aldine Pub. Co., 1964.
  Includes bibliographical references and index.
  ISBN 978-0-202-30934-7 (alk. paper)
    1. Industries—Great Britain. 2. Econometric—Case studies.
  I. Meyer, John Robert. II. Title.

HC53.C57   2007
338.0941—dc22   2006048042

ISBN 13: 978-0-202-30934-7 (pbk)

For

A. R. C.

and

L. S. M.

For

A.H.O.

and

M.S.M.

Preface

The historical essays in this volume, the first of which was drafted in the early 1950's, were consciously designed as experiments. We had been talking and arguing about evidence, explanation, and proof in history for several years, trying to find a link between the new techniques of econometric and numerical analysis that we were learning and the problems of explanation in the history we were reading. In the input-output study of British stagnation and in the slavery paper, we attempted to test econometrically two venerable historical theses. Then, after these first experiments, we tried, more diffidently, to set down our methodological position, in what is now the first chapter of this book.

In editing and adding to these essays in the past few months, we frequently asked ourselves whether our basic position had changed since their first appearance. We have reconsidered a few of the arguments and attempted to develop some others, but in general we are able to stand by our earlier conclusions. This stability is not due to an exaggerated attachment to that small virtue, consistency, nor is it the result of a lack of criticism. However, Chapter 2 expands upon and clarifies some of the points in the earlier methodological paper. Some of the computations in the input-output and slavery studies have been redone on newer, more efficient computing equipment. There are two additions in the income growth chapter that are intended to expand the original argument. The final postscript reconsiders a few of our earlier assertions, but does not, we believe, change any of our conclusions.

Two of these essays were originally published individually: "An Input-Output Approach . . . ," by John Meyer, and

"Income Growth and Structural Change," by Alfred Conrad. Chapter 2 was first drafted by Alfred Conrad and an early version was presented by him at the Colloquium of the Center for Cognitive Studies, Harvard University, in November 1962. The basic argument of the section "Public Policy and the Structure of Enterprise" in Chapter 4 is due to John Meyer. All the other chapters represent our joint effort. They come out of a long conversation and it would be difficult now for either of us to identify the specific authorship of different sections or successive drafts.

A number of our friends, who have in several cases been our colleagues and teachers, were generous and sometimes firm in offering criticism and advice, before and after the first publication of these papers. Henry Rosovsky and Barry Supple made a substantial contribution to the quality of this work by their perceptive reading and careful criticism over many years and several drafts. Many participants in the Economic History Seminar at Harvard University have helped at specific points, and in particular we must acknowledge the contributions of Paul David, Albert Fishlow and Stanley Lebergott. The methodological arguments were subjected to the usually genial but always astringent discussions of an informal seminar on the philosophy of history that met in Cambridge during 1957-59, when Pieter Geyl and Maurice Mandelbaum were visiting professors. We are presuming upon the continuing generosity of several others, who may recognize some beneficial results of their careful reading of earlier drafts.

Our greatest debt, which we hope will be evident and pleasing to him, is to Professor Alexander Gerschenkron. Four of the six chapters were first presented in the stimulating atmosphere of his graduate seminar. Many of the arguments were first advanced in his office. Most of the assertions that he branded as particularly vulnerable have since disappeared, or, hopefully, have been sufficiently strengthened to justify airing before a wider audience. An academic generation of Harvard-trained economists and historians will understand and in some specific places perhaps recognize our debt to him. We acknowledge with pleasure and gratitude his contribution to these essays as our teacher and critic.

The original version of Chapter 1 was presented at the annual meetings of the Economic History Association in September, 1957, and was published in the *Journal of Economic History* (December, 1957). Chapter 3 and Douglas Dowd's "Comment" were read at the National Bureau of Economic Research Conference on Income and Wealth at Williamstown, Massachusetts, in September, 1957, and were published in the *Journal of Political Economy* (April and October, 1958). John Moes' "Comment" and our reply were published in the same journal in April, 1960. Chapter 4 was published in its original version in *American Economic History* (edited by Seymour E. Harris; New York: McGraw-Hill, 1961). The first version of Chapter 5 was published in *Explorations in Entrepreneurial History* (Volume 8, Number 1). We are grateful to the several institutions and publishers for their kind permission to present the material again here. We are especially grateful to Professors Dowd and Moes for allowing us to include their comments and for the fruitful, continuing correspondence we have had with them on the economics of slavery.

Cambridge, Massachusetts

ALFRED H. CONRAD
JOHN R. MEYER

Contents

Contents

ONE

ONE

It is a truth perpetually, that accumulated facts lying in disorder begin to assume some order when an hypothesis is thrown among them. HERBERT SPENCER

If we were not ignorant there would be no probability, there could only be certainty. But our ignorance cannot be absolute, for then there would no longer be any probability at all.

HENRI POINCARÉ

1

Economic Theory,

Statistical Inference,

and Economic History

I

This chapter is an attempt to examine critically the function of theory in historical research and particularly in economic history. We shall take as our starting point the assertion that the historian is not interested simply in collecting facts or true statements about some segment of previous experience. He wants to find causes and to explain what happened. Our purpose here is to introduce some of the problems attached to the concepts of historical causality and explanation in a stochastic universe and to suggest how the analytic tools of scientific inference can be applied in economic historiography.

We wish to avoid *methodenstreit* and will therefore avoid arguments about precedence or relative importance. The literature is already overburdened with the logbooks of intellectual voyages inspired by the false charts of the history-theory dichotomy. We reject the possibility of such a dichotomy from the outset. Instead, we shall assert simply that economics as a science deals with historical processes and is dependent upon historical research. In any position other than the extreme of antiquarianism, therefore, the tools of economic analysis must have some function in the handling of the historical material that deals with economic processes. These tools—theory, statistical inference, and general laws of nature and causality—have seemed to many historians to be unnecessary or useless, even antithetical to a historical point of view. The elements of this negative argument will provide us with an outline from which to propose the affirmative position.

First, it is frequently argued that causal order cannot be defined among singular historical statements. This is the "randomness" approach, which faces, at the other extreme, the determinist position epitomized by Marx and Schumpeter. The second element is the assertion that historical hypotheses cannot be stated in probabilistic terms. The possibility and necessity of employing formal, that is, objective, probabilities is the central issue here. The third ground for the rejection of statistical inference for economic history is the proposition that the scarcity and quality of the data make quantification practically impossible. It is not our intention simply to argue these issues but also to examine some of the peculiar problems of scientific explanation in economic history.

II

Let us consider first what we do when we write "history" or the history of a period in a particular place. We are concerned not only with statements about the characteristics of the economy (and/or the state, the church, the family, etc.) at times t_1, t_2, t_3, . . . , but about relationships of a sequential type in which the variables have specific calendar-time subscripts. History or historiography, then, is the writing of a story. Just as we expect a story to have a beginning and an end, and that the beginning and the end should be connected, similarly we expect the sequence or ordering of the states in a history to have causal significance.

This concentration upon order and sequence—and ultimately upon causal ordering—is not intended simply as a contrast or alternative to the recording of facts about some block of experience. Histories are written about 1848 or the American Revolution or the cotton-slave culture of the antebellum South. The recording of detail about some single clearly bounded period is a valuable occupation. But it is also an endless occupation, since the historian is faced with infinitely many true statements about his period. The concentration upon causal ordering in the present argument is intended to illuminate the ways in which historians must choose among the true statements. Within a sequence or among the conjunctions of contemporaneous details, the historian must find those characteristics which are most fertile for explanation. When Ranke urged the description of things "as they actually happened" as a goal for historians, he could not have meant to exclude from the description how they got that way and what became of them. Recognizing this is sufficient justification for our emphasis upon causal ordering. In addition, it gives us a criterion for the choice among true statements: it is the "causal fertility" of the sequence or conjunction which should guide our search among historical data.[1]

There are, however, serious and quite special difficulties inherent in the attempt to explain singular historical events and to find causes among them. These difficulties have led one group of historians to draw sharp distinctions between historical and scientific explanation. In the extreme, a second important group of historians have been led to deny that the deliberate search for causes is meaningful in historical study. The first position may be represented by the following quotations from Popper and Rickert, respectively:[2]

Generalization belongs simply to a different line of interest, sharply to be distinguished from that interest in specific events and their causal explanation which is the business of history.

Historical laws are not just more or less difficult to find—the very concept of historical law carries an inner contradiction. Historical and nomothetic science are mutually exclusive.

The more extreme position is reflected in the following statements of Croce and Collingwood, respectively, both of which carry a strong Idealist bias:[3]

The fact historically thought has no cause and no end outside itself, but only in itself, coincident with its real qualities and with its qualitative reality.

For history, the object to be discovered is not the mere event, but the thought expressed in it. To discover that thought is already to understand it. After the historian has ascertained the facts, there is no further process of inquiring into their causes. When he knows what happened, he already knows why it happened. . . . The history of thought, and therefore all history, is the re-enactment of past thought in the historian's own mind.

The difficulty, perhaps the impossibility, of generalizing about historical events is usually attributed to the special characteristics of past events. This is a reference to their irretrievable pastness, that is, the experiential and unreproducible, as opposed to experimental, nature of historical knowledge. Another way of discussing this is to cite the uniqueness or particularity of historical events, the likelihood of falsifica-

tion in any attempt to reduce the infinite richness of detail
that defines each block of past experience. The renunciation
in history of causality in its usual scientific sense stems also
from the belief that human motives and individual judgments,
the proper subjects of historical research from the Idealist
point of view, are not amenable to quantification or scientific
generalization. In addition, some historians, such as Croce,
are overwhelmed by the putative necessity of infinite regress
in historical explanation, that is, by the view that the causes
of every historical event extend into the infinite past.

These assertions have been quoted heuristically, not in
any spirit of conflict. The problems of defining or assigning
causal relationship between singular statements have not been
solved finally in any branch of science; in history they appear
to be more difficult of solution than elsewhere. We shall proceed by defining causality and matching to the definition the
special characteristics of historical sequences.

A causal explanation is an answer to the question "Why?"
This seems a perfectly sensible, acceptable definition until
we consider the various ways in which "why?" questions are
answered. They can sometimes be answered—acceptably from
a pragmatic point of view—simply by asserting authority:
children and some adults use "why?" when they are really asking for confirmation. More often, however, only an answer
that contains "because" will be acceptable. But even this
requires stiffening if we are to base a strong definition of
causal explanation upon it. "Because" implies the conjunction
of properties or states, either in sequence or simultaneously,
and a generalization or assertion about the permanent connection between these properties. Causal explanation requires, in addition to the constant conjunction implied in
the answer "because," that the connection or the relationship should be asymmetrical, that is, the statement "A caused
B" should not be reversible. A causal explanation, then, involves (1) invariant relationship and (2) asymmetry. The

asymmetry, which may be but is not necessarily to be associated with sequence in time, is the part of the definition that gives us causal ordering.

Is there any inherent necessity implied when we add the asymmetry to the constant conjunction? If there is, we shall of course be in trouble with David Hume, who has taught us not to waste our time looking for the demons or forces which run between states. All that is required, however, is (1) that we be able to assign some probability to the assertion that a "first" set of conditions will be followed by a "second" and (2) that it can be demonstrated that the order cannot be reversed. The operational significance of this asymmetry —the ordering element—has been considered by Herbert Simon and Guy Orcutt in the context of econometric models. When we assign causal order, we are, in effect, identifying exogenous and endogenous variables. This means that any intervention—either altering the coefficients in the equations that describe the system or observing such alterations historically—can be specifically associated with subsequent changes in the values of some of the variables. "The causal ordering specifies which variables will be affected by intervention at a particular point (a particular complete subset) of the structure."[4] Simon offers a helpful example in the relationships among the amount of rainfall, the size of the wheat crop, and the price of wheat. Alteration in the amount of rainfall, by cloud-seeding perhaps, will probably affect the wheat crop and the price of wheat. The crop may be directly varied without subsequently influencing the weather, of course, but the price of wheat is likely to respond. An autonomous change in the price, however, obviously cannot influence the weather and can influence the wheat crop only if new variables and relationships are introduced into the system. The association of particular interventions with changes within the complete subsets defines the causal ordering among these relationships. Causal ordering is an operational concept and does not require the introduction of any unseen forces or inherent necessities.

Stochastic or random elements have been introduced twice in the preceding paragraph. First, estimating the probability of constant conjunction in a nonexperimental system requires that we state a hypothesis about the distribution of the random variables in the data. (It can be shown that distinctions between experimental and experiential systems on this score are erroneous and that experimental studies must also face this requirement.) Second, the operational significance of causal ordering in a nonexperimental context depends upon the provision, by history or nature, of sufficient variation among the conditional states so that the ordering can be identified. It is here that we are brought up sharply against the limitations imposed by the uniqueness and pastness of historical events. These limitations have appeared to most historians who have given much thought to their tools, not simply as a handicap but as characteristics that make history a discipline *sui generis,* beyond the help of the enumerative, experimental procedures of science.[5] Frequently historians react to these limitations by asserting that history is a "consumer of theories" but cannot pretend to generalize or even to test generalizations.[6] Even in this case, however, they are extremely chary of exercising their consumer sovereignty. Popper, for example, after implicitly limiting historical explanation to only "trivial universal laws," goes on to limit history further to those preconceived theories that determined which facts are deemed sufficiently interesting to be recorded.

Anyone who has attempted to explain what happened from historical evidence or to present in an orderly fashion a set of historical data is not likely ever again to underestimate the seriousness of the difficulties which history imposes upon the search for causes. But the step from this recognition to a denial that the rules (that is, the tools) of scientific explanation hold for historical explanation is a false and unnecessary step. First, the distinction between disciplines that consume theories and those that produce theories is misleading. The more sophisticated version—that there are pure generalizing sciences that *test* universal hypotheses, applied generalizing sciences that *predict* specific events, and history that tries to *explain* specific events—is a similarly empty distinction.[7] Explanation is prediction; an explanation links a subsequent event or prognosis to a set of initial conditions, using some statement of invariant relationship to make the link. And testing a universal hypothesis consists in using the least general, lowest-level hypothesis in a deductive system as a predictor, applying it to a particular empirical case. All three, then, have in common the application of hypothetico-deductive systems to empirical material; no scientist or economic historian can consume a theory without testing it. Second, repetition is not the distinction between the natural, that is, experiential (that is, historical) sciences, on the one hand, and the experimental sciences, on the other. Historical events, in their infinite complexity, cannot be reproduced. But experiments cannot be repeated with all the variables the same, either. As Harold Jeffreys points out, if repetition were the important element in testing scientific hypotheses, "astronomy would no longer be regarded as a science, since the planets have never even approximately repeated their positions since astronomy began."[8] Nor is the control of the experiment a distinction of principle. An experiment is a fact, a realized state. From a set of initial conditions, nature—which does not give second chances or alternative courses in a deterministic world—sets the course. It can make no fundamental difference in our reasoning processes whether the conditions have been set by an experimenter or by nature.

Finally, it is frequently asserted that, while historians may use theories or generalizations as searchlights or road maps, they cannot be submitted to precise tests to determine whether they are or are not applicable. The putative reasons for this have to do with "the difficulty of formulating the underlying assumptions with sufficient precision and at the same time in such a way that they are in agreement with all the relevant empirical material available."[9] In short, it is argued that historical events are unique and that the evidence, including the length of Cleopatra's nose and the presence of the Archduke at Sarajevo, cannot be reduced to fit the "underlying assumptions" of a generalization or universal hypothesis. In formal terms, this implies that, while historical explanation does presuppose regularity, it must be assumed that the random elements will dominate the causal system and that the random elements are differently distributed at every moment of historical time. The language in which this problem is generally discussed—the "infinite subject matter" of history, the imponderables, etc.—simply masks the fact that explicit assumptions about the random variables must be made in historical explanation as elsewhere.

The view that everything is unique, that there is no repetition or constancy in human behavior patterns, has had a pronounced influence upon the selection of material for studies in economic history. This is evidenced by the preoccupation with biographies, the preference for narrow case studies of unusually prosperous or influential persons and groups, and the concentration upon very limited periods in historical time. Modern examples of this tendency in economic history can be found in the studies conducted under the heading of entrepreneurial research. That the entrepreneurial approach, with its acknowledged debt to Schumpeter (one of the most positive builders of complete and pervasive models to have graced the economic profession), should have taken this direction is particularly intriguing. There is nothing inherently wrong with this kind of historiography; it is extremely useful if related to general historical patterns or theories of economic behavior. The difficulty is that these relationships, which are per se inimical to the professions of uniqueness, are specified in only a few of the better entrepreneurial studies.

It is not the fact that "in history anything can happen" that makes it so difficult for historians to generalize or, by extension, to test hypotheses. It is wordmongering to suggest that historians can interpret, assess, make judgments, but not conclude or test or generalize. When one says "in history anything can happen" and therefore that the student of history can attend only to the particular event which has indeed occurred, one means to say that there are too many random variables in the available generalization and that, since we do not know the distributions of these variables, we had better give up explanation and concentrate upon recording facts about specific events. But explanation in a historical system can be interpreted as the estimation of probabilities of transition from one state to a succeeding state, given the initial conditions and a causal law or generalization. In that interpretation the task of the economic historian is to search out the variations in the exogenous variables, that is, to add to the set of empirically realized independent conditions. Unfortunately, data are not found with neat labels—"condition" and "observation sentence" or "exogenous, endogenous, and random." The response to this fact has too often been to fall back upon uniqueness and to deny the possibility of establishing causal hypotheses. In the luxuriant diction of Croce: "The material of history is the singular in its singularity and contingency, that which is once and then is never again, the fleeting network of a human world which drifts like clouds before the wind and is often totally changed by unimportant events."[10] The resignation implied in this statement is, of course, neither universal nor necessary. Consider a stochastical causal system, containing two sets of variables which, if statistically identified, will be labeled "exogenous" and "endogenous" or perhaps "cause" and "effect," and a third set, the random variables. This third set provides us with the proper meaning of the uniqueness of historical events; within this set is included the "singularity and contingency" of history, chance, and the differential value of the individual. Historical, stochastical systems have been described as incomplete causal systems, implying that the distribution of the excluded variables must be made an arbitrary function of time.[11] Economic generalization from this approach depends upon the economic historian not for the accumulation of infinite detail about some period but for the conscious, deliberate identification of variables and the estimation of transition probabilities.

Does this view simply force the economic historian into the position of being a miner of cases and facts for the econometrician? Not at all. If his intention is indeed to know about and explain specific, historical events, then it is our contention that he must follow the rules of scientific explanation. To explain an event, one must be able to estimate a range of admissible possibilities, given a set of initial conditions and a causal or statistical law. The phrase "in history anything can happen" can hardly be a satisfactory estimation of the range of admissible developments for many economic historians. Like other economists and other scientists, it must be their aim to narrow the range of possibilities, to explain why the particular realized development did in fact occur. It is not necessary, however, to read this as an insistence upon strict determinism. There have been brilliantly ambitious attempts by economists to establish completely determined or total explanations of economic behavior. But these economists have been too often loath to admit the possibility of deviations or exceptions to their hypotheses; they have sought to encompass within one model all the necessary materials to explain in its entirety the social behavior under study. Outstanding examples of total hypotheses about economic behavior can be found, of course, in the work of Marx, Tawney, Schumpeter, and Selig Perlman, although in some cases more ambition was attributed to these writers by critics seeking appropriate straw men than by the originators themselves. The extreme of determinism may be found in the following statement of Engels: "In default of Napoleon, another would have filled his place, that is established by the fact that, whenever a man was necessary, he has always been found."[12] A particular cause is neither a wholly random event nor a sequence rigidly ordained through all time.

At the extreme of determinism, it might be thought that history, since it involves purposive behavior, that is, motivations and goals, can often be explained only teleologically. Most teleological explanations, however, as has been pointed out by Hempel and Oppenheim and by Braithwaite, can be reduced to causal explanations in which (1) intentions and (2) the belief, before the action, that a course of action will achieve the intended result provide sufficient antecedent conditions.[13] Where intention cannot be made evident (a more frequent and serious problem in the biological sciences), goal-directed activity, that is, teleological causal chains, can be demonstrated if, but only if, it can be shown that there are many alternative activities, clearly directed toward a single goal, operating under varying preconditions. In any event, teleological explanation, however attractive in suggesting that we "understand" historical behavior, has very little predictive power. It is difficult to imagine that many economic activities require to be explained in terms of inherent tendencies toward distant goals.

Narrowing the range of admissible possibilities may sound deceptively like what historians mean when they assert their interest in finding particular causes by gathering more and more data about specific events. But knowing more about an event increases our chance of explaining the event only if we can connect the information causally. And these connections depend upon our ability to subsume the data, the event, under appropriate causal regularities; that is, explanation depends upon the availability and proper use of theoretical generalizations. Furthermore, explaining a specific event means the fitting of some aspect of a specific time and place (in our case an economic aspect) into the narrowest possible causal sequence. Specific explanation cannot usefully mean that we should be able to predict from the set of initial conditions all the complex contemporary characteristics of the time slice. An economic historian interested in finding explanations for specific events has for his goal the ability, given a set of historical data, to predict the likelihood of the most explicit set of admissible outcomes.[14]

III

Argument over the nature of historical causality has had a peculiar impact on the statement of historical findings and the nature of historical investigations, as we have just seen. In essence, it has bred unnecessary extremes.

The continued existence of these extremes is curious because both are rejected today by modern philosophy and science. This rejection holds true regardless of whether the data are of historical or experimental origin.[15] The presently accepted scientific objective is to seek as complete explanations as possible but to deny total exactitude as, indeed, even being attainable. Total explanation remains a goal, sought for but never fully attained.

With this admission of human imperfections, the statement of a hypothesis becomes, to take an oversimplified example, in notational form as follows:

$$X = a + bY + e,$$

where the X and Y can be interpreted as observable variables, the a and b as behavior parameters, and the e as a random error term. The important conceptual change is contained, of course, in the addition of the final or e term. In the jargon of modern statistics, it changes the statement of a functional relationship from that of an "exact" hypothesis to a "stochastic" hypothesis. The existence of errors represented by the e term is commonly attributed to the influence of omitted variables or errors of observation in the X variable, although this distinction is sometimes difficult to make in practice and is perhaps even philosophically indefensible as well. Thus the e term represents in historical hypotheses the impact of those influences that have a sporadic, unsystematic influence on the dependent or X variable; e can also represent the errors due to human frailties of observation or, in experimental situations, the influence of certain variables that have a slight influence on X but are not under experimental control. Much of modern statistics is concerned with identifying and deducing the consequences of different behavior patterns on the part of error terms. However, the almost universal behavioral assumption, and certainly the most important from the standpoint of the present discussion, is that e is randomly or unsystematically distributed. To attain this objective, one must have a model that includes all the systematic influences as explanatory variables, that is, as Y terms. Indeed, the existence of an error term that has systematic or nonrandom behavior indicates that a model is incomplete, that it has an insufficient number of independent or Y-type variables.

The importance of this seemingly slight modification in the formulation of empirical hypotheses is tremendous. It means essentially that one can encompass deterministic or systematic factors and unique or unsystematic factors within a single and also consistent model; both influences have a role in the stochastic formulation of hypotheses and both help explain behavior.

The systematic factors explain the central tendencies of behavior, that is, the

$$X' \equiv a + bY \equiv X\text{-}e$$

"part" of the above function. The term "central tendency" is applied to the systematic components because these influences are construed as explaining some sort of mean, average, or median of behavior.

The remainder, or nonsystematic component of behavior represented by the error term, has been in essence the preoccupation of the noncausal school. An emphasis upon the random, exceptional, or deviant experience perhaps makes sense in the study of social, military, and political history because in these fields the play of individual factors and strong personalities is likely to be more pronounced and important. However, even there a tendency toward analyzing specific unique instances has been grossly overdone. Whatever the merits of the causal approach may be in these other historical studies, it is absolutely certain that the exceptional, unique, or nonsystematic experience is not what the economist is seeking in historical data. As a social scientist with a strong orientation toward public policy problems, the economist seeks to establish theories with at least some generality and timelessness. He is interested therefore in the systematic, repetitive aspects of economic behavior. Consequently, the economic historian should not be surprised if the economist shows little interest in the social competence and family relationships of some nineteenth-century merchants—*unless it is previously or concomitantly established* that social competence and family relationships help to explain the successes or failures of individuals in general. The economic historian, in sum, should seek the limited generalization that is the objective of all science; only if that course is adopted can economic history expect to influence the development of economics.

IV

Undoubtedly the most frequently cited objection to the employment of more formal quantitative techniques in historical studies is that the intrinsic nature of historical data and hypotheses absolutely prevents such quantification. This objection has been made in two basic forms: (1) there are simply not enough data of a quantitative nature to permit the formal testing of quantifiable hypotheses; and (2) even if these data were available, historical hypotheses are very often of a qualitative or subjective nature and are therefore untestable by quantitative methods and data.

The existence or nonexistence of historical data in a quantitative form is, of course, a question essentially of fact, the negative attitude being that such data do not in fact exist. Since those who make these statements are usually reputable historians, familiar with the sources of their particular period or periods of study, it is rather difficult not to give their statements credence. However, there are some fairly obvious reasons why one might contest the accuracy of their historical finding in regard to data. In the first place, the training of historians does not tend to orient investigators toward the discovery of quantitative records; for example, the economic historian who has received his basic training in history (often from a social, political, or military historian) tends to adopt the historian's preoccupation with diaries, letters, and contemporary journal articles as source documents. By contrast, quantitative records are likely to be found in different places; in the records of government offices, business firms, savings institutions, insurance societies, agricultural societies, etc. The interpretation of such documents will often require, moreover, certain technical skills that the ordinary historian does not possess. For example, nineteenth-century accounting documents often require the skills of a reasonably well-trained accountant, preferably one who is well versed in the history and development of accounting techniques.

In support of the contention that the lack of quantitative data may be as much a function of the historical viewpoint as of actual circumstances there is also mounting evidence that quantitative historical data are available. The work of Hoffman, Hansen, Cole, Evans, Beveridge, Gerschenkron, Kuznets, and many others provides fine earlier examples of such availability.[16] In short, the scarcity of quantitative historical data may be more imagined than real and rather readily remedied by a slight redirection of historical training and outlook.

The contention that the qualitative or subjective nature of historical hypotheses rules out testing by quantitative data poses substantially more subtle problems that are also somewhat more difficult to answer. Unfortunately, the subject has been badly obscured by a number of misconceptions. Thus the most rewarding approach to answering this assertion would appear to be essentially negative, stating what quantification does not mean or require and only implicitly what it does mean.

To begin, quantification does not require, as is often thought, a continuous scale of measurement for all the variables involved. It is only necessary that there be classes, that is, that certain of the observations are differentiable from the others. There need be, moreover, no more than two classes; thus an investigator might need to know only whether the answer is yes or no, or the color is black or white, etc. A large number of historical hypotheses involve only such elementary classification schemes. A common difficulty has been that one man may concentrate on counting the items in one box and another man will count only the items in the other box. As in the story of the blind men and the elephant, the result is, not surprisingly, very different interpretations. Two good examples of this difficulty can be cited. First, the difference of opinion between Selig Perlman and Sumner Slichter about the bases of union organization might be explained by the fact that, whereas Perlman's investigations usually concentrated on declining industries, Slichter focused his attention upon expanding sectors of the economy. The conflict of interpretation between the Hammonds and Ashton is similarly reducible to their concentration upon different boxes of evidence on the English industrial revolution. Clearly, a good investigator should count all classes— and introduction of this simple principle into historical studies would be a significant methodological advance in and of itself.

Quantification also does not require observation of every state of mind, every motive involved in the particular aspect of human behavior under study. Such insistence on direct data about qualitative or subjective mental states is akin to what has been appropriately called "questionnaire myopia," which leads those so afflicted to insist that the only way to find out what people are thinking is to ask them. For example, the reliance upon diary and personal letter sources that characterizes a good deal of historical writing is basically equivalent to a questionnaire approach. As social psychologists have pointed out many times and as modern poll-takers have discovered on several occasions, the questionnaire procedure may be one of the worst ways of finding out people's real motivations.

Because of the difficulties involved in directly measuring subjective mental states or attitudes, a major preoccupation of modern psychology has been to infer or measure mental states indirectly. Factor and principal component analysis, scaling techniques, and much of modern learning theory are aimed at achieving this objective. With these techniques an attempt is usually made to infer backward from certain objective or observable measures. such as test scores. The historian cannot, of course, set up such tests to measure the attitudes of the deceased individuals with whom he is dealing. This deficiency does not, however, constitute any final or absolute deterrent because objective evidence of mental attitudes is often available in forms other than test scores. Such evidence is commonly generated, for example, in the normal course of daily business events. Thus the behavior of certain accounting values, such as the level of liquid assets, the rate of investment, and the utilization of different financial sources, may yield excellent objective evidence on the mental preoccupations and attitudes of businessmen. In fact, the way in which businessmen respond to these values is as likely to be indicative of their attitude toward liquidity preference and sales expectations, etc., as what they enter in their diaries.

All these techniques are equivalent, of course, to nothing more or less than the utilization of indirect evidence to verify a hypothesis that cannot be directly verified. Thus in a large number of cases a historical investigator can deduce the quantitative consequences of behavioral hypotheses even if the hypotheses themselves are qualitative; or, in the same vein, he can very often deduce certain indirect quantitative consequences of behavioral hypotheses that may be quantitative in character but lack direct quantitative evidence. The first case, the use of quantitative evidence to verify a qualitative hypothesis, is perhaps the most important to the economic historian. Let us illustrate the technique by citing specific examples.

EXAMPLE 1. In a paper on Negro slavery in the antebellum South presented before the National Bureau of Economic Research Conference on Research in Income and Wealth, the present authors were faced with the problem of quantitatively testing the old historical question about whether the typical southern gentleman planter could bring himself to indulge in the slave trade. Diaries have been searched many times with different searchers arriving at very different results. In essence, these differences developed from the fact that it was considered something less than genteel and refined for a southern gentleman to engage in slave breeding and trading. Consequently, slave transactions in diary entries were often euphemistically described as operations to get rid of some troublemakers or young laggards. Those who like to retain notions about the superior refinement and gentility of the southern plantation culture usually chose to interpret these diary entries at face value; those who denied any such qualities in the antebellum South chose, of course, to look upon these diary entries as mere euphemisms. Within the context of the diary data there was obviously no way of resolving these differences. One could, however, deduce the type of age and sex distribution of the Negro population that would be likely if slave breeding and trading was widely indulged and what pattern would be likely if it was not indulged. Data on such population distributions are available in early American censuses and when obtained were found to verify the skeptics, hence justifying the use of the word "euphemism" as descriptive of the diary entries.

EXAMPLE 2. Michael Lovell, in an article on the Bank of England in *Explorations in Entrepreneurial History*,[17] reconsidered the often debated question of whether the Bank of England was engaging in central banking practices in the early eighteenth century; here the diary entries, in this case the deliberately edited record of bank board meetings, are confusing and inconclusive. However, there are available time series on eighteenth-century bankruptcies, bank reserve ratios, and discount rates. Lovell has inferred the results that might be expected in the behavior of these series if a central banking policy had been followed and tested his deductions against the actual data. He found, contrary to others, that central banking apparently emerged at a very early date in eighteenth-century England.

The agreement of certain actual conditions with deduced conditions does not imply, of course, that the original hypothesis is necessarily correct. This is so because there may be other initial hypotheses from which the same observed conditions can be deduced. We are able, in short, to reject a hypothesis but not to accept one hypothesis over all others. In agreement with the principle enunciated in the last section, it is highly probable that a particular hypothesis was formulated and tested in the first place because it was suggested by other established information about the subject. The empirical test in that case serves essentially to strengthen at a minimum our subjective beliefs in the truth of the hypothesis. And that is no little or mean advance.

It is also worth noting that once the consequences of a hypothesis have been thoroughly recognized, data problems are likely to prove less severe than first believed. Thus working out the consequences of a hypothesis often reveals that the behavior of a larger number of available quantitative series is relevant to testing a hypothesis than was initially believed to be the case when the hypothesis was considered in its simple undigested state.

The inverse of this problem of the indirect deduction of consequences is the logical issue of the counterfactual conditional. It has been recently argued by some historians and philosophers of history that the inability to reduce all lawlike conditional statements in history to verifiable propositions makes causal explanation and generalization impossible in history.[18] For example, to assert that "If the Civil War had not occurred, the South would have abolished Negro slavery in an orderly fashion within one generation" is to propose a counterfactual or subjunctive conditional for which no procedure of verification or falsification is possible. However, granted that counterfactuals cannot be directly tested, it is possible to consider the statement within a valid deductive system, independently of the acknowledged falsity of the conditional clause. Then, without being able to demonstrate any given instance of the counterfactual, it may be possible to verify or falsify some other proposition higher up in the deductive chain. The question of whether the negative of the (falsified) higher level conditional is cotenable with the subjunctive prediction can then be asked. In the slavery example we examined the higher level hypothesis that slavery was not profitable in the antebellum South, from which the conditional sentence above is derived. The falsification of the higher-level hypothesis, while it may not provide final proof, will support something stronger than an indefinite interpretation. It is not our intention to try to argue away the logical problem of the counterfactual conditional for historical causality, but simply to assert that it is not in principle necessary to treat historical counterfactuals as always irreplaceable. If we recognize the position of a subjunctive conditional in its hypothetico-deductive system, we can frequently devise at least a test of cotenability.[19]

V

A more scientific approach to the study of economic history has been advocated in the preceding discussion. This raises the inevitable question of whether such advocacy extends to the introduction of the very formal and complex techniques of modern probability statistics into historical studies. Answering that question in a simple categorical fashion is difficult, since there are at issue such complex problems as the central disagreements separating the so-called subjective and objective probability schools.

The objections to using formal probability tests may be broadly classified into two major categories. First, there is a serious question about the appropriateness of using probability models with historical data. Although all the randomness, normality, and other assumptions which commonly underlie probability models might be met in the scientific laboratory or in a well-designed sample or questionnaire study, there is little doubt but that the assumptions are not met by most historically generated economic data.

Even with the many recent advances in the development of analytical tools for use with economic time series, the application of formal econometric or statistical techniques to the analysis of such data remains fraught with hazard. For example, the economic statistician must usually behave, for want of better knowledge, as if his total degrees of freedom equal the total number of available observations; because of the lack of randomness in the generation of his data, this assumption is rarely met. Similarly, most probability tests are based upon the assumption that sampling is from a large universe and involves techniques for inferring the properties of the universe from a small sample. But the economic statistician-*cum*-historian usually cannot be selective; he has in fact so few observations that he must employ all that are available. Nor is this problem solved either by the mere passing of time and the accumulation of additional data on new years or by the extension of research into the past and the accumulation of new data on old years. Such extensions can make an empirical study apply to a far wider range of economic structure than can usually be encompassed within a tractable statistical hypothesis or model. That is, the greater the number of years covered by the empirical study, the fewer institutional or structural conditions that can be considered fixed, and consequently the greater the need for expanding the number of specific explanatory variables included in the model. This is essentially the difficult problem of "structural change" that makes the economic theorist's box of *ceteris paribus* conditions something else than fixed. This problem has plagued many modern econometric applications, even though these studies have usually been confined to limited time spans of between twenty and thirty years.

The limitation on the years included in these studies has not, of course, been due either to mere capriciousness or to the admitted limitations on available data. Even when longer time series are available, it is not uncommon to find the investigator limiting his attention to a few specific years; war years, drought years, severe depression years, or years of similar catastrophic occurrences are commonly eliminated. This selection of data is obviously dictated by the fundamental scientific precept of trying to control as many influences extraneous to a hypothesis under test as possible. As was pointed

out in Section III, the modern scientist seeks the most simple
explanatory hypothesis obtainable that is consistent with his
objective of including all systematic influences in his model.

By contrast, it has been frequently asserted by historians
and others that the necessity to explain not only *how* the individual or group behaved but *why* involves a long chain of
causes infinitely far back into the past.[20] This harping on an
infinite regress of explanation back to some first cause is really
a confusion between the necessity of a complete explanation,
a total cause, as opposed to the specification of the sufficient
antecedent conditions and appropriate general laws and, possibly, a necessary condition. The criterion for suppressing
"causal ancestors" (and causal laws) should be, in keeping
with general scientific objectives, the effect upon the predictive power of the explanation. This is what Popper referred
to when he spoke of the fact that we "tacitly assume a host
of rather trivial universal laws" and concentrate upon a
sufficient condition, assuming "certain initial conditions hy-
pothetically."[21] Most journalistic causal explanations, cling-
ing to the canon that there is nothing so dead as yester-
day's news, have little predictive power; at the other extreme,
it is not necessary to demonstrate the sequence between the
rise of Protestantism and the development of capitalism in
order to explain the Great Depression of the last quarter of
the nineteenth century. There is obviously no single rule to
be offered; also obviously, a condition that cannot reasonably
be assumed should not be omitted from mention. First causes
aside, insufficiency in explanation is more likely to occur where
conditions are catalogued in detail and the necessary empirical
regularities are not made explicit. But all this is small com-
fort to the empirical investigator attempting to give his hypotheses tests of more formal content. He is obviously caught
in a dilemma wherein his efforts to obtain more quantitatively
reliable tests will often involve him in unwanted, intractable
complexity.

However, even if this dilemma and the related difficulties

created by the "unrealistic" assumptions of objective probability models could be handled, and there are many ingenious devices available today to make handling them more nearly attainable, most of the formal statistical probability tests for hypotheses are overly stringent. Above all, they assume no prior knowledge about the probable accuracy of a hypothesis under test. This is obviously a rather dubious assumption, since an investigator would rarely test a particular model if he did not attach an a priori probability greater than zero to its chances of being correct. A strict mechanical application of probability tests therefore raises the serious possibility of rejecting hypotheses when they should not be rejected (although it should be recognized that this tendency toward too easy rejection may be partially or more than offset by counterbalancing influences, such as overestimation of the degrees of freedom contained in historical time series).

Despite these many drawbacks to formal tests, there are substantial and, in our view, almost compelling advantages to using objective probability tests wherever there is at least reasonable approximation between the assumptions of the probability models and the actual circumstances that generated the data. Unquestionably the greatest of these advantages is that the tests are widely known and well understood. This greatly simplifies the communication of scientific findings, since the very formality or rigidity of the tests minimizes the role of personal predilections or a priori attitudes in assessing the empirical results. Phrases such as "a significant difference," "a significant finding," "a reliable predictor," and many others that regularly occur in empirical studies, whether or not they are formal in character, have a definite meaning when interpreted in terms of objective probability tests. (Though such phrases are freely used in the absence of formal techniques, their meaning in such applications is frequently less than universally understood.) In addition, there is at least a heuristic gain arising from the fact that the formal tests are quantitative. Explicitly, the formal tests

attach an actual numerical probability to the correctness of
the hypothesis in the light of the observed results. This introduces the question of relative plausibility into the empirical
procedure and consequently helps the investigator to scale
the degree of belief, an intrinsically ordinal concept at the
very least, that should be placed in the hypothesis.

There are, in sum, substantial advantages as well as dis-
advantages to the introduction of more formal procedures in
the evaluation of historical hypotheses. The question therefore arises: Is there a satisfactory compromise that embodies
maximum advantage with minimum disadvantage? Ideally,
the best procedure would appear to be one in which the formal
tests were adapted or altered to take account of a maximum
of a priori information. This leads, admittedly, to an essentially Bayesian approach to statistical inference. The difficulty
of the Bayesian approach is, of course, that it bogs down in
a morass of subjectivism unless the prior notions and probabilities are fully stated. These are difficult matters to com-
municate effectively and completely. As such, one may won-
der whether the ideal can ever be achieved.

Short of the ideal, the formal tests do constitute at least
some guide, furthermore a well-understood and objective
guide, to determining the kind of confidence that should be
placed in a given hypothesis. If the overly stringent nature
of most of the tests is remembered, and if proper allowance
is made for the discrepancies between the underlying probability assumptions and the conditions existing in the actual
world of historical data, hypotheses that pass the formal test
should gain, at a minimum, substantial intuitive attraction.

> If we take from history the discussion of why, how
> and wherefore each thing was done and whether the
> result was what we should reasonably have expected,
> what is left is a clever essay but not a lesson, and while
> pleasing for the moment of no possible benefit for the
> future.[22]   POLYBIUS

NOTES TO CHAPTER 1

1. See Morton G. White, "Toward an Analytical Interpretation of History," in Marvin Farber (ed.), *Philosophic Thought in France and the United States* (Buffalo, N. Y., 1950), pp. 705–26.

2. Karl Popper, *The Open Society and Its Enemies* (Princeton, 1950), II, 251, and Heinrich Rickert, *Die Grenzen der naturwissenschaftlichen Begriffsbildung*, quoted in F. C. Lane and J. C. Riemersma, *Enterprise and Secular Change* (Homewood, Illinois, 1953), p. 432.

3. Benedetto Croce, *The Theory and History of Historiography* (London: George G. Harrap, 1921), p. 76, and R. G. Collingwood, *The Idea of History* (Oxford: Clarendon Press, 1946), pp. 214–15.

4. Herbert A. Simon, *Models of Man* (New York, 1957), chap. i, "Casual Ordering and Identifiability," p. 26, see also chap. iii, "On the Definition of the Casual Relation," and Guy H. Orcutt, "Toward Partial Redirection of Econometrics," *Review of Economics and Statistics*, XXXIV (August, 1952), 195–200.

5. See, e.g., the arguments discussed in Patrick Gardiner, *The Nature of Historical Explanation* (Oxford, 1952), pp. 28–64.

6. See, e.g., Popper, *op. cit.*, pp. 246–56, and Lane and Riemersma, *op. cit.*, pp. 522–34.

7. See Popper, *ibid.*

8. Harold Jeffreys, *Scientific Inference* (2d ed.: Cambridge, 1957), p. 191. Much of the argument of this section is derived from the analysis of probability and statistical methods in scientific explanation by Jeffreys, *op. cit.*, and R. B. Braithwaite, *Scientific Explanation* (Cambridge, 1955), esp. chaps. vi, viii, ix.

9. Quoted in Gardiner, *op. cit.*, p. 91, from Carl Hempel, "The Function of General Laws in History," *Journal of Philosophy*, XXXIX (January, 1942), 35–48. The quotation is cited because Gardiner, having almost answered the argument by anticipation when he considered the proposition that history is *sui generis*, in a later chapter swallows it whole, "sufficient precision" and "relevant empirical evidence" included.

10. Quoted in G. Salvemini, *Historian and Scientist* (Cambridge: Harvard University Press, 1939), p. 88.

11. This approach is developed in greater detail starting in Sec. III below. See Paul A. Samuelson, *The Foundations of Economic Analysis* (Cambridge, 1947), pp. 311–20, for an interesting attempt to define causal, historical, and stochastical systems.

12. F. Engels to H. Starkenburg, January 25, 1894, quoted in Gardiner, *op. cit.*, p. 100.

13. C. G. Hempel and P. Oppenheim, "Studies in the Logic of Exploration," *Philosophy of Science* (April, 1948), 135–75, esp. p. 145; Braithwaite, *op. cit.*, esp. pp. 322–25.

14. See C. G. Hempel and P. Oppenheim, *op. cit.*, and W. W. Leon-

tief, "Note on the Pluralistic Interpretation of History and the Problem of Inter-disciplinary Cooperation," *Journal of Philosophy*, XLV (November, 1948), 617–24.

15. Even in the experimental sciences there is always some chance or probability that a new experiment will disprove a hypothesis that has previously stood up to all experimental tests. The fate of Newton's law is an obvious example in this regard.

16. It is interesting to note that when one lists the good quantitative work done in the field of economic history, it has more often than not been done by someone originally trained in economics.

17. "The Role of the Bank of England as Lender of Last Resort in the Crises of the Eighteenth Century," *Explorations in Entrepreneurial History*, October, 1957, pp. 8–21.

18. See, e.g., Stuart Hampshire, "Subjunctive Conditionals," *Analysis*, IX (October, 1948), 9–14.

19. Excellent treatments of the counterfactual conditional may be found in Nelson Goodman, "The Problem of Counterfactual Conditionals," *Journal of Philosophy*, XLIV (February, 1947), 113–28, and in Braithwaite, *op. cit.*, pp. 295-317. The slavery examples are from Alfred H. Conrad and John R. Meyer, "The Economics of Slavery in the Antebellum South," presented at the Conference on Research in Income and Wealth, National Bureau of Economic Research, at Williamstown, Mass., September, 1957, and printed as Chapter 3, below.

20. See, e.g., Frank H. Knight, "The Limitations of Scientific Method in Economics," in Rexford G. Tugwell (ed.), *The Trend of Economics* (New York, 1924), esp. pp. 251–52; see also Croce, *op. cit.*, p. 65.

21. Popper, *op. cit.*, p. 250.

22. Quoted on p. 440 of the *Times Literary Supplement* (London), July 19, 1957.

2

Statistical Inference

and Historical Explanation

I. What Do We Know Historically?

In the first chapter, we discussed the role of theory in historical reasoning and considered some of the problems of quantifying and testing historical hypotheses. In this brief and somewhat speculative chapter, we will pick up the reference to "the Bayesian approach" and examine more closely some of the technical aspects of statistical explanation in history.

Faced by the *bête noire* of the social sciences—insufficient evidence—historians have frequently reacted by defining historical knowledge as something larger, more splendid, than the scientific conception of knowledge. The grand, overarching, full determined schema of Marx, Spengler, or Toynbee are at the "historicist" end of the spectrum of response to the problems of explaining history. At the other end, opposed to determinism in particular and scientism or materialism in general, stand Dilthey, Rickert, and, more recently, Collingwood and Berlin. They have argued that history, being non-repetitive, cannot be read statistically: historical thinking should be a kind of redoing. The historian must recreate the past experience, even to the point of re-experiencing somebody else's thought. Dilthey and the late-nineteenth-century Romantics called this approach *Verstehen*—understanding, the intuitive involvement of the historian in the situation. The past situation, they argued, cannot really be analyzed but must be experienced in its "wholeness."

We are attempting something different. Starting from the assertion that the historian is concerned ultimately to explain what happened, we argue that he should use his evidence purposefully toward that end. But the historian is faced with the difficult problem of insufficient evidence. (The "special" nature of historical evidence was examined and disputed in the previous chapter.) Having so little data, he could not possibly amass a statistically valid weight of evidence. He has too small a sample. But then the historian ought not to engage in crude and implicit statistical inference. He cannot proceed as if three letters arguing that slavery was inefficient in Virginia and two letters arguing that it was efficient simply sum to one vote, net, for the inefficiency position. That is neither *Verstehen* nor good statistical inference.

The point of view of this chapter, like that of the previous one, looks upon the world as a stochastic universe. "Stochastic" means probabilistic; it means that the historical process is not determined exactly. There are accidents and errors, and *some* of the accident, at least, is fundamentally random. In the physical sense, "stochastic" means that there is a certain amount of irreducible "noise" in the universe; in the statistical sense, it suggests that the error term in a regression equation is not simply an admission of ignorance, but that it represents, at least in part, a random disturbance.[1] The kind of causal explanation that fits this view of the universe suggests a third way of dealing with evidence in history.

But first, what is the evidence? What do we know historically? We may have some facts—or artifacts—in the records and documents of written history. These are the durable goods of historiography. Ranke is the philosopher of facts in this sense, and Namier is the virtuoso. The material ranges from censuses and laundry lists to recorded testimony; it may be contemporary or historiographic. It may include the outlined streets and bathing tanks of unearthed ancient cities.

Second, we may know in the *verstehen* sense, at various levels: at the journalistic or cinematographic level, as in books that "re-create" a day or an event, like Wall Street's Black Thursday or the sinking of the Titanic; at the Williamsburg Reconstruction level, where a compressed or foreshortened physical environment is put together, with a nice degree of selection that includes the miscreant in the stocks but not the smells or the slums. More seriously, we may *understand* in Collingwood's sense of re-enacting the past thought by putting to the facts only the contemporary *why?* (cf. chapter 1, part II).

Finally, we can know something about an event in the sense that we might be prepared to predict, perhaps even to place a bet upon, its occurrence. It is also possible to predict backward, as the argument of the first chapter suggests.[2] We might be willing to place bets that something did or did not happen, that a condition did or did not prevail. Seen from this point of view, new evidence generally involves us in changing the odds, or perhaps changing the degree of confidence with which we describe (or explain) a passage in history.

For instance, consider a historian about to open a tax roll or a packet of letters—a moment comparable to the beginning of an experiment. He will draw conclusions about the social structure or some diplomatic maneuver, perhaps, on the basis of the evidence he finds. He may change the odds in the hypothetical bet of the last paragraph. The new odds, however, depend upon the old odds, upon the initial probabilities he assigned to some reconstruction of the past event, upon the likelihood that if the hypothesis were true he could have expected to find what he did in fact find. But in what sense can the historian *know* these earlier, or older, probabilities? Are they based entirely on the earlier scraps of evidence he has observed? And could he have assigned probabilities before he had any observational evidence of the event? These are questions that will disturb the historian who, if he has got past the vocabulary of the gaming table, yet wishes to avoid the apparent definiteness of thinking in terms of precise, numerical probabilities. However, we can start by thinking of probabilities simply as "degrees of reasonable belief" and go on now to consider where they come from and how we might use them in reading history.[3]

II. BAYESIAN STATISTICS

The basic theorem in the inductive system that we are discussing is the progeny of an eighteenth-century dissenting minister, Thomas Bayes, of Tunbridge Wells. Bayes's fundamental theorem, which is sometimes referred to as the "Principle of Inverse Probability," tells us that the probability to be assigned to an unknown or hypothesized event, *after* some evidence has been observed, is proportional to the initial probability we attached to the event, multiplied by the likelihood (or the conditional probability) that we should assign to the occurrence of the new datum if we knew that the hypothesized event had in fact occurred. (The factor of proportionality is the probability of observing the datum at all, i.e., its unconditional or marginal probability.)

In mathematical symbols, we may write the theorem in the following form:

$$Pr(y|x) = \frac{Pr(y)Pr(x|y)}{Pr(x)}$$

On the left hand side, we have the probability that y is true, given the observed datum x. In other words, this term represents the betting odds or the degree of belief with which we hold a hypothesis, y, if we are in possession of some evidence, x. We may, for example, be trying to decide whether the Nazis did engineer the Reichstag fire, given some new piece of circumstantial evidence. What are the consequences of the new datum? How do we reach a new, tentative conclusion about that crucial event from the piece of evidence we are considering?

The right-hand side of the equation defines the relationship between the datum and the conclusion that the historian may draw from it. The first term in the numerator, $Pr(y)$, is the initial probability he assigned to y being true, *prior* to finding the evidence. He might have had a completely open mind with regard to the conflagration, as he often claimed, even though the Nazi leadership made such effective use of it. Or he may have suspected, on the basis of other evidence, that the Communists had indeed foolishly worked to the Nazis' advantage by committing a provocative action. Judgments or estimates or simply hunches of this kind about isolated events are sufficient to assign broad ranges of probability. In other cases, we may be able to draw the probabilities on the basis of rough statistical evidence; for example, in most of the cases in which these conditions were present, civil disorder aimed at a minority broke out, whether there was any provocative occurrence or not. And finally, as we shall see in the next example, theories or deductive relationships may enable us to define the probabilities, just as they often give us valuable leads in searching for evidence.

The second term on the right, $Pr(x|y)$, is called the "likelihood." It is a somewhat weaker measure of credibility in that it depends upon the hypothesis. It is the conditional probability of finding the datum, given the hypothesis y. That is, should we have expected to find that Karl Ernst and his party of Storm Troopers were engaged, as they evidently were, in the tunnel between Goering's house and the Reichstag, if we were convinced (up to a high degree of probability) that the Communists had started the conflagration?[4]

However ill defined and subjective these two estimates— the prior probability and the likelihood—may be, it will become evident in the next example that their product yields a more widely acceptable, precise measure of credibility than the initial personal probability. The denominator in the Bayesian equation, $Pr(x)$, is the unconditional probability of observing the piece of evidence. It makes the final estimate, $Pr(y|x)$, stronger or weaker as the chance of observing x, under *any* circumstances, is slight or great.

Now suppose that from our reading about slave institutions in general and the auction blocks in particular we find it extremely difficult to say whether the market for slaves was efficient in the antebellum United States, in the sense that it enabled Southern planters to move slaves from regions where they were not needed to those where there was a shortage of labor. On the whole, however, the available testimony seems to be weighted on the side of rigidity and inefficiency, and we might feel that the odds were, *at best*, fifty-fifty that we should be correct in describing the slave block (and the coffle, etc.) as an effective capital market. Then, on reading the price lists and the advertisements in old southern newspapers, suppose we observe that these rather dry pieces of evidence show that prices in New Orleans and in Charleston moved in parallel fashion over a fairly long period, though the New Orleans averages were generally higher than the Carolina listings. (It should be kept in mind that this is not much in the way of evidence about the functioning of a market as complicated as the one for slave labor.) But could we reasonably expect to find parallel price behavior in two markets, almost twelve hundred miles apart by sea and separated by almost 750 miles over land, if the market were inefficient?

Economic theory, as well as observation of other situations, tells us that between isolated markets, with imperfect communication, we should not expect to find parallel price movements unless the supply and demand conditions in the two markets moved in exactly parallel fashion. This was certainly not the case in the situation we are examining, as we shall see in a moment. An answer to the question, then, could take the form of the "likelihood" in our more formal statement in the paragraphs above. In this case it is a statement of the probability of finding the specific evidence of parallel price behavior, conditional upon the hypothesis that the inter-regional slave market was inefficient. The low value of that conditional probability reduces the degree of reasonable belief that we should attach to the inefficiency position, *after* the observation. Recall that the fifty-fifty odds represented our original estimate *before* we observed the price listings. Multiplying the two—the initial probability, made prior to reading the price data, times the likelihood of finding parallel price movements in an inefficient, rigid market situation—gives us a new estimate of the credibility of the inefficiency argument, revised in the light of the price evidence.

Now consider the factor of proportionality. The value of a piece of historical evidence—that is, whether it provides a crucial link in the story—depends upon the relationship between the Likelihood $Pr(x|y)$ and the factor of proportionality in the denominator of our equation. If the probability of observing the datum in any event, whether the hypothesis were true or not, is great relative to the probability of observing it given the hypothesis, then any belief that depends upon the observation must be weaker. If our chance of observing some evidence were very small *except* under the hypothesized condition, then probabilities directly based upon the observation would become greater. This is an important result for the problem of selection in history, for it tells us that the significance of a variable, or of an isolated piece of evidence, depends upon the range of conditional probabilities of observing the particular piece of evidence, which we have been calling the "likelihood."[5]

In our present example, the probability of finding parallel prices is greater in general than it would be under the specific condition of inefficiency. As the value of the denominator becomes larger, then, the value of the whole expression becomes smaller. The fact that it was very unlikely that we should have found such evidence of regional arbitrage if the markets were rigid and isolated and if the transfer mechanism were inefficient and unresponsive to regional demands for labor, makes the posterior (*after-the-evidence*) probabilities very different from the original fifty-fifty odds.

Now, suppose we read further and learn that the yield of cotton per hand was perhaps two-thirds higher in the growing region near New Orleans, compared with the older, more settled and populous seaboard area. The likelihood that we should assign to finding parallel price behavior under these conditions, given an inefficient market, is now even lower. The higher productivity in the West ought to have forced prices up in that area, while the abundant slave population in the East, combined with the unit-cost disadvantage of the seaboard producers, ought to have had a depressing effect upon Carolina prices. The second revision of the degree of reasonable belief that we could attach to the inefficiency thesis is further reduced below the original fifty-fifty odds. Recall that the fifty-fifty assessment was minimal, based upon the weight of conventional wisdom. The inference of efficiency is correspondingly strengthened. Each revision has been a *posterior* probability in the Bayesian sense, posterior to the observation of a specific, singular piece of historical evidence. It has the same status as a probability statement made after a sample has been tested or a scientific experiment performed.

What made the Principle of Inverse Probability useful here is precisely what strikes terror into many philosophical hearts, namely, that the initial probabilities may be arbitrary or personal. But that is also what ought to make it attractive to historians, since the assignment of probabilities apparently does not depend crucially upon a weight of frequencies that the historian could not hope to gather. There is an alternative argument, that the prior probabilities, being subjective, cannot be consistently assessed. It has been the purpose of this chapter to show that argument to be demonstrably not true.

What we have been demonstrating here is that historical inference of the kind that reconstructs past events from isolated scraps of evidence is an activity very much like the reasoning that we engage in when making and testing predictions. But one must be careful: we are not talking about predictions that *were* made, obviously. Neither are we talking about predictions that *could* have been made. We are saying of observed events only that they would have confirmed predictions that *might* have been made.[6] Following directly upon this, we can ask the question: Under what conditions, with the evidence in hand, might we have predicted the observed outcome? In this way, we can use the little evidence that we are lucky enough or skillful enough to find, as the basis for a reconstruction, much as an archeologist reconstructs a temple on the basis of some pediments and portals, or the paleontologist reconstructs a dinosaur from a few scattered bones and teeth.

NOTES TO CHAPTER 2

1. See F. M. Fisher, "On the Analysis of History and the Inter-dependence of the Social Sciences," *Philosophy of Science,* Vol. 27, No. 2, April, 1960.

2. Cf. W. W. Leontief, "When Should History Be Written Backwards?" *Economic History Review,* 2d ser., Vol. XVI, No. 1 (1963), pp. 1–8.

3. Harold Jeffreys, *Scientific Inference,* chap. 2.

4. See William L. Shirer, *The Rise and Fall of the Third Reich* (London, 1961), p. 192.

5. Cf. Jeffreys, *op. cit.,* p. 30, and Fisher, *loc. cit.,* p. 154.

6. See Gilbert Ryle, *Dilemmas* (Cambridge, 1954), chap. 2.

TWO

OWT

3

The Economics of Slavery
in the Antebellum South

I. OBJECTIVES AND METHODS

The outstanding economic characteristics of southern agriculture before the Civil War were a high degree of specialization and virtually exclusive reliance on a slave labor force. Large-scale, commercial dependence upon slave labor was to distinguish the antebellum South not only from other regions in its own time but from all regions at all other times in American agricultural history. Because of this unique historical status, antebellum southern agriculture has been a subject for special historical attention. Above all else, attention has been focused upon the proposition that, even without external intervention, slavery would have toppled of its own weight. This allegation has its source in the assertions of slave inefficiency to be found in the writings of men who lived with slavery: American or English liberals like G. M. Weston, H. R. Helper, or J. E. Cairnes and southern slaveowners who, in a religious, self-righteous age, could find every motive for the protection of the slave system except that it was personally profitable. The argument is to be found most strongly stated in the work of later southern historians, especially C. W. Ramsdell and U. B. Phillips, who take the position that the Civil War, far from being an irrepressible conflict, was an unnecessary blood bath. They argue that slavery had reached its natural limits and that it was cumbersome and inefficient and, probably within less than a generation, would have destroyed itself. To the question why emancipation was not resorted to, they reply that slavery was for the southerners an important (and evidently expensive) duty, part of their "unending task of race discipline." On the other side, Lewis Gray and Kenneth Stampp have strongly contested this view, contending that southern plantation agriculture was at least as remunerative an economic activity as most other business enterprises in the young republic.

The evidence employed in this debate has been provided by the few, usually fragmentary, accounting records that have come down to us from pre-Civil War plantation activities. The opposing parties have arranged and rearranged the data in accordance with various standard and sometimes imaginary accounting conventions. Indeed, the debate over the value of the different constituent pieces of information reconstructs in embryo much of the historical development of American accounting practices. Virtually all the standard accounting valuation problems have been discussed with relation to the slave question, including the role and meaning of depreciation, the nature and accountability of interest charges, and the validity of distinctions between profits and payments of managerial wages. Still, despite the fact that the problem is ostensibly one in economic history, no attempt has ever been made to measure the profitability of slavery according to the economic (as opposed to accounting) concept of profitability. This study is an attempt to fill that void.

Specifically, we shall attempt to measure the profitability of southern slave operations in terms of modern capital theory. In doing so, we shall illustrate the ways in which economic theory might be used in ordering and organizing historical facts. An additional methodological point is also made evident by this exercise, namely, how the very simple statistical concepts of range and central tendency as applied to frequency distributions of data can be employed in interpreting or moderating inferences from historical facts.[1]

In executing these tasks, we must ask, first, what is it we are talking about? and, second, can we say anything that can be proved or disproved? For example, we must ask what the slave economy was. Was it cotton culture? Was it cotton and sugar and tobacco? Was it all the antebellum southern agriculture? In answering, we shall define slavery in terms of two production functions. One function relates inputs of Negro slaves (and the materials required to maintain the slaves) to the production of the southern staple crops, particularly cotton. The second function describes the production of the intermediate good, slave labor—slave-breeding, to use an emotionally charged term which has affected, even determined, most of the historical conclusions about this problem.

What do we mean by "inefficiency"? Essentially, we shall mean a comparison of the return from the use of this form of capital—Negro slaves—with the returns being earned on other capital assets at the time. Thus we mean to consider whether the slave system was being dragged down of its own weight, whether the allocation of resources was impaired by the rigidity of capitalized labor supply, whether southern capital was misused or indeed drawn away to the North, and finally, whether slavery must inevitably have declined from an inability of the slave force to reproduce itself.

The hypothesis that slavery was an efficient, maintainable form of economic organization is not a new one, of course. Nor are we, by one hundred years at least, among the first to conclude that Negro slavery was profitable in the antebellum South. What we do believe to be novel, however, is our approach. Postulating that American Negro slavery was characterized by two production functions, we argue that an efficient system developed in which those regions best suited to the production of cotton (and the other im-

portant staples) specialized in agricultural production, while
the less productive land continued to produce slaves, exporting the increase to the staple-crop areas. It is this structure
that we are examining.

We propose to test the hypothesis by putting appropriate
values on the variables in the production functions and computing any present value over cost created by the stream of
income over the lifetime of the slave. These returns must, of
course, be shown to be at least equal to those earnable elsewhere in the American economy at the time. It is further
necessary to show that appropriate slave markets existed to
make regional specialization in slave-breeding possible and
that slavery did not necessarily imply the disappearance or
misallocation of capital. Evidence on the ability of the slave
force to maintain itself numerically will be had as a corollary
result. To accomplish all these assessments, it is necessary to
obtain data on slave prices and cotton prices, the average
output of male field hands and field wenches, the life-
expectancy of Negroes born in slavery, the cost of maintaining slaves during infancy and other nonproductive periods,
and finally, the net reproduction rate and the demographic
composition of the slave population in the breeding and using
areas.

Looked upon simply as a staple-commodity agriculture,
the southern system must appear to have been burdened—
possibly even to have been on the verge of collapse—under
the weight of areas of inefficient, unprofitable farming. We
submit that this view is in error and that the error arises
from the failure to recognize that an agricultural system
dependent upon slavery can be defined operationally only in
terms of the production function for both the final good—
in our case, cotton—and the production function for the intermediate good—Negro slaves. Considered operationally, in
terms of a neoclassical two-region, two-commodity trade system, it must be seen that a slave system produces labor as
an intermediate good. The profitability of the system cannot

be decided without considering the system's ability to produce chattel labor efficiently.

There are also nonhistorical reasons for taking up once again the economics of antebellum southern slavery. A detailed re-evaluation of the profits of plantation slavery in the American South might help us evaluate the possibilities, first, that the near-slavery existing today in many highly agricultural, underindustrialized lands is an institution that can be expected to disappear automatically or, second, that dislodging it will require substantial governmental pressure or interference. These are, of course, often key policy questions in former colonial countries that are just beginning to develop modern industrial economies.

The possible relevance of the American experience in this connection increases, moreover, as the underlying economic motivations of a slave system are analyzed and established. This happens primarily because, once these motives are recognized, it becomes possible better to understand and predict the political structures that will accompany slavery. In other words, the interrelationships between certain economic and political goals of slavery can be better understood once the underlying economic factors are understood.

II. THE ECONOMIC RETURNS ON SLAVEHOLDING

From the standpoint of the entrepreneur making an investment in slaves, the basic problems involved in determining profitability are analytically the same as those met in determining the returns from any other kind of capital investment. The acquisition of a slave represented the tying-up of capital in what has appropriately been called a roundabout method of production. Like the purchase of any capital, a slave purchase was made in the anticipation of gaining higher returns than are available from less time-consuming or capital-using methods. This model is perhaps particularly applicable in the slave case, because slave investments, like the forests or wine cellars of classic capital theory, produced a natural increase with the passage of time.

A. *Longevity of Slaves*

Slave longevity corresponds, of course, to the period for which a slave investment was made. We shall limit attention here to the purchase of twenty-year-old Negroes in the immediate pre-Civil War era and shall deal only with the typical or median life-expectancy for this group. These limits greatly simplify the problem and still include the vast majority of relevant cases.

Investment returns can be computed by using the capital-value formula, $y = x_t/(1 + r)^t$, where y is the present value of the investment, x_t is realized net return t years hence, and r is the interest rate.[2] (As an alternative, the internal rate of return can be calculated by setting y equal to the cost of the investment and solving the equation for r; such a procedure is not quite as appropriate in some cases as the present value procedure, but for completeness and ease of comparison, results using both methods are reported subsequently.) When returns are realized over a number of years, the total present value of the capital can be found by simple summation in this formula. The criterion for a profitable investment is that the present value exceeds the current cost of the investment or that the ratio of the present value to cost exceeds unity; this ratio will be subsequently referred to as the "benefit-cost ratio." From this statement of the problem, it is obvious that the following information is needed to determine the profitability of slaveholding from the slaveholder's point of view: (a) the longevity of slaves, (b) the costs of slaves and any necessary accompanying capital investments, (c) the interest rate, and (d) the annual returns from slave productive activities, defined to include both field labor and procreation. We shall consider each of these in turn and then put the pieces together to determine the approximate profitability of slave investments.

There is a scarcity of good longevity data for the period, but it is known that in 1850 Negroes lived just about as long as whites in the two states for which acceptable data are available. The available figures are given in Table I. Doubt

TABLE 1

EXPECTATION OF LIFE AT BIRTH IN YEARS FOR WHITE AND
COLORED MALES, UNITED STATES, 1850*

State	White	Colored
Massachusetts..................	38.3	39.75
Maryland......................	41.8	38.47
Louisiana......................	....	28.89

*Reported in L. I. Dublin, A. J. Lotka, and M. Spiegelman, *Length of Life* (New York: Ronald Press Co., 1949) p. 54, where the source is given as the L. W. Meech table based on the records of the 1850 Census and first published in J. C. G. Kennedy, *The Seventh Census—Report of the Superintendent of the Census, Dec. 1, 1852* (Washington, D.C., 1853), p. 13. The Maryland colored data are for slaves only; the Louisiana, for slaves and free together.

exists about the quality of these estimates because they show Negroes in New England expecting a longer life than whites. This is not the case today, nor was it the case in 1900, when the first good data became available. Also, Negroes appear in this table to have had a longer life-expectancy in 1850 than they had fifty years later. Although surprising, this may be perfectly correct. Negroes could have received better care under slavery than in freedom because the plantation owners had an economic interest in keeping Negroes alive. Furthermore, the Negro in the period after emancipation generally lacked the means to participate equally in the new medical advances, in contrast to his position of roughly equal medical care in the period before 1860.

Life-expectation at birth does not tell us much, of course, about the expectation of a twenty-year-old man. Actually, there are no data on Negro life-expectancy at different age levels in the prewar period except for some imperfect estimates made by Sydnor for Mississippi slaves.[3] Using the average reported age at death of those over the age of twenty who died in 1850, he estimated a life-expectancy of twenty-two years for a twenty-year-old Mississippi slave. This figure is probably low for two reasons. First, the estimating procedure tells more about life-expectancy in the years preceding 1850 than after, unless we make the dubious assumption that there was no advance in medical and dietary knowledge around the middle of the last century. Second, estimates from deaths reported at the end of ten-year intervals and averaged back over the decade would tend to underestimate life-spans at the younger ages. Doubts about the quality of the Sydnor data are borne out by consideration of the Massachusetts life-expectancy of 40.1 years for twenty-year-old males, white and Negro, in 1850.[4] Looking back at the data in Table 1, there is no reason to expect twenty-year-old Massachusetts Negroes to have a lower life-expectancy than Massachusetts whites, though both clearly lived longer than southern Negroes of the period. Taking all these factors into account, an estimate of thirty to thirty-five years of life-expectancy seems most plausible for twenty-year-old Negroes working as prime cotton hands on southern plantations in the period 1830-50, and a thirty-year life-expectancy will generally be used in the succeeding calculations.

B. Cost of the Capital Investment

The capital investment in plantation operations included both slaves and the land and equipment on which they worked. The price of slaves fluctuated widely, being subject to the waves of speculation in cotton. The price also depended, among other things, upon the age, sex, disposition, degree of training, and condition of the slave. In order to hold these variables roughly constant, the present analysis is confined to eighteen- to twenty-year-old prime field hands and wenches. Some summary data on slave prices were compiled by U. B. Phillips on the basis of available market quotations, bills of transactions, and reports of sales in most of the important slave markets of Georgia. His estimates of the best averages for several years between 1828 and 1860 are presented in Table 2. On the basis of these data it would

TABLE 2

ESTIMATED AVERAGE SLAVE PRICES IN
GEORGIA, SELECTED YEARS, 1828–60

Year	Average Price of Prime Field Hands
1828	$ 700
1835	900
1837	1,300
1839	1,000
1840	700
1844	600
1848	900
1851	1,050
1853	1,200
1859	1,650
1860	1,800

Source: U. B. Phillips, "The Economic Cost of Slave-holding in the Cotton Belt," *Political Science Quarterly*, XX, No. 2 (1905), 267.

appear that both the median and the mean price for prime field hands were in the range of from $900 to $950 in the period 1830–50. Because of the substantial price increases in the last antebellum decade, these averages would run substantially higher for the entire slave period after 1830—specifically, between $1,000 and $1,200. Since the prices of field wenches usually averaged about $100–$150 less than those of hands, they were probably in a range of $800–$850 in the years 1830–50 and between $900 and $1,100 for the entire period 1830–60. (Phillips' averages are substantially confirmed by the detailed tabulation of slave transactions shown in Table A of the appendix to this chapter. This is a reasonably exhaustive list of such transactions as reported in the standard references on antebellum southern agriculture.)

By far the most important nonslave capital was the investment in land. Since the land values varied widely, depending on the quality of the soil and the type of agriculture pursued, attention is confined to cotton culture. The range in cotton-land prices in the period 1830–50 was fairly well bracketed by the $6 per acre paid for poor upland pine land in Alabama and the $35–$40 per acre paid for cleared Mississippi alluvium. Such a range even encompassed the costs of new lands in the Southwest. Although such land was obtained for a nominal original cost, the usual costs of clearing, draining, and otherwise preparing for cultivation, plus the transportation of slaves and supplies, amounted to $20–$30 per acre. There was also variation in the number of acres needed per hand. Counting garden land and woodlots, as well as productive fields, the usual number of acres per field hand was between 15 and 35, the exact figure depending primarily on the quality of the land. This meant an original land investment per hand of somewhere between $90 and $14,000, with $180–$600 bracketing the vast majority of instances.

The price per acre also was related to the durability of the land. Cotton lands lasted between ten and forty years, depending upon original quality and fertilization. In the land-rich, labor-scarce economy of the nineteenth-century United States, fertilization was a rare practice. Furthermore, planters had a choice between operating less capital intensively on low-durability land or more capital intensively on high-durability land. For example, poor Alabama pine land might be expected to last ten years and require 30–35 acres per hand; this meant that $180–$210 had to be reinvested every ten years to utilize the slave force properly. Assuming thirty-year slave longevity and an 8 per cent interest rate, the present value of the land investment for one slave's lifetime was $302–$350 for an upland-pine operation. On the alluvium, by contrast, the land would typically outlast the slave in usefulness; assuming, though, that both lasted the same number of years and that 16 acres of cleared and 10 of uncleared land (at $10 per acre) were used per hand, a total investment of $660 per hand is indicated. This difference in value of the land investment was presumably a function of different yields. At any rate, the typical case was probably halfway between these two, involving a land investment of about $450 per hand.

Similar problems arise in estimating the investment in plows, gins, wagons, cabins, and miscellaneous implements. Such investments ran about $25 per hand in original outlay and had to be renewed every fifteen years. This gives a total present value per hand in such items (again on the assumption of thirty-year slave longevity and 8 per cent interest) of about $33. A small investment was required in work horses and oxen, but in this case the stock was likely to be self-replenishing, reducing the costs to interest on the investment at most. Putting all these capital costs together indicates that $1,400–$1,450 was a fair approximation of the typical or average total investment per male slave in terms of present values. The range ran from $1,250 to $1,650.

C. Interest Rate

Determining the relevant rate of interest—the rate with which the cotton-slave returns must be discounted or compared—is perhaps empirically the easiest and conceptually the most difficult of the tasks in computing the economic returns on slave investments. While there is a relative abundance of data on interest rates in this period, none corresponds exactly to the desired rate. Probably the most relevant rate of interest would be that which plantation owners or other investors in southern agriculture could have earned on their money in other pursuits if slavery had gone out of existence. This is difficult to estimate on historical evidence, since it assumes circumstances contrary to fact. A close substitute might be earnings on other investments that were *least* dependent upon cotton and southern agriculture. Given the importance of cotton in the American economy prior to the Civil War and the general interdependence of economic systems, even in an economy as primitive as that of the United States in the first half of the nineteenth century, it is difficult to find any conceptually correct figures. The figures that follow are offered in complete recognition of their fallibility, yet they are probably as good as are available.

In the contemporary chronicles southerners and northerners alike considered 6–8 per cent a reasonable rate of return and a reasonable asking price for loans. Figures in this range are repeated over and over again. These figures also are consistent with reported rates charged on prime commercial paper and other debt instruments in the principal money markets before 1860, as shown in Table 3.[5] Similarly, rates on New York Stock Exchange call loans, New England municipal issues, and rail debentures, shown in Table 4, fall for the most part within, or below, this same 6–8 per cent range. While the average annual rates fluctuated widely in the years between 1830 and 1850 and the distribution of rates is skewed, the central tendency was clearly close to

TABLE 3

AVERAGE ANNUAL INTEREST RATES ON PRIME COMMERCIAL
PAPER FROM 1831 TO 1860

	New York*	Boston†		New York*	Boston†
1831	5.1	6.5	1849	10.0	12.0
1832	5.3	6.5	1850	8.0	7.5
1833	6.9	6.0	1851	9.7	7.0
1834	14.6	14.5	1852	6.6	6.0
1835	7.0	5.0	1853	10.2	10.7
1836	18.4	20.3	1854	10.4	12.0
1837	14.1	6.0	1855	8.9	7.0
1838	9.0	7.0	1856	8.9	10.0
1839	13.2	9.0	1857	12.9	9.0
1840	7.8	6.0	1858	5.0	4.5
1841	6.9	6.0	1859	6.8	7.0
1842	8.1	7.8	1860	7.0	6.0
1843	4.5	3.0	1861	6.5	....
1844	4.9	5.0	1862	5.8	....
1845	6.0	6.0	1863	5.0	....
1846	8.3	8.0	1864	6.0	....
1847	9.6	6.0	1865	7.6	....
1848	15.1	15.0			

Sources: *New York data:* Federal Reserve Bank of New York. *Monthly Review,* March 1, 1921, p. 3. The figures are also reproduced in A. O. Greef, *The Commercial Paper House in the United States* (Cambridge, Mass.: Harvard University Press, 1938), p. 79. *Boston data:* Joseph G. Martin, *One Hundred Years' History of the Boston Stock and Money Markets* (Boston: The Author, 1898), pp. 52–53.

* Two-name sixty–ninety-day paper.

† "First class three to six months, bankable paper." The rate reported is either one sustained for a major portion of the year or an arithmetic average.

the 6–8 per cent range. Specifically, the New York average was 9.2 per cent, the median was 8.0, and the mode was between 6.0 and 7.0 per cent.

TABLE 4

YIELDS ON VARIOUS ECONOMIC
ACTIVITIES, 1857–65

Year	New England Municipal Bond Yields (January Index Numbers)	Call Money Rates at the New York Stock Exchange (Arithmetic Average of Months)	Railroad Bond Yields (January Average for All Railroads)
1857	5.2	9.3	8.1
1858	5.3	4.2	8.7
1859	4.8	5.4	7.4
1860	4.8	6.0	7.5
1861	4.9	5.8	7.4
1862	5.2	5.2	7.5
1863	4.4	6.2	5.6
1864	4.7	6.6	6.0
1865	5.2	6.2	6.2

Source: Frederick R. Macaulay, *The Movements of Interest Rates, Bond Yields and Stock Prices in the United States since 1856* (New York: National Bureau of Economic Research, 1938), pp. A172–A173 and A34–A38.

The interest rates for the Civil War years, although they lie outside the slavery period of this investigation, may be conceptually the most pertinent figures in Tables 3 and 4. The Civil War rates represent an approximation of what investment returns in the North might have been in the pre-war period under complete divorce from the plantation economy—but only an approximation because many other structural changes took place concomitantly with the withdrawal of the southern cotton economy. A most significant change was that the Lincoln administration adopted the very essence of Keynesian expansionary fiscal policies. It simultaneously ran a large deficit budget and closed the economy with high tariffs and buy-American clauses in government contracts. On the supply side of the money market, the war meant that the southern withdrawal was consummated without any flow of capital out of slavery and into other ventures.

Consequently, returns on northern investments unquestionably remained higher than they would have been if southern cotton had been withdrawn without offsetting government action and with a flow of southern capital into northern money markets. Of course, there might have been compensatory government action even without the war, and the loss of southern funds was at least partially offset by the loss of southern opportunities. Still, the 6–7 per cent average returns realized in the period 1860–65 can be viewed as indicative of at least what might have been achieved in the United States in the absence of cotton investment opportunities.

The realization on short-term, high-quality commercial paper might normally be expected to be below the realization on longer-term investments of the type represented by ownership of a cotton plantation. However, in the period 1840–60 banking practices were rather lax and potentially or actually inflationary, as indicated by the recurrent financial panics of the time. Such unstable financial conditions may have given equity a premium that it might otherwise not have enjoyed. Furthermore, the existence of well-established slave and real estate markets made most plantation investments highly negotiable, thereby reducing the time commitment in such investments. There are some reports available on the realizable returns on longer-term investments; for example, Table 4 presents the rates at which some municipal and railroad development bonds were floated in the prewar period. In addition, Davis reports returns of 16.76 per cent on total capital stock in the 1844–48 period and 5.75 per cent in the 1848–53 period for nine of the larger and more prosperous Massachusetts textile firms.[6]

From these many disparate sources it seems safe to estimate that a wholesale withdrawal of capital from slave operations in southern agriculture would not have depressed marginal investment returns in the prewar United States economy much below 4.5–5 per cent. Similarly, it seems safe to conclude that the withdrawn capital could not have expected to earn returns much in excess of 8 per cent. Between these high and low estimates, a return of 6 per cent seems the most probable.

D. Annual Returns

The appropriate annual-return figure to enter as the numerator in the capital equation is the net return on current account, or the difference between gross sales and all out-of-pocket expenses. The expense deduction is limited to out-of-pocket expenses, since all the book charges that complicate the usual accounting procedures are taken into account in the process of constructing the capital cost estimate.

Estimates of plantation expenses have been taken primarily from three excellent, exhaustive records of the available material: J. L. Watkins' *The Cost of Cotton Production*,

TABLE 5

TYPICAL ANNUAL OUT-OF-POCKET COSTS OF MAINTAINING AND WORKING
PRIME FIELD HANDS ON SOUTHERN PLANTATIONS
IN THE PERIOD 1840–60

A. Food and clothing
   (1) Out-of-pocket costs where most food was produced on
       plantation and most clothing was hand-sewn......... $ 2.50–$ 3.46
   (2) Cash costs if purchased......................... $25.00–$40.00
   (3) Out-of-pocket costs where some ready-made clothing
       and meat, fish, and other food "delicacies" were pur-
       chased... $ 7.00–$10.00
B. Medical care..................................... $ 1.50–$ 2.00
C. Taxes... $ 0.39–$ 1.20
D. Supervision...................................... $ 5.00–$15.00

   Total, based on means of the estimates above and option (3)
   under A... $20.00–$21.00

Principal sources: J. L. Watkins, *The Cost of Cotton Production* (United States Department of Agriculture, Division of Statistics, Miscellaneous Series, Bull. 16 [Washington, D.C.: Government Printing Office, 1899]); Lewis C. Gray, *History of Agriculture in the Southern United States to 1860* (Washington, D.C.: Carnegie Institution, 1933), pp. 529–67; Kenneth Stampp, *The Peculiar Institution* (New York: A. A. Knopf, Inc., 1956), chaps. vi, vii, and ix.

Lewis C. Gray's *History of Agriculture in the Southern United States to 1860*, and Kenneth Stampp's *The Peculiar Institution*.[7] A reasonably thorough check of these secondary sources against some primary sources and against one another for consistency indicates that these surveys have been reliably and accurately made. A digest of the estimates is presented in Table 5. The figure of $20–$21 annual out-of-pocket slave maintenance costs is used in subsequent calculations, being subtracted from the annual gross return figures on slave activities.

For a male field hand, returns depended on sales of products realized from his field labor; in the case of a female hand, an addition must be made for the returns realized on the labor and sale of her children. These basically different production functions for the two sexes must be treated separately.

For the male field hand, limited to the returns on his field labor, the gross proceeds depended on the price of cotton and the quantity of his annual output. The output, in turn, was crucially dependent on the quality of the land on which the slave was employed and, to a much lesser degree, upon the quality and amount of capital goods with which he was equipped. The figures in Table 6 illustrate possible variations in productivity per hand. These estimates agree with

TABLE 6

REPORTED YIELDS PER PRIME FIELD HAND

Location	Year	Bales per Hand	Source
South Carolina coastal.........	1849	$4\frac{1}{3}$	Watkins
Mississippi (De Soto County)....	1849	4	Watkins
Unidentified.................	1844	7	Watkins
Alabama (Cherokee County).....	1855	4	Watkins
Mississippi (Vicksburg area).....	1855	8	Watkins
New Southwest land...........	1850's	5	Gray, p. 912
South Carolina upland.........	1852	3	Gray, p. 912
Texas........................	1859	10	Stampp, p. 408
Arkansas River...............	1859	7	Stampp, p. 408

frequent statements in contemporary journals that in the typical case a prime field hand could be expected to raise from 3.5 to 4 bales per year. The maximum seems to have been 7–8 bales on the best lands, and 2–3 bales was the minimum on the poorest land.

The relevant price of cotton for valuing these yields would be the net price realized at the farm (in order that price and cost data be comparable). This means that export prices at the major ports must be adjusted downward by the amount of freight, insurance, storage, drayage, and factor's commission charges that were properly chargeable to the planter. Gray estimates that these costs generally ran between $2.50 and $4.00 per bale. Somewhat more detailed information is presented by Watkins, whose findings are summarized in Table 7. The Gray and the Watkins findings are fully compatible, and a marketing cost of from 0.7 to 0.8 cent per pound appears to be properly deductible from the export price in determining the price f.o.b. farm.

TABLE 7

COTTON MARKETING COSTS PER BALE
CHARGEABLE TO PLANTERS IN 1840

	At Mobile	At Charleston
Freight in...............	$1.50*	$1.25†
Drayage................	0.125	0.13
Weighing...............	0.125	0.06
Storage (1 month)......	0.20	0.24
Insurance (1 month)....	‡	0.25
Factor's commission (2–2.5 per cent).........	0.80	0.60–1.61
Total per bale........	$2.75	$3.03§
Total cents per pound‖	0.69	0.76§

Source: Watkins, *op. cit.*, pp. 38, 39.
* By river.
† From Columbia.
‡ Not reported. Note that the higher (Charleston) figures have been used in the profit computations to follow.
§ Assuming $1.10 factor's commission.
‖ Four hundred pounds to a bale.

The export price of cotton fluctuated widely over the period, as can be seen from Table 8. New Orleans cotton prices averaged almost 50 per cent higher in the thirties and

TABLE 8

WEIGHTED YEARLY AVERAGE PRICES OF SHORT-STAPLE COTTON (USUALLY
LOUISIANA OR MISSISSIPPI MIDDLING OR SECOND GRADE) AT
NEW ORLEANS FOR THE CROP YEARS 1830–60

Year	Price	Year	Price	Year	Price
1830.........	8.4	1840..........	9.1	1850..........	11.7
1831.........	9.0	1841..........	7.8	1851..........	7.4
1832.........	10.0	1842..........	5.7	1852..........	9.1
1833.........	11.2	1843..........	7.5	1853..........	8.8
1834.........	15.5	1844..........	5.5	1854..........	8.4
1835.........	15.2	1845..........	6.8	1855..........	9.1
1836.........	13.3	1846..........	9.9	1856..........	12.4
1837.........	9.0	1847..........	7.0	1857..........	11.2
1838.........	12.4	1848..........	5.8	1858..........	11.5
1839.........	7.9	1849..........	10.8	1859..........	10.8
				1860..........	11.1
Decade average price.......	11.2		7.6		11.2

Source: Gray, *op. cit.*, Table 41, pp. 1027–29.

fifties than in the depressed forties. Even in the forties, however, the export price level was sufficient to insure an average
net farm price of not much less than 6.5 cents. Since prices
at any given port were usually equal to the Liverpool price
minus ocean shipping rates, the New York and Mobile prices
were generally somewhat higher. Taking all this into consideration, 7–8 cents seems a realistic and conservative estimate of the average realized farm price for the whole period.

These price, productivity, and capital cost estimates can
be combined to estimate the actual profitability of investments in male slave labor for cotton production. In lieu of a
single computation, several cases involving different capital
outlays, yields per hand, and realized farm prices have been
constructed; the results are given in Table 9.[8] Cases 1, 2, and
3 are the most typical; cases 4, 5, and 6 represent the situation on somewhat better land. These first six cases, with
benefit-cost ratios almost invariably above unity, at 4 and 6
per cent interest rates and internal rates of 4, 5, and 8 per
cent, encompass the majority of antebellum cotton plantation
operations. Cases 7, 8, and 9 represent the minimum of profitability, or what might be expected on poor upland pine coun-

try or the worked-out lands of the eastern seaboard. Operations on these lands were apparently profitable only if money could be borrowed at 4 per cent or if income could be supplemented by breeding slaves. By contrast, cases 10, 11, and 12 show the upper range of profitability realized on the best lands of the new Southwest, the Mississippi alluvium, and the better South Carolina and Alabama plantations.[9] These were quite obviously highly profitable by any standards.

The calculations in Table 9 pertain to estimates of potential returns for the relatively simple production activities of prime field hands. With the female hand or prime field wench the situation is much more complex; in addition to her own field productivity, the field productivity of her children and the returns realized on their sale must be evaluated. Also, the extra cost of maintaining the children and the maternity and nursery costs associated with their births must be counted.

To simplify the calculations in this rather complex situation, the following assumptions are useful:

1. Each prime field wench produced five to ten marketable children during her lifetime. (The computations for the ten-child or upper-limit case are shown in Table 10, while those for the lower limit of five children are shown in Table 11.) Furthermore, successful pregnancies were spaced two years apart. It must be recognized that these figures represent as-

TABLE 9

REALIZED RETURNS ON PRIME FIELD HANDS UNDER VARIOUS HYPOTHESIZED CONDITIONS

Case	Present Value of Capital Outlay per Hand	Yield per Hand (Bales)	Average Net Farm Price (Cents)	Benefit/Cost Ratios			Approximate Internal Rate of Return (Per Cent)
				@4%	@6%	@8%	
1.	$1,350–$1,400	3¾	7	1.07	0.85	0.70	4.5
2.	$1,350–$1,400	3¾	8	1.26	1.00	0.82	5.2
3.	$1,350–$1,400	3¾	9	1.45	1.15	0.94	6.5
4.	$1,600	4½	7	1.15	0.91	0.74	5.0
5.	$1,600	4½	8	1.34	1.07	0.87	7.0
6.	$1,600	4½	9	1.54	1.22	1.00	8.0
7.	$1,250–$1,300	3	7	0.87	0.69	0.55	2.2
8.	$1,250–$1,300	3	8	1.00	0.82	0.67	3.9
9.	$1,250–$1,300	3	9	1.19	0.95	0.78	5.4
10.	$1,700	7	7	1.79	1.43	1.16	10.0
11.	$1,700	7	8	2.08	1.65	1.35	12.0
12.	$1,700	7	9	2.36	1.88	1.53	13.0

sumptions more about what was achievable than about actual happenings. Slave infant mortality data are too poor to permit inferences about the latter.

2. The prime field wench was one-half to two-thirds as productive as a prime field hand when she was actually at work in the field. This estimate is based on the fact that, when prime field hands and wenches were hired out, the hiring rate on the latter was usually one-half to two-thirds the hiring rate on the former. Thus, it is assumed that the market hiring rate reflects the relative productivity of the two sexes. On the assumption that wenches in late pregnancy were not for hire, adjustment also must be made for the time lost by the female during the pregnancy and postnatal periods. It is assumed here that three months' productive field time was lost for each successful pregnancy; the entire deduction has been made in the year in which the successful birth took place, despite the fact that it would probably be more realistic to assume that one month and a half was lost on each unsuccessful as well as each successful pregnancy. This allowance for "lost time" is probably too generous, since the only births that really cost any important productive field time were those occurring during the peak agriculture seasons, planting and picking times.

3. The wench's children became productive in field labor at age six, with the males becoming self-sustaining by age nine (that is, they then earned the adult maintenance charge of $20 per year), while females became self-sustaining by age thirteen. This can be represented by letting the male productivity go up $5 every year between ages six and nine and letting female productivity increase by $2.50 for every year between the ages of six and thirteen. These rates are in keeping with the previously stated principle that females were roughly half as productive in field labor as males. After reaching a self-sustaining status at these ages, it is further assumed that the children's productivity continued to rise linearly until they reached their full adult productivity

to age eighteen; thus, male productivity is assumed to rise $10 per year between ages nine and eighteen and female productivity $5 per year between ages thirteen and eighteen.

4. The typical wench had as many male as female children. For purposes of computation, the productivity, sales price, and other data for children of the two sexes have been averaged. For example, the final sales price of a typical child

TABLE 10

ANNUAL RETURNS ON A PRIME FIELD WENCH INVESTMENT (WORKING ON LAND WHICH YIELDED 3.75 BALES PER PRIME MALE FIELD HAND, ASSUMING A 7.5-CENT NET FARM PRICE FOR COTTON AND TEN "SALABLE" CHILDREN BORN TO EVERY WENCH)

Year from Purchase Date	Personal Field Returns	Child Field Returns	Child Sale Returns	Personal Upkeep	Child Upkeep	Net Returns
1............	$56	....	....	$20	....	$ 36
2............	40	....	....	20	$ 50	−30
3............	56	....	....	20	10	26
4............	40	....	....	20	60	−40
5............	56	....	....	20	20	16
6............	40	....	....	20	70	−50
7............	56	....	....	20	30	6
8............	40	$ 3.75	,...	20	80	−56.25
9............	56	7.50	....	20	45	−1.50
10............	40	15.00	....	20	95	−50.00
11............	56	22.50	....	20	60	−1.50
12............	40	37.50	....	20	110	−52.50
13............	56	52.50	....	20	75	13.50
14............	40	75.00	....	20	130	−35.00
15............	56	97.50	....	20	95	47.50
16............	40	127.50	.....	20	150	−2.50
17............	56	157.50	....	20	115	78.50
18............	40	195.00	....	20	165	55.00
19............	56	232.50	....	20	130	134.30
20............	40	195.00	$875	20	170	920.00
21............	56	232.50	....	20	130	138.50
22............	56	195.00	875	20	120	986.00
23............	56	232.50	....	20	120	148.50
24............	56	195.00	875	20	110	996.00
25............	56	232.50	..:.	20	110	158.00
26............	56	195.00	875	20	100	1,006.00
27............	56	232.50	....	20	100	168.00
28............	56	187.50	875	20	90	1,008.50
29............	56	225.00	....	20	90	171.00
30............	56	180.00	875	20	80	1,011.00
31............	...	210.00	....	...	80	130.00
32............	...	157.50	875	...	60	972.50
33............	...	180.00	....	...	60	120.00
34............	...	120.00	875	...	40	955.00
35............	...	135.00	....	‹..	40	95.00
36............	...	67.50	875	...	20	922.50
37............	...	75.00	....	...	20	55.00
38............	...	....	875	...	....	875.00

is assumed to be $875, halfway between the average price of $825 for prime field wenches and the average price of $925 for prime field hands.

5. Nursery costs were about $50 per successful pregnancy.

Using these assumptions, hypothetical annual returns for a typical prime field wench can be determined; such calculations are shown in Tables 10 and 11. In constructing these tables, it was assumed that the prime field wench and her children worked on land that returned 3.75 bales of cotton per year for every prime male hand employed; that is, the land is slightly below average fertility. Also, a 7.5-cent net farm price for cotton has been used. The first successful preg-

TABLE 11

ANNUAL RETURNS ON A PRIME FIELD WENCH INVESTMENT (WORKING ON LAND WHICH YIELDED 3.75 BALES PER PRIME MALE FIELD HAND, ASSUMING A 7.5-CENT NET FARM PRICE FOR COTTON AND FIVE "SALABLE" CHILDREN BORN TO EVERY WENCH)

Year from Purchase Date	Personal Field Returns	Child Field Returns	Child Sale Returns	Personal Upkeep	Child Upkeep	Net Returns
1	$56	....	....	$20	...	$ 36
2	40	....	....	20	$50	−30
3	56	....	....	20	10	26
4	40	....	....	20	60	−40
5	56	....	....	20	20	16
6	40	....	....	20	70	−50
7	56	....	....	20	30	6
8	40	$ 3.75	....	20	80	−56.25
9	56	7.50	....	20	45	−1.50
10	40	15.00	..	20	95	−50.00
11	56	22.50	....	20	60	−1.50
12	56	37.50	....	20	60	13.50
13	56	52.50	....	20	65	23.50
14	56	75.00	....	20	65	46.00
15	56	97.50	....	20	75	58.50
16	56	127.50	....	20	75	88.50
17	56	157.50	....	20	85	108.50
18	56	191.25	....	20	85	142.25
19	56	225.00	....	20	90	171.00
20	56	180.00	$875	20	75	1,016.00
21	56	210.00	....	20	75	171.00
22	56	157.50	875	20	60	1,008.50
23	56	180.00	....	20	60	156.00
24	56	120.00	875	20	40	991.00
25	56	135.00	....	20	40	131.00
26	56	67.50	875	20	20	958.50
27	56	75.00	....	20	20	91.00
28	56	....	875	20	...	911.00
29	56	....	....	20	...	36.00
30	56	....	....	20	...	36.00

nancy has been assumed to occur in the second year after the prime field wench is purchased; further successful pregnancies occur at regular two-year intervals. The children were sold at age eighteen, and the annual maintenance cost per child was assessed at the rate of $10 per year for children between ages one and six, $15 per year for seven- to twelve-year-olds, and $20 per year, the full adult maintenance cost, for those age thirteen and over. The maternity costs have been included in the annual charge for the children's upkeep; similarly, the $16 decline every other year for the first few years in the wench's own field returns represents the allowance for time lost because of pregnancy. Benefit-cost ratios and rates of returns were computed on the streams of net returns shown in the far right-hand columns of the tables on the assumption that the total investment in the prime field wench, land, and equipment was between $1,200 and $1,300, figures which would appear to be very good averages. A benefit-cost ratio of 1.62 at a 6 per cent interest rate and an internal rate of return of 8.1 per cent were obtained for the mother bearing ten children; a ratio of 1.23 and a return of 7.1 per cent were estimated for the mother with five children.

These returns are somewhat higher than those calculated for the prime field hands. A proper working of the market mechanism would suggest that the attainable returns on the two sexes should be approximately equal. That is, the sales price differential between males and females should be such that the rate of return on the two types of investment turns out to be roughly equal in the typical case.

The higher rate of return for the females might be explained, however, in several different ways. First, it may have taken a somewhat higher return on the females to attract capital investment into that type of productive activity. Slave-breeding and slave-trading were not generally considered to be high or noble types of activity for a southern gentleman. Indeed, many plantation owners would stoop to considerable subterfuge to disguise engagement in any part of the slave-trade or breeding operations. Second, the investment in the female was a longer-term affair than with the male; from Tables 10 and 11 it is apparent that the bulk of the returns on a female were realized twenty or more years after the investment was made, when the children had grown to marketable ages. To the extent that more distant developments are more uncertain, investments in female slaves could be expected to demand a higher return. Finally, the over-all average price of prime field wenches quoted from Phillips may be too low for proven "childbearers"; as is evident from Table A of the appendix to this chapter and contemporary comments, a female who had proved herself fertile was worth more than a female who had yet to bear her first child.

But these qualifications do not change the principal conclusion that slavery was apparently about as remunerative as alternative employments to which slave capital might have been put. Large or excessive returns were clearly limited to a few fortunate planters, but apparently none suffered excessively either. This general sharing in the prosperity was more or less guaranteed, moreover, if proper market mechanisms existed so that slaves could be bred and reared on the poorest of land and then be sold to those owning the best. Slavery in the immediate antebellum years was, therefore, an economically viable institution in virtually all areas of the South as long as slaves could be expeditiously and economically transferred from one sector to another.

III. Reproduction, Allocation, and Slave Markets

It thus remains to be determined whether an efficient supply mechanism—efficient in both its generative and its allocative functions—existed in the antebellum South. That the slave force might reproduce itself was not sufficient; there must also have been a capital market capable of getting the labor to the areas where production was expanding if slavery was to be profitable. The several arguments that, together, form the orthodox opposition to the present hypothesis are as follows (in every case accompanied by a citation as a talisman against any possible charge that we are setting up straw men):[10] (i) slaves are notoriously inefficient and unwilling workers; (ii) slave property, unlike wage labor, must be supported in the years before and after the slave is economically productive; (iii) slaveholding absorbed plantation earnings; (iv) slave economies are constantly threatened by decline because they cannot in general maintain the number of slaves; and (v) capitalization of the labor force inhibits the efficient allocation of labor.

The first and second of these arguments are implicitly tested in the computation of the rate of return on slave capital. We are not concerned with efficiency per se, however that might be measured, or with the efficiency of slaves as opposed to free white laborers. The more sophisticated version of this efficiency argument—that slave ineptness forced the planters to use a particularly wasteful form of agriculture—is probably untestable because of the difficulties of identification when impetus or motives are being considered. It might be suggested as a partial answer, however, that extensive farming was not peculiarly a characteristic of slave agriculture or even of plantation cotton culture. It was common to all North American colonial agriculture and, as late as the end of the nineteenth century, was reputed to be characteristic of farming in the Northwest wheat lands. It is, generally, a salient feature of agriculture when labor is scarce relative to land.[11] But, insofar as slaves were inefficient, the inefficiency must be reflected in the returns computed in our model. Similarly, the costs of maintaining slaves in infancy and dotage are accounted for in our cost of production.

The third argument—that the South lost from the payment of interest and the constant enhancement of slave prices (and therefore overcapitalization of the labor force)—rests in part upon two misapprehensions, attributable to U. B. Phillips: (1) that capitalization involves a net loss through the payment of interest and (2) that slaves were, somehow, a fictitious form of wealth. We have already shown that slave capital earned returns at least equal to those earned by other contemporary forms of capital. For the overcapitalization part of the argument, it remains to be shown that slave prices did not run away from cotton values.

The last two of the assertions state the negative of our principal secondary hypothesis, which is that an efficient market system existed for the supply of slaves to the rapidly growing cotton industry of the Southwest through transfer from the exhausted land of the Old South. It will be shown that the slave population, in all but the Louisiana sugar area, more than reproduced itself. It will also be shown the border states were not depleted to provide for western needs, since only the natural increase was exported. Finally, avoiding the emotion-wracked testimony of the time, we will attempt to demonstrate the existence of regional specialization and an efficient market by comparing the demographic composition of the cotton and border states and by examining the price behavior in the market for Negro slaves.

A. *Reproduction of the Slave Labor Force*

The history of slavery is full of examples of slave economies that could not reproduce their population and collapsed because of a failure of supply. Frequently, as in the Roman case, the supply was dependent upon a steady flow of military prisoners. The Augustan peace and the stabilization of the borders of the empire are credited with the decline of Roman slavery for this reason. Similarly, the labor supply in the Caribbean sugar islands could be maintained only by importation. It is generally argued that slavery disappeared from Jamaica, not because of abolition in 1834, but because of the inability of the slave population to reproduce itself once the slave trade had been closed.

By contrast, the antebellum cotton-slave economy of the

southern states managed to maintain and allocate its labor supply by a system of regional specialization that produced slaves on the worn-out land of the Old South and the border states for export to the high-yield cotton land of the Mississippi and Red River valleys. For the whole nation the Negro rate of increase in the six decades before the Civil War was only slightly below the rate for the white population; for most of the period the slave rate was very much above that for free Negroes. In the South the disparity between Negro and white rates of increase favors the Negro; considering the relative rates of immigration of whites and Negroes after the first decade of the nineteenth century, the discrepancy in natural increase is even more striking. The evidence in Table 12 does

TABLE 12

PERCENTAGE DECENNIAL INCREASE IN WHITE
AND NEGRO POPULATION, 1790–1860

Census Year	Total	White	Negro — Increase During Preceding Ten Years		
			Total	Slave	Free
1800	35.1	35.8	32.3	28.1	82.2
1810	36.4	36.1	37.5	33.1	71.9
1820	33.1	34.2	28.6	29.1	25.3
1830	33.5	33.9	31.4	30.6	36.8
1840	32.7	34.7	23.4	23.8	20.9
1850	35.9	37.7	26.6	28.8	12.5
1860	35.6	37.7	22.1	23.4	12.3

Source: Bureau of the Census, *Negro Population in the United States, 1790–1915* (Washington, D.C., 1918), Tables 2 (chap. ii) and 1 (chap. v) and pp. 25 and 53. The sharp declines in the rate of increase for slaves in the decades ending in 1840 and 1860 probably reflect the generation cycle following the increase in importations, mostly of mature Negroes, in the years just prior to 1808.

not admit of any doubt that the slave population was capable of producing a steady supply of labor for the plantation economy.[12]

B. *Slave Markets and Allocation*

The more important issue, however, is whether or not the slave force could be allocated efficiently. The natural rate of increase was more than sufficient in the Old South to meet the needs of agriculture in the region, but in the West it was less than sufficient to meet the demands for increased cotton production. By direct export and by the migration of planters with their work forces, the eastern areas supplied the needs of the Southwest. In every decade before the Civil War the increase of slaves in the cotton states was much above, and in the Atlantic and border states much below, the rate of increase for the whole slave population. Indeed, in the decades ending in 1840 and 1860 the net rate of population increase in the Old South was only slightly above the level sufficient to maintain the population at a constant level, 4.5 per cent and 7.1 per cent (see Table 13). From 1790 to 1850 the increase of slaves in the Atlantic states was just 2 per cent

TABLE 13

PERCENTAGE RATE OF POPULATION INCREASE, BY RACE, IN THE COTTON AND BORDER STATES, 1790–1860

DECADE ENDING	COTTON STATES*		BORDER STATES†	
	White	Negro	White	Negro
1800...........	42.9	47.4	27.9	24.4
1810...........	37.5	61.3	23.5	23.4
1820...........	38.8	48.0	19.5	15.5
1830...........	40.0	46.8	19.0	14.0
1840...........	31.3	37.6	21.1	4.5
1850...........	34.1	35.6	34.5	11.0
1860...........	27.6	29.0	39.2	7.1

Source: Ernst von Halle, *Baumwollproduktion und Pflanzungswirtschaft in den Nordamerikanischen Sudstaaten* (Leipzig, 1897, p. 132. His sources were Tucker, *Progress of the United States* (to 1840), *Census of Population* (1850 and after), and H. Gannett, *Statistics of the Negroes in the United States.*
*North Carolina, South Carolina, Georgia, Florida, Alabama, Mississippi, Louisiana, Texas, Arkansas, and Tennessee.
†Delaware, Maryland, District of Columbia, Virginia, West Virginia, Kentucky, and Missouri.

per annum, while in the Gulf states (including Florida), Arkansas, and Tennessee the rate was 18 per cent per annum. A rough but probably conservative estimate of the export from the selling states between 1820 and 1860 is given by W. H. Collins. Taking the difference between the average natural increase and the actual rate in the selling states, Collins arrived at the following estimates:[13]

1820–30 124,000
1830–40 265,000
1840–50 146,000
1850–60 207,000

Collins estimated that at least three-fifths of the removals from the border states were due to emigration to the Southwest rather than to export. While this has little bearing upon the issue of allocative efficiency, it does have significance for the corollary assertion that the slaveowners of the border states, consciously or unconsciously, were engaged in a specialized breeding operation, producing chattel labor for the growing Southwest. In 1836 the *Virginia Times* estimated that, "of the number of slaves exported [from Virginia], not more than one-third have been sold, the others being carried by their masters, who have removed."[14] Ruffin supposed that the annual sale in 1859 "already exceed in number all the increase in slaves in Virginia by procreation."[15] Bancroft goes beyond these estimates and states that "in the 'fifties, when the extreme prejudice against the interstate traders had abated and their inadequate supplies were eagerly purchased, fully 70 per cent of the slaves removed from the Atlantic and the border slave states to the Southwest were taken after purchase or with a view to sale, that is, were the objects of slave-trading."[16] Whatever the accuracy of these several estimates, which range from two-fifths to four-fifths of total exports of slaves from the border and the Atlantic states, it is clear that sales of slaves provided an important capital gain for the exporting states. There is ample documentary evidence that planters in the Old South were aware of this, that some welcomed it and depended upon it, and that others were fearful of its effect upon the agriculture of the area and upon the tenability of slavery. Some spoke frankly about Virginia as a "breeding state," though the reply to such allegations was generally an indignant denial. Whether systematically bred or not, the natural increase of the slave force was an important, probably the most important, product of the more exhausted soil of the Old South.

The existence of such specialization is evident in the demographic composition of the cotton and breeding areas and in the price behavior in the markets for slaves. Table 14 demonstrates that the selling states contained, in 1850 and 1860, a greater proportion of children under fifteen years and a substantially greater proportion of slaves above the age of fifty than did the buying states. While the disproportions are not great enough to characterize the selling states as a great nursery, the age composition is in the direction which our hypothesis would lead one to expect. The relationship between the prices of men and women in the slave market, when compared with the ratio of hiring rates for male and female field hands, gives an even stronger indication that the superior usefulness of females of breeding age was economically recognized. The relative hiring rates for men and women in 1860, shown in Table 15, can be taken as a measure of their relative values in the field.[17]

To be compared to these rates are the purchase prices of male and female slaves in the same markets in 1859 and

TABLE 14

SLAVE POPULATION BY AGE

(Per Cent)

AGE (YEARS)	TOTAL	1860		TOTAL	1850	
		Selling States*	Buying States†		Selling States*	Buying States†
Under 15.........	44.8	45.6	43.8	44.9	45.6	44.3
15–19............	11.4	11.5	11.4	11.1	11.3	11.0
20–29............	17.6	16.5	18.9	18.0	17.0	18.9
30–39............	11.7	10.7	11.8	11.3	10.5	12.1
20–49............	36.4	34.4	38.1	36.4	34.6	38.1
50 and over.......	7.5	8.5	6.7	7.5	8.5	6.6

Source: J. C. G. Kennedy, *Population of the United States in 1860* (Washington, D.C., 1864), "Classified Population," Tables No. 1, by state; J. D. B. DeBow, *Statistical View of the United States, . . . Being a Compendium of the Seventh Census* (Washington, D.C., 1854), Part II, Table LXXXII, pp. 89–90.

* Virginia, Maryland, Delaware, South Carolina, Missouri, Kentucky, District of Columbia.

† Georgia, Alabama, Mississippi, Florida, Texas, Louisiana.

NOTE.—The exclusion of Tennessee and North Carolina is explained in n. 14. Missouri was included with the selling group because of its apparent net selling position in this period.

1860. Purchase prices should reflect the relative usefulness of the sexes for field work. More than this, however, if there is any additional value to slave women—for breeding purposes, presumably—there should be a premium in the form of a narrower price differential than is found in the hiring

TABLE 15

ANNUAL HIRING RATES FOR MALE AND FEMALE
SLAVES (INCLUDING RATIONS AND CLOTHING),
BY STATES, 1860

State	Men	Women	Ratio (Men : Women)
Virginia........	$105	$ 46	2.28
North Carolina.	110	49	2.25
South Carolina.	103	55	1.87
Georgia........	124	75	1.65
Florida.........	139	80	1.74
Alabama.......	138	89	1.55
Mississippi.....	166	100	1.66
Louisiana......	171	120	1.43
Texas.........	166	109	1.52
Arkansas......	170	108	1.57
Tennessee.....	121	63	1.92

rates. The prices shown in Table 16 are taken from Table A in the Appendix. Whenever possible, 1860 is used; wherever necessary, 1859. Table 16 includes age designations and, when available, a description of the grade or class represented in the average price.[18] This evidence is a striking confirmation of the validity of the model. In every case but one, the purchase-price differential is narrower than the hiring-rate differential. The price structure clearly reflects the added value of females due to their ability to generate capital gains. It is especially interesting in this regard to note that the price ratios in Virginia and South Carolina, the two breeding states represented in the list, show practically no differential. This evidence clearly shows that the Old South recognized in the market the value of its function as the slave-breeding area for the cotton-raising West.

C. "Overcapitalization" of the Labor Force

The aspect of slave economics that causes the most confusion and outright error is that which relates to the capitalization, and, in the antebellum southern case, the presumed overcapitalization of slave labor. Phillips speaks of an "irresistible tendency to overvalue and overcapitalize" and argues that slaveholding had an unlimited capacity for absorbing the planters' earnings through the continual payment of interest and the enhancement of prices. For the Cotton Belt this was presumably aggregated into a continuous public drain of wealth, first, to England and New England and, later, to the upper South.[19] Moreover, a series of writers from Max Weber down to the most recent theorists of economic growth have argued that capitalization tends to rigidify the pattern of employment. "Free labor is necessary to make free transfers of labor possible. A production organization cannot be very flexible if it has to engage in the purchase or sale of slaves every time it changes its output."[20] But this is really a question of how good the market is; no one, after all, claims that manufacturing is made suicidally inflexible by the fact that expanding sectors must buy the capitalized future earnings of machinery. There are three issues to be

TABLE 16

SELECTED PRICES OF MALE AND FEMALE SLAVES, 1859 AND 1860

State (Year)	Age	Condition	Male Price	Female Price	Ratio
Virginia (1859)	17–20	Best	$1,350–$1,425	$1,275–$1,325	1.07
South Carolina	....	Prime	$1,325	.... }	1.03
	....	Wench	......	$1,283 }	
South Carolina (1859)	....	Field hand	$1,555	...... }	.91
	....	Girl	......	$1,705 }	
Georgia	21	Best field hand	$1,900	...... }	.88
	17	(9 mo. inf.)	......	[$2,150] }	
Georgia (1859)	....	Prime, young	$1,300	...... }	1.04
	....	Cotton hand, houseservant	......	$1,250 }	
Alabama (1859)	19	....	$1,635	...... }	1.37
	18, 18, 8	....	......	$1,193 }	
Mississippi	....	No. 1 field hand	$1,625	$1,450	1.12
Texas	21, 15	....	$2,015	$1,635	1.23
Texas (1859)	17, 14	....	$1,527	$1,403	1.09

distinguished in this argument: first, the alleged tendency toward overcapitalization; second, the inflexibility of chattel labor and the difficulty of allocating it, geographically and industrially; and third, the loss of wealth.

First, was the southerner his own victim in an endless speculative inflation of slave prices? The assertion of an irresistible tendency to overvalue and overcapitalize must mean that he was so trapped, if it means anything. Phillips answered the question by comparing the price of cotton with the price of prime field hands, year by year. He found, or believed he found, a permanent movement toward over-capitalization inherent in American slaveholding. But speculative overexpansion is capable of reversal; from the inflation of 1837 to the bottom of the depression in 1845, slave prices fell as sharply as cotton prices. If the rise from that lower turning point is a demonstration of speculative mania, it was a mania solidly based on the increase in the value of the crop per hand, owing to the concentration of production in more fertile areas, the greater efficiency of the American-born slaves, lowered transportation costs, and the development of new high-yield varieties of cotton from the fourth decade of the century on.[21] Finally, the choice of the initial period in Phillips' analysis exaggerates the decline in cotton prices relative to the price of slaves. At the turn of the century the demand for cotton was increasing rapidly, supporting remarkably high prices, while the unrestricted African slave trade kept domestic slave prices well below the level that might be expected in view of the level of profits. Table 17 and Chart 1 demonstrate the relationships among slave prices, cotton prices, and the value of cotton output per slave (of field-work age, ten to fifty-four). Several things become clear in this comparison. To begin, the relationship between slave and cotton prices is significant for Phillips' purposes only if there is no increase in productivity. While he is struck by the fact that slave prices rose more rapidly than did cotton prices in

TABLE 17

VALUE OF COTTON PRODUCTION AND SLAVE POPULATION, 1802–60, NEW ORLEANS PRICES

Year	Crop (Thousands of Pounds)	Average Price (Cents per Pound)	Value (Thousands)	No. of Slaves, Aged 10–54 Years*	Crop Value per Slave	Price of Prime Field Hand	Crop Value per Hand per Dollar Slave Price
1802.......	55,000	0.147	$ 8,085	550,708	$ 14.68	$ 600	.02
1803.......	60,000	.150	9,000	568,932	15.82	600	.03
1804.......	65,000	.196	12,740	587,157	21.70	600	.04
1805.......	70,000	.233	16,310	605,381	26.94	600	.05
1806.......	80,000	.218	17,440	623,606	27.97	600	.05
1807.......	80,000	.164	13,120	641,831	20.44	600	.03
1808.......	75,000	.136	10,200	660,055	15.45	640	.02
1809.......	82,000	.136	11,152	678,280	16.44	780	.02
1810.......	85,000	.147	12,495	696,505	17.94	900	.02
1811.......	80,000	.089	7,120	717,376	9.93	860	.01
1813.......	75,000	.155	11,625	759,118	15.31	600	.03
1814.......	70,000	.169	11,830	779,989	15.17	650	.02
1815.......	100,000	.273	27,300	800,860	34.09	765	.05
1816.......	124,000	.254	31,496	821,731	38.33	880	.04
1817.......	130,000	.298	38,740	842,602	45.98	1,000	.05
1818.......	125,000	.215	26,875	863,473	31.12	1,050	.03
1819.......	167,000	.143	23,881	884,344	27.00	1,100	.03
1820.......	160,000	.152	24,320	905,215	26.88	970	.03
1821.......	180,000	.174	31,320	933,517	33.55	810	.04
1822.......	210,000	.115	24,150	961,818	25.11	700	.04
1823.......	185,000	.145	26,825	990,120	27.04	670	.04
1824.......	215,000	.179	38,485	1,018,421	37.99	700	.05
1825.......	255,000	.119	30,345	1,046,723	28.99	800	.04
1826.......	350,000	.093	32,550	1,075,024	30.28	840	.04
1827.......	316,900	.097	30,739	1,103,326	27.86	770	.04
1828.......	241,399	.098	23,657	1,131,627	20.91	770	.03
1829.......	296,812	.089	26,416	1,159,929	22.77	770	.03
1830.......	331,150	.084	27,817	1,208,034	23.03	810	.03
1831.......	354,247	.090	31,882	1,247,489	25.56	860	.03
1832.......	355,492	.100	35,549	1,275,061	27.88	900	.03
1833.......	374,653	.112	41,961	1,302,633	32.21	960	.03
1834.......	437,558	.155	67,821	1,330,206	50.99	1,000	.05
1835.......	460,338	.152	69,971	1,357,778	51.53	1,150	.05
1836.......	507,550	.133	67,504	1,385,350	46.79	1,250	.04
1837.......	539,669	.090	48,510	1,412,923	34.38	1,300	.03
1838.......	682,767	.124	84,663	1,440,495	58.77	1,220	.05
1839.......	501,708	.079	39,635	1,468,067	27.00	1,240	.02
1840.......	834,111	.091	75,904	1,507,779	50.34	1,020	.05
1841.......	644,172	.078	50,245	1,568,022	32.04	870	.04
1842.......	668,379	.057	38,098	1,611,269	23.65	750	.03
1843.......	972,960	.075	72,972	1,654,516	44.11	700	.06
1844.......	836,529	.055	46,009	1,697,762	27.10	700	.04
1845.......	993,719	.068	67,573	1,741,009	38.81	700	.06
1846.......	863,321	.099	85,469	1,784,256	47.90	750	.06
1847.......	766,599	.070	53,662	1,827,503	29.36	850	.04
1848.......	1,017,391	.058	59,009	1,870,750	31.54	950	.03
1849.......	1,249,985	.108	134,998	1,913,996	70.53	1,030	.07
1850.......	1,001,165	.117	117,136	1,979,059	59.19	1,100	.05
1851.......	1,021,048	.074	75,558	2,034,482	37.14	1,150	.03
1852.......	1,338,061	.091	121,764	2,080,554	58.53	1,200	.05
1853.......	1,496,302	.088	131,675	2,126,626	61.92	1,250	.05
1854.......	1,322,241	.084	111,068	2,172,698	51.12	1,310	.04
1855.......	1,294,463	.091	117,796	2,218,770	53.09	1,350	.04
1856.......	1,535,334	.124	190,381	2,264,843	84.06	1,420	.06
1857.......	1,373,619	.112	153,845	2,310,915	66.57	1,490	.05
1858.......	1,439,744	.115	165,571	2,356,988	70.25	1,580	.04
1859.......	1,796,455	.108	194,017	2,403,060	80.74	1,690	.05
1860.......	2,241,056	0.111	$248,757	2,460,648	$101.09	$1,800	.06

Source: *Crops:* Computed from the data on number of bales and average weight of bales in James L. Watkins, *Production and Price of Cotton for One Hundred Years* (U.S. Department of Agriculture, Miscellaneous Series, Bull. 9 [Washington, D.C., 1895]). *Price:* Gray, *op. cit.,* Table 41: "Weighted Yearly Averages and Monthly Prices in Cents per Pound of Short-Staple Cotton at New Orleans for the Crop Years 1802–1860." *Slaves:* Bureau of the Census, *Negro Population in the United States, 1790–1915,* "Slave and Free Colored Population at Each Census by Sections and Southern Divisions: 1790–1860," p. 55, and "Negro Population in Years Specified, Classified by Sex and Age Periods; 1830–1910," p. 166. *Slave prices:* Estimated visually from the chart "Approximate Prices of Prime Field Hands in Hundreds of Dollars per Head: . . . at New Orleans . . . ," in U. B. Phillips, *Life and Labor in the Old South* (Boston, 1935), p. 177.

* To estimate the slave population in the intercensal years, the increase over each decade was divided into equal parts and assigned to each year in the decade. The proportion of Negroes in the field-work age brackets (between the ages of ten and fifty-four) was .641 in 1860, .635 in 1850, .621 in 1840, and .610 in 1830. The census-year proportions at the beginning and end of each decade were averaged for use in the intervening years. For the years before 1830, an estimate of .60 was used. There is no implication that we have measured the number of field hands, but it should be noted that the range .60–.65 brackets several contemporary estimates of the proportion of the slave population employed in cotton agriculture (see, e.g., P. A. Morse, "Southern Slavery and the Cotton

CHART I

SLAVE POPULATION AND PRICES AND THE VALUE OF COTTON PRODUCTION, 1802-60

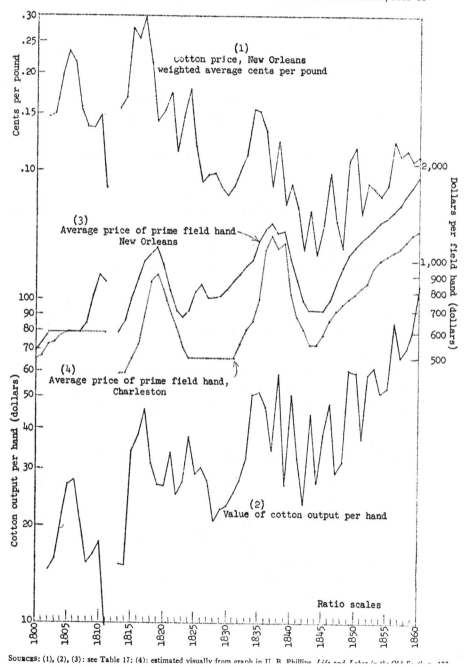

SOURCES: (1), (2), (3): see Table 17; (4): estimated visually from graph in U. B. Phillips, *Life and Labor in the Old South, p. 177*

the long upswing starting in the early 1840's, it is equally striking to observe that (New Orleans) slave prices rose about one and one-half times between the low point in 1843-45 to 1860, while values of cotton production per hand rose more than three times from the low in 1842. This was recognized in the *New Orleans Daily Crescent* in 1860, as follows:

> Nor do we agree with our contemporaries who argue that a speculative demand is the unsubstantial basis of the advance in the price of slaves. . . . It is our impression that the great demand for slaves in the Southwest will keep up the prices as it caused their advance in the first place, and that the rates are not a cent above the real value of the laborer who is to be engaged in tilling the fertile lands of a section of the country which yields the planter nearly double the crop that the fields of the Atlantic States do.[22]

Furthermore, it would appear that slave prices fluctuated less than did cotton prices. This and the less clear-cut lag of the slave prices make it difficult to accept the image of unwary planters helplessly exposing themselves in a market dominated by speculators. It would make more sense to argue simply that the rising trend of slave prices coupled with a growing slave population is, in and of itself, strong evidence of the profitability of slavery.

D. The Efficiency of Allocation

The second point relates to geographic allocation and, to a lesser extent, to the mobility of the slave labor force among crops. The slave prices in all regions move very closely with cotton prices and products per hand. It is clear, too, that the eastern prices move directly with the cotton-area slave prices, although in the last two decades the rate of increase of prices fell behind in the breeding area. If the market were extremely imperfect and the transfer between the breeding and consuming states inefficient, in contradiction to our hypothesis, then there should be much less evidence of regional arbitrage than is found here. In response to the western demand, Virginia and the other eastern states shipped their natural increase to the cotton areas. Indeed, it is frequently argued that the transfer was too efficient and that the Old South was being continuously depressed by the high price of labor occasioned by western demand. Edmund Ruffin, particularly, took this position and argued that slave trade could not bring profits to Virginia but could result only in the paralysis of her industry. If true, this argument would be supported empirically by increasing real estate values on the western lands and decreasing values in the Atlantic and border states. That is, the chain of high cotton profits— high slave prices—increased cost of farming in the Old South should have depressed land prices in the latter area. Emigration, by reducing demand, should have meant more downward pressure. The only influence that operated in the direction of maintaining the value of land in the older states was the profit to be had from the increase and sale of slaves. Indeed, in 1850 and 1860 the value per acre of farm land and buildings in the border states was $7.18 and $12.33 and, in the lower South for the same two census years, $4.99 and $8.54. Undoubtedly, the western cotton land earned a considerable rent in farming over the older land. It was this rent that maintained the flow of migration to the Cotton Belt. But that migration depended upon and supported the prosperity of the breeding states. It also is not clear that slavery was able to continue only by skinning the topsoil and moving on, leaving exhausted land and low slave and land value in its wake. Quite the contrary, the evidence can plausibly be interpreted as indicating a unified, specialized economy in which the settlers on the naturally superior western lands (superior even before the deterioration of the older regions by single-crop cultivation of tobacco and cotton) were able to bid slave labor away from general farming and to make wholesale abandonment of the older areas unnecessary, if indeed there had ever been such a necessity.

E. Slavery and Southern Economic Growth

Finally, there are two economic arguments about slavery and potential southern growth to be considered. The assertion that slavery per se was inimical to economic growth rests in part upon the alleged inefficiency of slave labor in industrial pursuits and in part upon the loss of capital that might otherwise have gone into industrialization and diversification.

The inefficiency argument is not supported very securely. There were slaves employed in cotton factories throughout the South. Slaves were used in the coal mines and in the North Carolina lumbering operations. In the ironworks at Richmond and on the Cumberland River, slaves comprised a majority of the labor force. Southern railroads were largely built by southern slaves. Crop diversification, or the failure to achieve diversification, appears to have been a problem of entrepreneurship rather than of the difficulties of training slaves. In the face of the demand for cotton and the profits to be had from specializing in this single crop, it is hardly difficult to explain the single-minded concentration of the planter.[23]

In what ways was slavery allegedly responsible for the drain of capital from the South? The lack of diversification, to the extent of a failure even to provide basic supplies, made necessary the import of much food and virtually all manufactured articles from the North. But half of this assertion, the argument that laid the responsibility for the single-crop culture upon slavery, has been found questionable already.

The major avenues by which wealth is said to have been drained from the cotton states were the excessive use of credit (through dependence upon factors' services) and the "absorption" of capital in slaves. Good crop years bring the temptation to expand production; bad years do not bring any release from the factors. But resort to factoring is characteristic of speculative, commercial agriculture, whether or not the labor force is organized in slavery. It is also frequently argued that slavery gave southern planters a taste for extravagant, wasteful display, causing the notorious lack of thrift and the relative lack of economic development, compared to that experienced in the North and West. This is a doubtful inference, at best. Slavery did not make the cavalier any more than slavery invented speculation in cotton. However, insofar as successful slave management required military posture and discipline, the southerner's expensive image of himself as a *grand seigneur* was encouraged. It is beyond the scope of this paper to offer hypotheses about the reasons for the relative degrees of entrepreneurship in Charleston and Boston; in this context it is sufficient to state that slavery per se does not seem to have been responsible for the excessive reliance upon factoring and external sources of credit.[24]

There remains only the absorption of capital in slaves to set the responsibility for lack of growth in the South upon the peculiar institution. Earnings that might have gone out of the South to bring in investment goods were fixed in the form of chattel labor. For the early years, during the external slave trade, there is some plausibility to this argument, though it is difficult to see how the capitalization of an income stream, excellent by contemporary standards, can be said to count as a loss of wealth. In the later years there was, except to the extent that northern or English bankers drew off the interest, a redistribution of wealth only within the slave states: from the cotton lands back to the less profitable field agriculture of the older section. And, to the extent that the old planting aristocracy used the profits to maintain the real or fancied magnificence of the preceding century, capital was absorbed. But, as Russel pointed out, slavery also made the profits in the cotton fields and the resultant demand for eastern hands.

We are left with the conclusion that, except insofar as it made speculation in cotton possible on a grander scale than would otherwise have been the case and thereby weakened whatever pressure there might have been for diversification, capitalization of the labor force did not of itself operate against southern development.

IV. CONCLUSION

In sum, it seems doubtful that the South was forced by bad statesmanship into an unnecessary war to protect a system that must soon have disappeared because it was economically unsound. This is a romantic hypothesis, which will not stand against the facts.

On the basis of the computation of the returns to capital in our model of the antebellum southern economy and the demonstration of the efficiency of the regional specialization, the following conclusions are offered.

1. Slavery was profitable to the whole South, the continuing demand for labor in the Cotton Belt ensuring returns to the breeding operation on the less productive land in the seaboard and border states. The breeding returns were necessary, however, to make the plantation operations on the poorer lands as profitable as alternative contemporary economic activities in the United States. The failure of southern agriculture on these poorer lands in the postbellum period is probably attributable, in the main, to the loss of these capital gains on breeding and not, as is so often suggested, to either the relative inefficiency of the tenant system that replaced the plantations or the soil damage resulting from war operations. These factors were unquestionably contributing elements to the difficulties of postbellum southern agriculture, but they were of relatively small quantitative importance compared with the elimination of slave-breeding returns.

2. There was nothing necessarily self-destructive about the profits of the slave economy. Neither the overcapitalization argument nor the assertion that slavery must have collapsed because the slaves would not reproduce themselves is tenable. Slave prices did not outpace productivity, and the regional slave price structure would imply a workable transfer mechanism rather than the contrary.

3. Continued expansion of slave territory was both possible and, to some extent, necessary. The maintenance of profits in the Old South depended upon the expansion, extensive or intensive, of slave agriculture into the Southwest. This is sufficient to explain the interest of the Old South in secession and does away with the necessity to fall back upon arguments of statesmanship or quixotism to explain the willingness to fight for the peculiar institution.

4. The available productive surplus from slavery might have been used for economic development or, as in some totalitarian regimes of this century, for militarism. In spite of this good omen for development, southern investment and industrialization lagged. It is hard to explain this lag except on the social ground that entrepreneurship could not take root in the South or on the economic ground that the South did not really own the system but merely operated it. Furthermore, the American experience clearly suggests that slavery is not, from the strict economic standpoint, a deterrent to industrial development and that its elimination may take more than the workings of "inexorable economic forces." Although profitability cannot be offered as a sufficient guaranty of the continuity of southern slavery, the converse argument that slavery must have destroyed itself can no longer rest upon allegations of unprofitability or upon assumptions about the impossibility of maintaining and allocating a slave labor force. To the extent, moreover, that profitability is a necessary condition for the continuation of a private business institution in a free-enterprise society, slavery was not un-

tenable in the antebellum American South. Indeed, economic forces often may work toward the continuation of a slave system, so that the elimination of slavery may depend upon the adoption of harsh political measures. Certainly that was the American experience.

TABLE A

TABULATION OF REPORTED SLAVE TRANSACTIONS AND VALUATIONS

Year	State	Sex	Age	Grade or Condition	No. in Sale	Average Price $	Source, Page*
1800	S.C.			Prime field hands		500	P(PSQ)
1805	Ga.			Prime field hands		450	P(PSQ)
	S.C.			Prime field hands		550	P(PSQ)
1808	Ga.			Prime field hands		550	P(PSQ)
	S.C.			Prime field hands		550	P(PSQ)
1810	Ga.			Prime field hands		650	P(PSQ)
	S.C.			Prime field hands		500	P(PSQ)
	Va.			Prime field hands		500	P(PSQ)
	La.			Prime field hands (max.)		900	G.665
1813	S.C.			Prime field hands		450	P(PSQ)
	Ga.			Prime field hands		450	P(PSQ)
1818	Ga.			Prime field hands		1,000	P(PSQ)
	S.C.			Prime field hands		850	P(PSQ)
1819	Va.			Prime field hands		700	P(ANS).370
	La.			Prime field hands		1,100	P(ANS).370
	La.			African, "brute Negro"		400–500	G.664
	La.			Intelligent dom. Negro		1,000	G.664
1820	S.C.			Prime field hand		725	P(PSQ)
1821	Ga.			Prime field hand		700	P(PSQ)
1822	S.C.			Prime field hand		650	P(PSQ)
	Va.	F		Mother of 3		300	B.78
		M	4		1	200	B.78
		M	2		1	150	B.78
		F	1		1	75	B.78
1825	S.C.	F		Prime field hand	1	500	P(PSQ)
	Va.	F		Mother of 3 (see above)	1	200	B.78
		M	7		1	200	B.78
		M	5		1	125	B.78
		F	4		1	90	B.78
1826	S.C.			Prime field hand		475	P(PSQ)
1828	Ga.			Prime field hand		800	P(PSQ)
	S.C.			Prime field hand		450	P(PSQ)
	Ga.			Prime field hand		700	P(PSQ)

* SOURCES

P(PSQ): U. B. Phillips, "The Slave Labor Problem in the Charleston District," *Political Science Quarterly*, XXII, No. 3 (1907), 436.

P(Doc. II): U. B. Phillips, "Plantation and Frontier, 1649–1863," in *A Documentary History of American Industrial Society*, Vol. II (Cleveland, 1910).

P(ANS): U. B. Phillips, *American Negro Slavery* (New York, 1918).

G: Lewis Gray, *History of Agriculture in the United States to 1860* (Washington, D.C., 1933).

B: Frederic Bancroft, *Slave Trading in the Old South* (Baltimore, 1931).

O: Frederick Law Olmsted, *The Cotton Kingdom* (New York, 1953).

GMW: George Melville Weston, *Who Are and Who May Be Slaves in the United States* (pamphlet, undated, unsigned).

TABLE A—*Continued*

Year	State	Sex	Age	Grade or Condition	No. in Sale	Average Price $	Source, Page*
1829	S.C.	M	18-24	Prime field hand	Bid	475	P(PSQ)
	Va., Md.	F	18-24	First	Bid.	400- 450	B.30
			18-24	First		450	B.30
	Ala., La., Miss.			First	Est.	280	B.30
						"Nearly twice as much"	
1830	S.C.			Prime field hands		450	P(PSQ)
	La.			Sugar hands, 5:3 ratio, working: children and aged		550	G.542
1832	S.C.			Prime field hand		500	P(PSQ)
	Miss.			Price range: $300-$1,000	30	500	B.308
1835	S.C.			Prime field hand		750	P(PSQ)
	Ga.			Prime field hand		900	P(PSQ)
	Md.	M	18-25	Likely	Est.	500- 650	B.39
		F	18-25	Likely	Est.	300- 500	B.39
		F	18-25	Best field hand	Est.	300- 400	B.39
		F	7	Servant	Est.	250	B.39
				En route	75	533	B.55
	S.C.		1		1	100	B.55
	D.C.	M	7- 8		1	400	B.55
		M	18		1	750	B.55
		F			2	650	B.55
		M		First field hand	Est.	900	B.55
	Ky.	M		Mechanic	Est.	1,200	B.209
		M	7	"Boy"		350	B.209
		F		"Young"	1	630	B.209
		M	23	Coachman	1	710	B.303
	Miss.	F		Seamstress	1	950	B.303
		M		Field hand	Est.	750	B.308
		F		Field hand	Est.	800	B.308
				Bodyservant	Est.	600	B.308
		M		Good mechanic	Est.	1,000	B.308
		F		Seamstress	Est.	900-2,000	B.308
					Est.	700-1,000	B.308
1836	S.C.			Prime field hand		1,100	P(PSQ)
	Tenn.			(Aver. Tax Value)		414	G.666
1837	S.C.			Prime field hand		1,200	P(PSQ)
	Ga.			Prime field hand		1,300	P(PSQ)
	Va.			Prime field hand		1,000-1,200	G.666
	Tenn.					[1,350]	B.207
1844	La.	F{ }	(3 mos.)	Young mother	2	[700]	B.336
	S.C.	F{ }	(2)	Prime field hand	2	500	P(PSQ)
	Ga.			Prime field hand		600	P(PSQ)

TABLE A—*Continued*

Year	State	Sex	Age	Grade or Condition	No. in Sale	Average Price $	Source, Page*
1846	S.C.			Prime field hand	13	650	P(PSQ)
	Ala.			Mostly boys and women, equal to 10 good hands		446	G.542
1851	S.C.			Prime field hand		750	P(PSQ)
	Ga.			Prime field hand		1,050	P(PSQ)
1852	S.C.			Prime field hand		800	P(PSQ)
	Va.			Incl. aged and infrm	42	400	B.167
				Not above ordinary	21	553	B.350
					of which:		
		M		No trade	1	1,028	B.350
		F( )	(10 mos.)		1	[950]	B.350
		F	11		2	600	B.350
					1	700	B.350
1853	Ala.			Plantation sale			P(PSQ)
	S.C.	M	18–25	Prime field hand		900	P(PSQ)
	Ga.	M	18–25	Prime field hand		1,200	P(PSQ)
	Va.			Best		1,200–1,300	O.595
				Fair		950–1,050	O.595
				Boys, 5' tall		850–950	O.595
				Boys, 4'8" tall		700–800	O.595
				Boys, 4'5" tall		500–600	O.595
				Boys, 4' tall		375–450	O.595
				Young women		800–1,000	O.595
				Girls, 5' tall		780–850	O.595
				Girls, 4'9" tall		700–750	O.595
				Girls, 4' tall		350–450	O.595
		M	45–50	Scarred back	1	460	B.107
				(Unscarred, est.)		(750–800)	B.107
						[650]	O.41
1854	Ky.	F( )	30(2)	Very handsome mulatto	2	1,600	B.131
	Ala.	F	Ten under 7	"Highest prices"	18	788	B.350
					of which:		
		M	7		1	760	B.350
		M	12		1	710	B.350
		M	17		1	1,374	B.350
		F( )	37(2–7)		7	[5,000]	B.350
1855	S.C.			Prime field hands		900	P(PSQ)
1856	Va.			Ordinary field hand		1,467	GMW
		M	70			100	GMW
		M	55			1,610	GMW
		F	20	Likely, "highest pr."		1,700	GMW
		M	12			1,518	GMW
				Prime field hand	Est.	1,050	GMW
				Prime field hand	Est.	1,250–1,500	GMW

87

TABLE A—Continued

Year	State	Sex	Age	Grade or Condition	No. in Sale	Average Price $	Source, Page*
1856......	Tenn.	M	30-45	Aver. reported tax value		689	G.666
	Mo.			Common crop hands	5	1,380	GMW
		F				800-900	GMW
		F		Houseservant	1	1,040	GMW
		F		Houseservant	1	1,753	GMW
		F	Over middle age		2	700	GMW
	Ga.	F	15		1	1,280	B.83
		F	14		1	1,280	B.83
		F	14		1	1,305	B.83
		F	16		1	1,525	B.83
		F	18	Pregnant	1	1,500	B.83
		F( )	20		2	[1,840]	B.83
		M	18		1	1,290	B.83
		M	22		1	1,500	B.83
	La.			"Prices never been equalled"		1,500–1,635	GMW
						1,200–1,550	GMW
1857......	Md.	F	14		1	900	B.79
		F		Small girl	1	880	B.79
		F		Small girl	1	350	B.79
	Va.	F	10		1	800	B.116
		F	7		35	700	B.116
		F	12		1	725	B.357
		F	9		1	770	B.357
	Mo.	M	5		1	805	B.79
		M	2		1	487	B.79
		F( )	20(3, 4)		1	325	B.79
	La.	F( )	30(3)		2	[2,505]	B.83
		F( )	35(2)		2	[1,610]	B.83
		M	22		3	[1,325]	B.83
	Tex.	5M, 5F	11		10	1,855	B.356
				Prime field hand		716	B.358
1858......	S.C.	M			2	950	P(PSO)
	Ga.	4M, 5F			"Several"	1,350	B.362
					9	1,100	B.362
					7	1,170	B.362
	La.			*of which:*		1,538	B.356
		M	36		1	1,835	B.356
		M	26		1	2,050	B.356
		M	50		1	1,225	B.356
		F	20		1	1,300	B.356

TABLE A—*Continued*

Year	State	Sex	Age	Grade or Condition	No. in Sale	Average Price	Source, Page*
1859	S.C.			Prime field hand		$ 1,100	P(PSQ)
	Ga.			Prime field hand		1,650	P(PSQ)
	Va.	F	10			1,151	B.79
				Mostly children	39	566	B.79
		M	20–26	Number 1	Est.	1,450–1,500	B.117
		M	17–20	Best plough boys	Est.	1,350–1,425	B.117
		M	15–17	Best class	Est.	1,250–1,375	B.117
		M	12–15	Best class	Est.	1,100–1,200	B.117
		F	17–20	Best grown girls	Est.	1,275–1,325	B.117
		F	15–17	Best class	Est.	1,150–1,250	B.117
		F	12–15	Best class	Est.	1,000–1,100	B.117
		F	14	Tolerably tall	1	1,150	B.349
		M		"Enormously high", (price)	1	1,275	B.349
		F		"Enormously high", (price)	1	1,300	B.349
		M	15	"Very high" (price)	1	1,188	B.350
		M	18	"Very high" (price)	1	1,395	B.350
		F	10–16	"Very high" (price)		792–1,275	B.350
		M		Field hand—"should bring more than $2,000 in La. or Texas"	1	1,640	B.351
	S.C.	M	16		1	1,600	B.351
		F	16		1	1,400	B.351
		F( )			4	1,395	B.83
		F( )	10	Excellent houseservant	2	[2,700]	B.83
		F	12		1	[1,300]	B.84
		M			1	765	B.79
				Entire Pimlico stock	235	915	B.79
		F	18	Unsound, excellent cook	1	750	B.183
		F	16	Maid, seamstress	1	910	B.184
		F	14	Likely	1	1,000	B.184
					90	970	B.184
		F( )			2	1,000	B.341
		F( )		Girl	4	[1,900]	B.352
		F			1	[3,000]	B.352
			12 <8	Field hand	1	1,705	B.352
		M	3 >40		36	1,555	B.352
					1	1,000	B.352
		M	40	Common field hand	1	1,630	B.352
		M	21		1	1,795	B.352
		M	10		1	1,605	B.352
		F	10		3	1,150	B.352
					1	1,045	B.352
		M	13–16		2	1,053	B.352
		M	14–38		7	1,540	B.352

TABLE A—*Continued*

Year	State	Sex	Age	Grade or Condition	No. in Sale	Average Price $	Source, Page*
1859......	Ga.	....	....	Three of working age	8	1,250	B.83
					436, *of which:*	716	B.232
			126<10			...	B.232
			182<31			...	B.232
			88<50			...	B.232
			40>50	(Several crippled or superannuated)		...	B.232
					of which:		
		M	....	Carpenter, fair	1	1,750	B.232
		F	....	Cotton hand, houseservant	1	1,250	B.232
		M	24, 21	Prime, young		1,250–1,350	B.232
		3F, 2M	17, 15, 12	......	5	1,205	B.232
	Ala.	M, F		Plain smith and wife	2	[2,900]	B.232
		M		Very high, 12 mo. credit w/o interest	126	1,084	B.341
					1	1,859	B.351
		M	32	...	3	1,800	B.351
		M	30	...	1	1,300	B.299
		M	22	...	1	1,290	B.299
		M	19	...	1	1,605	B.299
		F	18, 18, 8	...	3	1,635	B.299
		M	12	...	2	1,193	B.299
		F	8	...	1	1,305	B.299
		M	14	...	1	800	B.299
		F	33	...	1	1,050	B.299
		F, 4M	35, 32, 11, 9, 7	...	1	920	B.299
		M	13	...	5	[5,220]	B.299
		F	28, 8, 6, 4	...	2	1,000	B.299
		F	15	...	4	[2,328]	B.299
		F	30–38	...	1	1,200	B.299
		M		Field hands and children	Several	900–1,500	B.299
					4	1,400	B.299
					Thigpen estate	1,309	B.356
	Tenn.	....	15	...	6	1,140	B.357
	La.	M		No infants. Sugar estate	55	1,000	B.341
	Tex.	M		Prime field (in above)		1,500	B.341
		M	38	Blacksmith	1	2,000	B.356
		F	14	...	1	1,308	B.358
		M	17	...	1	1,403	B.358
		F	12	...	1	1,527	B.358
		M	12	...	1	1,255	B.358
		M	8	...	1	1,155	B.358
				...	1	1,007	B.358

TABLE A—Continued

Year	State	Sex	Age	Grade or Condition	No. in Sale	Average Price $	Source, Page*
1859.......	Tex.	....	28	....	1	1,500	B.358
		....	26	....	1	1,650	B.358
		....	18	....	1	1,800	B.358
		....	9	....	1	1,056	B.358
		....	7	....	1	1,005	B.358
		....	13	....	1	1,005	B.358
1860.......	S.C.	....	.....	Prime field hand	......	1,200	P(PSQ)
	Ga.	....	.....	Prime field hand	......	1,800	P(PSQ)
	S.C.	F	14	Wench	1	970	B.84
		F( )	30( )	Houseservant, children	4	[2,200]	B.84
		F( )	18( )	With infant	2	[1,160]	B.84
		F( )	25(2, 4)		3	[1,470]	B.84
		F	17	Wench	1	1,400	B.84
		F	18	Wench	1	1,165	B.84
		F( )	20( )		2	[1,180]	B.84
		....	.....	Very prime	30	750	B.185
		....	.....		72	665	B.185
		....	.....	Sea Island cotton hands	34	703	B.188
		M	21	Sea Island cotton hands	20	795	B.188
		F	.....		1	1,205	B.188
		M	.....	Disabled	1	485	B.188
		F( )	18	Prime	2	1,325	B.188
			(7 mos.)	Likely	2	[1,160]	B.195
		F	9		1	700	B.195
		4F, 5M	1–40		68	586	B.205
		M	.....	Prime (5 under 10)	9	450	B.220
		M	8	Carpenter	1	3,500–4,000	B.353
	N.C.	M	12		5	600	B.357
	Tenn.	M	7		1	800	B.211
		M	4		1	400	B.211
	Ga.	M	21		1	300	B.211
		F( )	17 (9 mos.)	Best field hand	1	1,900	P(Doc. II).73
		F( )	18(3)		2	[2,150]	P(Doc. II).73
		F( )	30(6)( )		2	[2,500]	P(Doc. II).73
					4	[4,525]	P(Doc. II).73
				Far from prime	140	625	B.224
					536	1,025	B.354
					of which:		
		F	17		1	1,800	B.354
		M	20		1	1,800	B.354
		M	30	Field hand	1	2,005	B.354
		M	.....		Several	2,000	B.354

TABLE A—*Continued*

Year	State	Sex	Age	Grade or Condition	No. in Sale	Average Price $	Source, Page*
1860......	Ga.	M,F( ) 25 F and 10 children	......	Railway builders	3	[4,500]	B.354
					108	1,364	B.355
		60 F and children	......	Ordinary	81	1,100	B.355
		F	11		1	1,465	B.355
		F	11		1	1,385	B.355
		......	......		20	919	B.355
					of which:		
		......	......	(Excluding 5, old and children)	15	1,128	B.355
		......	......		Estate sale	1,148	B.355
	Fla.	......	3–50	Trader's purchase	53	834	B.223
	Miss.	M	......	No. 1 field hands	Est.	1,600–1,650	B.309
		F	......	No. 1 field hands	Est.	1,400–1,500	B.309
		......	......		17	1,200	B.357
	Ala.	......	......	High, but for 12 mo. credit	33	1,145	B.84
					of which:		
		M,F	4<6	......	6	[5,200]	B.84
		F( )	......	......	3	[2,600]	B.84
	Tex.	M	18	......	1	2,045	B.84
		F	21	......	1	2,015	B.358
		M	15	......	1	1,635	B.358
		M,F	10–12	......	1	1,236	B.358
		M,F	6, 3	......	2	500	B.358
		M	35	......	1	2,206	B.358

NOTES

Square brackets indicate total sale price rather than average price and have been used where the age range is extremely wide.

Parentheses have been used to indicate children sold with their mothers.

"Est." is used to indicate estimates of going prices in a market.

Where no entry is given under "No. in Sale," the average has been reported without indication of the size of the market or the number of observations. The Charleston and Middle Georgia averages, taken from U. B. Phillips, "The Slave Labor Problem in the Charleston District," *Political Science Quarterly*, XXII, No. 3 (1907), 436, and given as the first entry in almost all the reported years, are given without indication of number.

The grade or condition or other comment on the sale or valuation has been quoted in the language of the original report whenever possible.

A COMMENT BY DOUGLAS F. DOWD

Messrs. Conrad and Meyer have undertaken to re-examine the question of the economics of slavery in the antebellum South "and on the basis of the computation of the returns to capital in [their] model of the antebellum southern economy and the demonstration of the efficiency of regional specialization" to draw conclusions about the profitability of slavery, the viability of the slave system, the importance of slavery to the southern economic system (as measured by "the interest of the Old South in secession"), and the relationship of slavery to the economic development of the South. In varying degrees, I find myself at odds with their conclusions on all these matters, but my differences are sharpest with their views on the relationship between slavery and economic development, and it is this question that I shall emphasize here. My disagreements are both methodological and substantive.

The authors have undertaken a careful, useful, and imaginative ordering of the facts relevant to the profitability of slavery in the antebellum South. Had they stopped there, I should have no comment to make. But they also direct their attention, however briefly, to the broader implications of slavery. Brief though their qualitative conclusions may be, I am disturbed lest they go unchallenged. My essential criticisms are (1) that the breadth of their conclusions is not supported by the narrowness of their investigation and (2) that their conclusions concerning slavery and economic development are wrong.

There is every reason to welcome an attempt such as theirs—an attempt by the economist to explore the past to shed light on current questions. But, when he does so, the economist must also recognize that he is then wandering through a forest, not, as in conventional economics, exam-

93

ining a potted plant. This is particularly true when examining the nature and impact of as complex an institution as
slavery in America. There is every reason why contemporary
economists should be vitally concerned with questions of
economic development, for there are of course many questions involved in economic development programs which only
economists can answer. But this does not mean that the historical process of economic development—or of stagnation—
can be explained solely or even primarily in economic terms,
that economic institutions and processes are the outcome of or
have their impact solely or even primarily upon economic
affairs; it does not mean that one can meaningfully separate
out the "social" from the "economic" meaning of a particular
institution, for the "two" are in a continuous state of interaction. This is clearly true of slavery in the South, and my objection to the Conrad-Meyer position is that they do not seem
to have recognized it.

The authors contend that "the available productive surplus from slavery might have been used for economic development or, as in totalitarian regimes in this century, for
militarism. In spite of this good omen for development, southern investment and industrialization lagged. It is hard to explain this except on the social ground that entrepreneurship
could not take root in the South or on the economic ground
that the South did not really own the system but merely
operated it." It was not only entrepreneurship that could not
take root in the South; it was the basic elements of a capitalist society that could not take root. I do not think I am
alone in believing that slavery and all that it entailed was
fundamental in inhibiting industrial capitalism—and economic growth—in the South.[25] Whether slavery is looked upon
as a "social" or as an "economic" institution is, for present
purposes, irrelevant. The "available productive surplus from
slavery" could not exist apart from the social milieu required
for the maintenance of slavery. If profits were made from the

slave system, it was at a price: the domination of southern society by the slave issue. This in turn meant the suppression of that kind of social rationality which has been, for better or for worse, associated with the development of industrial capitalism.

Conrad and Meyer have read widely in the literature of slavery, and they must surely be aware of the pervasive impact of such an institution on the society in which it exists. This was certainly true of ancient Greece and Rome. It was true a fortiori of the antebellum South, because the institution of slavery was then, in the Western world, an anachronism. The authors argue as though slavery were merely another, more manipulable, form of labor; as though it were, one might say, institutionally neutral. And, working essentially within the methodology of neoclassical economics (with time allowed in occasionally), they have analyzed the "economic" meaning of slavery as though they were analyzing the representative firm in the long run (or even, at times, in the short run).

The authors' argument may be reduced to this: *either* slavery was profitable *or* it was a deterrent to economic development. My contention is that it was a deterrent to economic growth despite the fact of its profitability. The point may perhaps be made by asking a question: When Indian economic planners estimate that a proposed project will be profitable, do they thereupon assume that it will contribute to the economic development of India? In short, "economics" should be concerned with more than profitability, particularly short-run profitability.

Apparently impounded in *ceteris paribus* are what I have long thought were some accepted implications of slavery in the South: (1) an economy of (virtually) no markets, based as it was on a labor force isolated from the system of exchange, "paid" little and in kind if Negro, dominantly self-sufficient if white; (2) a society whose consumption-savings

standards were seigneurial, with implications for both capital accumulation and persistent indebtedness; (3) a society
whose notions of status elevated the aristocratic agrarian and
denigrated the mercantile-industrial pursuits.

There was nothing "irrational" or controversial about the
introduction of slavery in Colonial America. Nor was there
anything irrational about its continuation and expansion after
the cotton gin. But slavery had, by then, become a matter of
heated debate, even and perhaps particularly in the South.
Southern society up until about 1820 had not yet hardened into
the Cotton Kingdom; the economy was still relatively diversi-
fied (more so than during the rest of the century), and the
society was still relatively fluid. During and after the twenties,
cotton became king, and slavery became the *sine qua non* of
the economic well-being of the South as a region. But the
economic well-being of the South must be defined as having
meaning for a small percentage of the southern population.
A society whose wealth is derived from plantation economy
does not tend, as does an industrial society, to push its prosperity down through all layers of the population (albeit, in
the latter case, in waves of diminishing force). If southern
society was to be firmly cemented to the institution of slavery
and a plantation economy, an ideology had to be developed
to buttress that which was materially inimical to the well-
being of the mass of the people. That is, an essentially irrational ideology had to dominate the mind of the South (in
Cash's apt phrase), or the Old South would be destroyed by
internal and external pressures.

But taking the United States in the early nineteenth century, with all that connotes in terms of social, political, religious, and economic institutions and attitudes—a belief in
social mobility and human rights, political democracy, the
Christian ethic, economic individualism, and so on—what did
the American in the South have to "do" with his mentality,
his beliefs, his conscience, his behavior (to mention only

these) in order to allow, let alone enforce, the enslavement of human beings? All this, in a world which was self-consciously giving up the institution; in a nation which was leading the rest of the world in the development of democratic institutions and demonstrating the productive power (for that time and place, at least) of economic individualism; in a section which yielded to none in its expressed dedication to the word of God and the rights of man. For the southerner to convert himself to beliefs and behavior which would support and comport with slavery required a concentration so intense that all else became secondary—including the process of capital accumulation. Does economic development take place when economic questions are in the realm of the afterthought?

Who would be inclined to use the term "capitalist" to describe the owners of southern wealth? Apart from a William Gregg here and there, southern capital was *planter* capital. Planters were of course interested in profits; so were medieval "businessmen" (as jarring a term as "southern capitalists"). But neither group approached the question of capital accumulation in the sense in which the northern manufacturer did. In the South, slaves were never *just*, or even most importantly, capital, any more than a Cadillac car is just, or even most importantly, transportation to the modern American. This was true because slaves *were* slaves, a fact of such enormity in America at that time that it could be accommodated only by dedicating southern society to its perpetuation. And this meant that economic development was relegated to the back of the mind of the southerner, big or small.

If all this sounds too vague, perhaps too psychological or even metaphysical, it is partly because the requisite elaboration and specification would go beyond the limits of a "comment"; but it is partly because the process of economic development does not appear to be reducible to the neat categories of conventional economics.

REPLY BY THE AUTHORS

It would be extremely difficult for us to find any grounds for disagreement with Mr. Dowd when he argues that the economic meaning of slavery is not simply a problem in Marshallian long-run equilibrium. Nor will we take issue with his insistence that one must consider the interrelations between the "social" and the "economic" in the process of economic development. We would not agree with Dowd in all particulars, but we readily grant that these are issues worthy of consideration. However, these were not the issues we were considering. We were testing hypotheses about the profitability of slavery and the efficiency of the slave labor market. The brief discussion of slavery's relationship to development was clearly limited to two economic assertions that are frequently offered as explanations for the failure of development in the South. Dowd may feel that our definition of economics is too strict. But he should not, on that ground, reread the hypotheses and conclusions in the light of what he thinks ought to be tested.

Dowd's reduction of our argument is this: "*either* slavery was a deterrent to economic development *or* it was profitable." That statement is difficult for us to recognize and impossible for us to accept. We did not set up any simple dichotomy between deterrents to development and profitability. We were explicitly testing the hypothesis that slavery in the South must have fallen before very long *because* it was unprofitable. It was profitable—at least as profitable as most other enterprises of the time in the United States. Our demonstration of that fact means that the imminent demise of slavery in the antebellum South must be argued on grounds other than unprofitability from now on. With respect to economic development, we argue simply that there were profits available for accumulation, that there was an efficient market for allocating resources—including labor—and that the failure of entrepreneurship requires a more complicated explanation than our simple model was intended to offer. That profits were not effectively used for development in the South may be a question for psychology or even metaphysics. Many planters apparently chose to spend the returns on consumption rather than investment; it is to this observation that Dowd mainly devotes his remarks. As we said, we consider this problem to be interesting but "beyond the scope" of our immediate concern, which was simply to point out that the failure of southern development can no longer be explained by assertions of the unprofitability of slavery or the inefficiency of the slave labor market.

(Neither this *Reply* nor the *Reply* to John Moes, below, has been revised since the discussion originally appeared in the *Journal of Political Economy*. We have now, however, added to our earlier statement on the effects of slavery upon southern development in chapter 6, "A Polemical Postscript on Economic Growth.")

A COMMENT BY JOHN E. MOES

This comment takes issue with Messrs. Conrad and Meyer's statement that "*economic forces* may often work toward the continuation of a slave system." Historic evidence is generally contrary to this assertion, except insofar as the slave supply can be cheaply replenished from external sources.

The authors mention the case of Rome, where slavery declined when the Pax Romana was established and the major external sources of slave supply had dried up. But they are wrong in saying that slavery in Rome declined because the slave population could not reproduce itself. Slavery in Rome declined as a result of widespread manumission. Profitable deals could be made with the slave or with the freedman, who could be and usually was obligated to render services to his former master. A freedman often continued in the same employment or else was set up in business with funds supplied by the master, or, on the land, was given part of the estate to work as a tenant. Hence the slave in fact bought his own freedom, either by being given the opportunity to accumulate savings of his own, the "peculium," or afterward as a freedman, having received his freedom, so to speak, on credit. This system was to the advantage of the owner because it gave the slave an incentive to work well and in general to make himself agreeable to his master. Thus, while the owner did not (immediately) appropriate the entire surplus that the slave earned over and above the cost of his maintenance, he still got greater economic benefits in the long run.[26] And it should be emphasized that this occurred in a period in which slave prices were rising.[27] Therefore we should be leery of the notion that economic considerations are contrary to voluntary emancipation when slave prices are high and on the increase. Rather, the opposite is true: the most highly valued slaves were the most likely to be freed, for the full benefit of their talents could be obtained not under the whiplash but only by giving them the positive incentive of immediate or ultimate freedom. And, if this is so, the idea that slavery is profitable (and therefore likely to be maintained) when slave prices are high does not stand up against the modern notion of opportunity cost but is the result of overlooking the most relevant alternative opportunity: that of allowing the slave to buy himself. No doubt slaves would have been less valuable in Rome if this opportunity had not existed. Without freedom in the offing the slave could be made to produce more than his keep and hence would have commanded a price representing the capitalized value of these surplus earnings, but this would have been less than he was able and willing to pay for his own person. In a cynical vein we could say that, as a rule, the slave was able to outbid anyone else because he had a sentimental attachment to his person.

It is true that slaves in Rome were often highly skilled, and the discrepancy between a person's productivity when free and when a slave may be greater in such a case than if the person is an unskilled laborer required to perform routine operations. However, free labor largely replaced slave labor in Rome not only among the skilled occupations but also on the large estates. During the late Republic these "latifundia" were worked by slave gangs, but in imperial times, when the large influx of captive slaves ceased and slave prices rose, they were converted into conglomerations of free tenant holdings.[28]

This is not to suggest that in the South slavery was disappearing or would inevitably have disappeared in due time as a result of manumission by self-purchase. Self-purchase of slaves in the antebellum period was not a movement of quantitative significance relative to the natural increase of the slave population—that much should be made clear at the outset of any discussion of the subject. I shall offer a tentative explanation of this fact later, but first we should gain an impression of the phenomenon as it occurred in the American setting.

Most cases of self-purchase occurred in urban areas, where certain industrial plants that owned or hired slaves, for instance the Tredegar Iron Works in Richmond, recognized the advantage of giving the slave the incentive of eventual liberty and operated in such a way "as to encourage slaves who wished to buy their freedom."[29] Slaves were sometimes hired out by their masters against a stipulated rent, and employers made it a practice to pay the slave for extra work or satisfactory performance so that he was able to accumulate savings and, if his master agreed, purchase his freedom. One tobacco manufacturer said that in his plant almost every slave made at least $5.00 a month for himself, while some made up to $28.00.[30] In other factories skilled workers might receive even more: Emmanuel Quivers, a foreman at the Tredegar Iron Works, was paid $1.25 a day, enabling him to purchase himself, his wife, and four children within four years.[31] There was, moreover, a practice of hiring out slaves to themselves. This was done in the case of artisans who could not be supervised when plying their trade. The practice persisted in spite of the fact that white laborers who resented the competition of the Negro, whether slave or free, everywhere succeeded in having laws enacted to prevent it. A contemporary newspaper article in Athens, Georgia, says: "Everyone who is at all acquainted with the character of the slave race knows that they have great ideas of liberty, and in order to get the enjoyment of it *they make large offers for their time*" (italics mine). Since self-hire enabled the slave to accumulate savings, self-purchase might be the result if the master was willing to co-operate.[32] One master even permitted his slave to go to California to mine gold, from where the slave soon sent back $1,500 to pay for his freedom. There are also instances of slaves being given their freedom on credit. Alexander Hays, who had been bought by his master for $300, paid $550 plus interest after seven years of freedom.[33]

On plantations, also, slaves were sometimes given the opportunity to buy themselves: a Mississippi planter arranged a plan whereby his slaves could do so on installments.[34] Outstanding among the examples Phillips cites is the case of John McDonogh, a well-known philanthropist, and, at the same time, a very thrifty man,[35] who concluded a collective agreement with his entire slave force under which they were to earn their freedom and passage to Liberia. The slaves were given the Saturday afternoon to work for themselves, and they were enabled to purchase more of their time as they accumulated savings, until it was all their own. The plan was carried out according to schedule, and in 1842 some eighty slaves sailed for Liberia, followed by more later.[36] This action earned McDonogh the gratitude of his slaves as well as a great deal of extra income that he could not have obtained in any other way. Writing of his experience, he says:

> I will further observe that since the day on which I made the agreement with them (notwithstanding they had at all times previous thereto been well-disposed and orderly people), an entire change appeared to come over them; they were apparently no longer the same people; a sedateness, a care, an economy, an industry, took possession of them to which there seemed to be no bounds but in their physical strength. . . . The result of my experiment, in a pecuniary point of of view, is not one of the least surprising of its features, and is this: that in the space of about sixteen years which these people served me, since making the agreement with them they have gained for me, in addition to performing more and better labor than slaves ordinarily perform in the usual time of laboring, a sum of money (including the sum they appear to have paid me in the purchase of their time) which will enable me to go to Virginia or Carolina and purchase double the number of those I sent away.[37]

These individual instances of manumission by self-purchase in the South suggest that the liberation of slaves was as profitable to those owners who seized the opportunity as it had been in Rome, where this type of manumission became so general that slavery virtually disappeared when external supplies dried up as a result of peaceful conditions. And yet, although there were thousands of cases,[38] self-purchase by slaves in the South remained a very minor affair relative to the size of the slave force and its natural increase. To give an explanation of this is difficult and leads outside the realm of an economist's special competence, but some suggestions may be attempted. Racial prejudice and concern with white supremacy undoubtedly were basic underlying factors. The fact that masters and slaves belonged to different races and that the race of the slaves was considered inferior was an element in the American situation that was largely absent in antiquity, and it may be taken as a starting point for our considerations.

Free Negroes were looked upon as a most undesirable element in the population. Harsh political measures were adopted in every slave state to perpetuate slavery and to rid the individual states of newly freed Negroes: laws restricting the freedom of the masters to manumit their slaves and laws requiring that manumitted slaves be removed from the state in which they had been freed.[39] In the 1850's this legislation culminated in the absolute prohibition of manumission in Louisiana, Arkansas, and Maryland. Moreover, it is well known that everywhere free Negroes were in a very precarious legal and social situation: they might be subjected to all kinds of harassment and lived in constant danger of losing their liberty.[40]

If they had been rigorously enforced, these laws alone would be sufficient to explain the low rate of manumission in the antebellum South. However, exemptions from their provisions were sometimes granted by the state legislatures, and in some cases the laws were openly ignored. In addition, the device of benevolent Negro slaveholding developed under which a slave who wished to purchase his freedom gave the money to a free Negro he trusted, who then nominally held him as a slave.[41] Thus the laws that tended to restrict manumission were not in their effect absolutely prohibitive, but they were not innocuous either. The adoption of such a precarious device as benevolent slaveholding, which not only made a person completely dependent upon the good will and honesty of someone else but could lead to serious legal complications (especially in the case of inheritance, since slaves could not legally own property and hence not inherit), is evidence that the antimanumission laws did in many instances constitute a serious hindrance to the realization of a slave's liberty.

In addition to racial prejudice and the resistance among white laborers to Negro competition, there was a strong reaction against the agitation of northern abolitionists, which in later years led the South to acclaim slavery as something positively virtuous. It may be thought that under such circumstances the pressure of public opinion would effectively prevent any freeing of Negro slaves by making manumission unprofitable in real terms to the slaveowner (because of unfavorable repercussions on his business, his career, his social life, etc.); in addition the attitude toward free Negroes might reduce the attractiveness of freedom to a slave. Migration to Liberia might be a solution in some cases, but it can hardly be imagined that all slaves were interested in going there unless perhaps they could go in a large group that included all their friends and relatives. Few slaveowners were as systematic as McDonogh or owned as many slaves as he did, so there were few slaves who had this opportunity. We must therefore conclude that these considerations are relevant, but at the same time we must guard against attaching an exaggerated importance to them. For, while free Negroes did not have a very enviable status, they were, on the whole, tolerated and sometimes even achieved considerable success in their occupations or in business, compelling the esteem of their white co-citizens. Conditions varied widely among places and individuals (there are instances of free Negroes voluntarily seeking slave status to be safeguarded against the tribulations they were subject to when free);[42] there is, naturally, no way of estimating the importance of the preventive effect of the fear of social disapprobation. On the other hand, there are few indications that the manumissions actually consummated led to unfavorable repercussions for master or slave,[43] and, as we have seen, the "slave race" continued to entertain great ideas of liberty.[44] It appears, therefore, that many slaveowners refrained from freeing their slaves, not so much because of outward circumstances or because it would not have been profitable to do so, but because they themselves did not approve of such action or simply did not see the opportunity of financial gain that it offered. Their thinking was conditioned by the intellectual climate of their environment, and in such a climate it probably took uncommon perception to see a profitable opportunity in the freeing of one's slaves. To the average slaveowner it must have appeared that there were no good reasons for such action other than in the case of blood relationship, faithful service rendered, etc.

The relative inefficiency of the slave without the prospect of freedom[45] would have become more marked with the progress of time as a result of the greater diversification of the southern economy in agriculture and industry, for it is generally granted that the slave did best in the cultivation of staple crops with its repetitive routine operations. The production of these crops has, of course, declined in relative importance, and hence it would have become necessary to employ more slaves in occupations requiring initiative and positive co-operation. We have seen that where such conditions were present in the antebellum period, notably in the towns and in industry, there already existed an unmistakable awareness of the advantage of making arrangements that gave the slave considerable freedom. However, it is by no means certain that voluntary manumission could have gone very far without eliciting increasing opposition, perhaps leading to violence. Which side would then have gained the upper hand is a moot question. In this context it is interesting to note that in Rome also there was resistance to the manumission of slaves and that laws were enacted tending to restrict

the practice. But the feeling was probably not so strong, because racially the slaves were hardly distinctive.

REPLY BY THE AUTHORS

Professor Moes raises an interesting but somewhat peri-
pheral issue relating to our original discussion of the economics of slavery in the American South. Our main concern
was to test the hypothesis that slavery *as it existed* in the
antebellum American South was profitable according to the
private-enterprise standards of the period. We asserted that
slavery in the antebellum South was economically viable and
that this was a sufficient, though not a necessary, condition
for its continuation as a private enterprise.

Moes is concerned with a somewhat different hypothesis.
He is arguing that, if the slaveowners of the American South
had been "true" profit maximizers, they would have turned
to a reorganization of the slave market, which would have
had as a direct consequence the disappearance of slavery
without civil war. The reorganization with which he is concerned is a policy of widespread voluntary manumission. The
possibility of self-purchase, he believes, would have led to
such an increase in the productivity of the slave labor force
that enough extra income would have been generated to com-
pensate the planter class for the loss of property rights in
slaves without leaving the ex-slaves, in terms of their lifetime total of psychic and material income, any worse off than
they were under slavery. The increase in productivity would
be great enough, moreover, to extend the likelihood of self-
purchase beyond slaves of special skills and ability. In short,

Moes believes that, once the benefits of manumission had begun to be realized, the increased productivity would have created a surplus more than sufficient to eliminate the American slave system.

This is clearly an empirical question—an empirical question, moreover, about which neither we nor Moes now have sufficient information to say anything definitive. For example, early in his paper Moes claims that we are wrong in our interpretation of the decline of slavery during the Pax Romana. In his view, it was not the drying-up of the external sources of supply, as we claimed, but widespread manumission that caused the decline. He gives no specific source to support this assertion of our error; checking his references, all of them familiar sources on ancient slavery, we found no strong evidence to convince us that we should change our assertion. Indeed, Westermann (p. 120) lists the cessation of war as first among his causes for the decline of slavery and adds manumission, which had constantly occurred, with some later suggestions for the gradualness of the decline.

It is pertinent to the empirical issue, moreover, that we could find little evidence that Negro slave productivity in the antebellum South was markedly inferior to that of freedmen or free white labor. If a marked inferiority had existed, then substantial increases in slave productivity would have seemed more possible or readily attainable.

Of course, slaves striving for freedom might be more productive than free men, who must work without such "special" incentives. That is the point underlying Moes's argument that voluntary manumission was the most relevant alternative to slavery, in the opportunity cost sense. Let us examine that point briefly.

First, with the exception of the slave property of a thrifty philanthropist, the examples offered by Moes refer to artisans, generally in urban pursuits. But the slave system, as Moes recognizes, was built upon a staple-crop plantation agriculture. His examples recall to us an interesting fact about ancient slavery. Duff (p. 15) gives as a reason for the greater occurrence of manumission in Rome than in Greece that slaves in Greece were not often superior to their masters in culture or talent and therefore did not have the same opportunities to earn their purchase price or win their masters' favors as in Rome. The American situation was probably closer to the Greek than to the Roman in this respect.

A second limit to the economic prospects for manumission was the high return realized on slave-breeding in the South. The slave woman seeking freedom would have had to be sufficiently more productive to buy the residual value of both her field labor and breeding activities. It is somewhat easier to visualize how productivity might have been increased in field or factory activities than in childbearing. Since breeding returns often constituted a large proportion of the value of a prime field wench, prospective freedom would have had to be a very effective incentive.

This leads to one final comment on the pertinence of the Roman experience. In essence, Moes argues that the Romans, by recognizing the possibilities in manumission, showed greater imagination and entrepreneurship in conducting their slave business than did the antebellum southerner. Perhaps, though, this argument could be reversed. Roman civilization may have been incapable of visualizing or, if capable, unwilling to accept the rich potentials in the slave trade, and this led them, as a sort of second-best opportunity, to use manumission as a method of increasing the returns on slave enterprises. Why they made this choice gets us into areas of institutional and sociological study in which our competence as economists will not support us.

NOTES TO CHAPTER 3

1. A more thorough presentation of these methodological views was given in Chapter 1.

2. Computation of present value in this way is preferable to the usual accounting procedure of recording net profit rates on total plantation investment in slaves, land, and durable equipment because of the reproductive character and the limited durability of slave investments. Clearly, the same characteristics do not apply to nondepreciable investments in land. A nondepreciable investment in agricultural land is, however, quite rare.

3. Charles S. Sydnor, "Life Span of Mississippi Slaves," *American Historical Review*, XXXV (April, 1930), 556–74.

4. L. I. Dublin, A. J. Lotka, and M. Spiegelman, *Length of Life* (New York: Ronald Press Co., 1949), p. 51. It is worth noting that there is general agreement that labor on the rice and sugar plantations was sufficiently more arduous to reduce Negro longevity in such locations. Therefore the Louisiana estimates are probably inordinately pessimistic, and the Maryland figures are better estimates of conditions prevailing on the cotton plantations. This, in turn, means that the thirty- to thirty-five-year estimates used below are, if anything, a little conservative or too low.

5. In confirmation of these figures, Lance E. Davis, who is now completing a study of New England financial intermediaries (the essentials of which can be found in his Ph.D. dissertation on deposit in the Johns Hopkins University Library), reports that these New England firms consistently realized less than 6 per cent on three-signature prime commercial paper in the period before 1840; from 1840 to 1860, however, almost all loans were made at 6 per cent, which was the legal maximum under Massachusetts usury laws. He estimates that these intermediaries realized an over-all return of between 6 and 7 per cent in the period 1840–60 on their total investment: 6 per cent on the debt and 7–8 per cent on equity.

6. Lance E. Davis, "Sources of Industrial Finance: The American Textile Industry," *Explorations in Entrepreneurial History*, IX (April, 1957), 201. The figures are based on the companies' financial records to be found at the Baker Library of the Harvard Graduate School of Business Administration.

7. These three secondary sources carefully and consistently record the estimates available from three basic types of primary material. Gray's *History of Agriculture in the Southern United States to 1860* (Washington, D.C., 1933), esp. pp. 529–67, covers the cost estimates intermittently reported in the principal agricultural and business journals read by the planters and traders: *DeBow's Review, Farmers' Register, Farmer and Planter, Southern Planter, Southern Agriculturist,* and

Hunt's Merchants' Magazine. Watkins' The Cost of Cotton Production
(U.S. Department of Agriculture, Miscellaneous Series, Bull. 16 [Wash-
ington, D.C., 1899]) includes the estimates recorded in the Patent Office and the Commissioner of Patents' Annual Reports, especially for
the years 1844, 1849, 1850, 1852, 1854, and 1855. Stampp's The Peculiar Institution (New York, 1956), esp. chaps. vi, vii, and ix, reports the
estimates available from diaries and individual plantation records still
in existence.

8. No allowance has been made in these computations for the expenses of maintaining slaves in their dotage. This does not appear
to be a serious omission. Generally speaking, slaves were considered
to be virtually fully productive in field labor until reaching their fifty-fifth
year—which corresponds to the average life-expectancy on the purchase
of a twenty-year-old slave. Furthermore; the direct out-of-pocket costs
of simply maintaining a slave were only $10–$15, figures considerably
below productive value in field work. Given the possibility of specialized
use of older labor in such occupations as gardening, nursery operations,
and supervision, it seems doubtful that many slaves lived long enough
to be economic drains on current account.

9. A purist might ask how different returns can be realized in what
is ostensibly the same type of economic activity in a relatively competitive industry. The question overlooks the fact that it took a much larger
initial outlay to attain productive situations like those in cases 10–12.
This is all the more true, since the capital outlay in these cases would
be concentrated at the start of the undertaking, while in cases 7–9 some
of the outlay would be delayed ten or fifteen years until the land lost
fertility.

10. (i) J. E. Cairnes, The Slave Power (New York: Follett Foster
& Co., 1863), pp. 44–50; F. L. Olmsted, The Cotton Kingdom (New York:
Mason Bros., 1861), pp. 100–110 (1953 ed.; New York: A. A. Knopf);
W. A. Lewis, Theory of Economic Growth (Homewood, Ill.: Richard
D. Irwin, Inc., 1955), pp. 107–8; (ii) U. B. Phillips, Life and Labor in
the Old South (Boston: Little, Brown & Co., 1935), pp. 174–75; (iii)
U. B. Phillips, "The Economic Cost of Slaveholding in the Cotton-Belt,"
Political Science Quarterly, XX (1905), 257–75; (iv) Lewis, op. cit.,
pp. 111–13; (v) J. S. Duesenberry, "Some Aspects of the Theory of
Economic Development," Explorations in Entrepreneurial History, III
(1950), 9. This is, of course, intended only as a list of examples, chosen
on the grounds that they are particularly well stated.

11. M. B. Hammond, The Cotton Industry (New York, 1897), p.
82. See also United States Patent Office Report (Agriculture), 1852
(Washington, D.C., 1853), p. 374.

12. See Bureau of the Census, Negro Population in the United
States, 1790–1915 (Washington, D.C., 1918); Gray, op. cit., chap.
xxviii; Cairnes, op. cit., chap. iv; E. Halle, Baumwollproduktion und
Pflanzungswirtschaft (Leipzig, 1897), Vol. I, Book III, 5.3.

13. W. H. Collins, The Domestic Slave Trade of the Southern States
(New York, 1904), chap. iii. In the first decade the selling states include
Virginia, Maryland, Delaware, North Carolina, Kentucky, and the Dis-
trict of Columbia; the buying states are assumed to be South Carolina,
Georgia, Alabama, Mississippi, Tennessee, and Missouri. In 1830, Florida
and, in 1850, Texas were added to the buying group. Tennessee, Mis-

souri, and North Carolina are very uncertain assignments, since these states were far from homogeneous slave-marketing areas; some parts imported, while other parts exported, during the period (cf. Halle, *op. cit.*, pp. 282 ff., and Frederic Bancroft, *Slave Trading in the Old South* [Baltimore: J. H. Furst, 1931], chap. xviii, for similar estimates, consistent with those given by Collins).

14. Quoted in *Slavery and the Internal Slave Trade in the United States of North America* (London, 1841) (by the Executive Committee of the American Anti-Slavery Society), p. 13. On the same page the authors assert that four-fifths or more of the slaves brought into the buying states were supplied by the internal slave trade.

15. Edmund Ruffin, *DeBow's Review*, XXVI (1859), 650.

16. Bancroft, *op. cit.*, p. 398.

17. The rates are quoted in Hammond, *op. cit.*, p. 90, from *Report of the Commissioner of Agriculture, 1866* (Washington, D.C., 1867), p. 416. Three Virginia newspaper quotations in G. M. Weston, *Who Are and Who May Be Slaves in the United States* (undated pamphlet), give ratios ranging between 2 and 2.5, supporting Hammond's estimate. There is a possible overestimate in these ratios, if they are to be used to infer relative usefulness in the field, since some allowance was probably made for time lost for delivery by pregnant females. No evidence has been found on this point, however.

18. With one exception—the South Carolina, 1860, comparison—the pairings are taken from single sales. In addition, the pairings are made, as far as possible, with slaves of apparently comparable quality. The Virginia and Mississippi quotations are from average-price listings and are probably most useful for present purposes.

19. Phillips, "The Economic Cost of Slaveholding in the Cotton-Belt," *op. cit.*, pp. 271 ff.

20. Duesenberry, *loc. cit.*

21. Gray, *op. cit.*, chap. xxx; *DeBow's Review*, XVIII (1855), 332–34; Hammond, *op. cit.*, pp. 76–77, 113–19; T. P. Kettell, *Southern Wealth and Northern Profits* (New York, 1860), p. 48.

22. Quoted in Phillips, *Life and Labor in the Old South*, p. 180. Having quoted this, Phillips, without offering any evidence, asserts: "But surely a peak was being shaped, whose farther side must have been a steep descent, whether in time of peace or war."

23. See Robert R. Russel, *Economic Aspects of Southern Sectionalism, 1840–1861* (Urbana, Ill., 1924), esp. pp. 54–64, and "Slavery and Southern Economic Progress," *Journal of Southern History*, IV (February, 1938), 34–54. See also Gray *op. cit.*, pp. 458–61, 940–42, and Hammond, *op. cit.*, pp. 40–44, 94–96.

24. Hammond, *op. cit.*, pp. 107–12; Russel, *op. cit.*, pp. 49 ff.; M. B. Hammond, "Agricultural Credit and Crop Mortgages," in *The South in the Building of the Nation* (Richmond, Va., 1909), V, 457–61; Alfred H. Stone, "The Cotton Factorage System of the Southern States," *American Historical Review*, XX (1915), 557–65. For an excellent discussion of the seigneurial impediments to entrepreneurship see W. J. Cash, *The Mind of the South* (New York, 1941), pp. 42–70.

25. Nor was the inhibition confined to the antebellum period. I have argued elsewhere that the role imposed upon the Negro in the postbellum South served as the central factor in keeping the South

underdeveloped up to the modern period. See "A Comparative Analysis of Economic Development in the American West and South," *Journal of Economic History*, XVI (December, 1956), 558 ff.

26. See, for instance, A. M. Duff, *Freedmen in the Early Roman Empire* (Oxford, 1928), especially chaps. i and ii. It may be pointed out here that in the history of slavery the Roman Empire occupies a unique place in that it is the only case in which chattel slavery achieved an economic importance comparable to its importance in the New World. The fact that the relatively minor significance of slavery in other societies usually had nothing to do with ethical considerations does in itself strongly support my contention that slavery is not an efficient economic system. The size of the slave labor force has always been in balance between extensive manumission or excessive mortality, on one side, and fresh outside supplies, on the other. In Greece, for instance, the advantages of manumission were no less realized than in Rome, and the practice was as widespread. According to Westermann, manumission prices were in excess of the usual market prices for slaves. See William L. Westermann, *The Slave Systems of Greek and Roman Antiquity* (Philadelphia, 1955), p. 36. Also Duff, *op. cit.*, p. 14.

27. The recorded slave prices that have survived do not give a conclusive indication of a trend: they are not numerous, individual differences between the slaves were important, and we do not know enough about changes in the price level. Nevertheless, there is general agreement in the literature that during the Empire slaves were more valuable than they were during the heyday of slavery in the time of the Republic, an opinion that is based upon evidence indicating that in the later period slaves were regarded as valuable assets, and treated accordingly, whereas under the Republic they were recklessly exploited. See, for instance, Westermann, *op. cit.*, pp. 72, 76–77, and R. H. Barrow, *Slavery in the Roman Empire* (London, 1928), pp. 54, 83. Barrow contains a list of references to passages dealing with slavery by ancient authors.

28. See, e.g., Barrow, *op. cit.*, pp. 89–90; Tenney Frank, *An Economic History of Rome* (2d ed.; Baltimore, 1927), pp. 327, 436–39; Duff, *op. cit.*, pp. 93, 199. To avoid misunderstanding, it may be pointed out that, while slavery during the prolonged period of peaceful and orderly conditions of the early empire became economically insignificant, it never disappeared completely. Later, when the Empire began to crumble and border warfare was resumed on a large scale, it became more important again, and the remnants of this late Roman slavery were carried over into early medieval Europe.

29. Sumner Eliot Matison, "Manumission by Purchase," *Journal of Negro History*, XXXIII (April, 1948), 162. This article gives many interesting details regarding the manumission of slaves by self-purchase in the South.

30. *Ibid.*, pp. 161–62.

31. *Ibid.*, pp. 160–61.

32. See U. B. Phillips, *American Negro Slavery* (New York, 1918), pp. 412–14.

33. Matison, *op. cit.*, p. 157.

34. *Ibid.*, p. 162.

35. In his will McDonogh states that from early boyhood his soul

had been filled with a desire to acquire a fortune, which after his death was to be used for the education of the poor. See William Allan, *Life and Work of John McDonogh* (Baltimore, 1886).

36. The details are recorded *ibid.*, chap. iv.

37. *Ibid.*, p. 49.

38. Data upon which a justifiable over-all estimate could be based are not available. Matison gives the following partial figures: out of approximately 12,000 persons sent to Africa by the American Colonization Society, 344 had purchased their own freedom, 5,957 had been given their freedom, and 4,541 had been born free; on the basis of a census in two separate districts in Cincinnati taken in 1835, it was estimated that out of 1,129 persons who had been in slavery 476 had purchased themselves; a poll made among the 18,768 colored people of Philadelphia in 1837 revealed that 250 persons had purchased their own freedom; in two counties of Maryland at least 281 slaves became free by purchase prior to 1826. Benevolent Negro slaveholding, a device explained below, must also be considered, for self-purchase often took this form. See Matison, *op. cit.*, pp. 166–67.

39. See Lewis C. Gray, *History of Agriculture in the Southern United States to 1860* (Washington, 1933), I, 524–26; Matison, *op. cit.*, pp. 146–56.

40. Phillips, *op. cit.*, chap. xxi.

41. Matison, *op. cit.*, pp. 152–53.

42. Phillips, *op.cit.*, pp. 446–47.

43. Gray, however, does cite a case in North Carolina, where, after the Declaration of Independence, many Quakers emancipated their slaves. This led to violent opposition and repressive action by the legislature. See Gray, *op. cit.*, I, 525–26.

44. This is emphasized throughout in Kenneth M. Stampp, *The Peculiar Institution* (New York, 1956).

45. It should perhaps be stressed that, in evaluating a master's opportunity of making financial gain in providing his slaves with the freedom motive, the relevant comparison is not that between the productivity of a free man and a slave but between the productivity of a slave with and without the hope of freedom. It does not seem unreasonable to suppose that such a slave would work harder than a free man ordinarily does. And, of course, a slaveowner interested in maximizing his gain might exact more than the slave's market value, since he held absolute monopoly power in the matter of freedom or bondage.

4

Income Growth and Structural Change:

The United States

in the Nineteenth Century

I. INTRODUCTION

In the late summer of 1773, Dr. Samuel Johnson, oppressed by the foul air of an indifferent Scottish inn, derived in his irritation a remarkably unambiguous definition of economic growth:

> . . . The great mass of nations is neither rich nor gay: they whose aggregate constitutes the people, are found in the streets, and the villages, in the shops and farms; and from them collectively considered, must the measure of general prosperity be taken. As they approach to delicacy a nation is refined, as their conveniences are multiplied, a nation, at least a commercial nation, must be denominated wealthy.[1]

The mass of the English people in 1773 was neither rich nor gay. The first years of the Industrial Revolution did not bring any great change in the rate of improvement of living standards; there may well have been a decline in general prosperity before 1800. Overseas, in the American colonies, although his food would be described in the hindsight of 1885 as "coarse" and his clothing "abominable," the common laborer received a higher daily wage than his British counterpart. At the end of the eighteenth century, the American nonfarm laborer could earn $1 a day, which would buy a 14- or 15-pound turkey or as much "good butcher's meat" as double that wage could buy in London. In the humblest houses there were no meals without meat, although it was probably salt meat, and there was always butter or cheese for the bread. It is from this benchmark that the "approach to delicacy" must be described. More than description, however, the aim of this chapter is to give an explanation of the rate of change.[2]

The transformation of the American economy that took place during the nineteenth century was great enough to loom large in even the most impressionistic account of the period. But impressionism in economic history is not explanation. We know why salt meat, which would have seemed a daily luxury to the British laborer, seems coarse today. Economic history ought to tell us more than that, however; we should be able to say how we have approached this level of consumption. With the mass of data that has been turned out as a by-product of the industrial system and the flood of theories by which we try to explain ourselves, we ought to be able to describe more convincingly, if less colorfully than earlier historians, the process by which the conveniences of the American people were multiplied in the last century and a half. This chapter will attempt, therefore, to go beyond— or behind—the net product indices. An index of income growth, even one much better than what we have for most of the period, is not a history of income. We want to show the factors—economic and noneconomic, if the reader has a taste for parochial taxonomy—that determined the rate of growth of income. For an explanation, we shall borrow heavily from theories of economic development that explain sudden jumps in the rate of growth as the results of sharp changes in the structure of the economy. The classic among these theories is Joseph Schumpeter's hypothesis that innovation is the driving force of economic development. Innovations are not simply inventions or new products, for the innovation is a structural change that destroys old profitabilities (for firms, industries, and perhaps even regions), introduces new industrial inter-relationships, and lifts the economy as a whole to new levels of output and of productive efficiency. The structural change may be institutional or organizational; it may be a series of corporate mergers or a major shift in the pattern of population movements to the frontier. For the statistics to illustrate and test the explanation, we are almost totally in the debt of Simon Kuznets.[3]

Two different measures, or at least, two different problems, have been suggested in what has just been said. We shall want a measure that can describe the multiplication of conveniences, that is, a measure of economic well-being. The net product or national income series comes close to being a measure of economic welfare. It is an index of the sum total of goods and services available for final consumption: the *final* output of the economy. But to know *how fast* income has grown, or perhaps how rapidly some index of welfare has risen, is not thereby to understand *how* we have grown. It is necessary to break open the sum if we are to answer the *how* question. We may choose to estimate welfare as the ability to consume or to produce. But we suspect strongly that the growth of the system, the increase in the capacity to produce, is to be explained largely by the ability or willingness of a nation to forgo present consumption, that is, to save and invest. Explanation requires that we try to find out how fast capital accumulated and how resources were used, whether for present consumption or the expansion of future output. In addition, the changing industrial composition of a growing economy and the different rates of productivity increase among the major sectors must be considered.

II. Some Caveats: A Digression

Before we start talking about explanation, we will take up a more basic question: Can the national income series be used as a means of comparing levels of well-being over long stretches of time? The next few paragraphs, which attempt an answer, form a digression from the main line of argument. It is a brief review, intended to clear some definitional ground rather than to isolate for later handling a few subtleties in welfare measurement. We are not going to display any of the biases or ambiguities as they occur historically; they are introduced here simply as warnings to be kept in mind by the reader.

There are two major problem areas in the use of national income statistics as measures of economic welfare. First, current net output must be defined. Defining *output* means identifying or delimiting the scope of economic activity; defining *netness* means eliminating the double count of outputs that are absorbed in the course of production. What is being sought is a measure of the flow of goods to final consumption and to capital formation. The second problem is that of assigning values to the physical products so that they can be summed and compared as totals across periods of time.[4]

We tend, for any moment of time, to delimit output or product statistically in terms of the market place. Goods and services that pass legally through some market or have a marketable counterpart are counted as part of the product of the economy. We do not count ubiquities, keeping in mind that the residents of Los Angeles might think bitterly of a classification that counts pure air a free good. We do not count prohibited commodities, however they may be priced in the illicit market. Finally, we do not count goods and services that are produced in the home for home consumption. For the historian, this last is the most difficult limit to accept. The process of development is achieved with a massive readjustment of the industrial composition of the economic system. In the course of these readjustments, many productive activities are taken out of the home, to be performed in market-oriented parts of the economy. The classic short-run illustration of this source of bias is the case of the man who marries his housekeeper, thereby subtracting her product, which is presumably not materially altered upon the exchange of vows, from the national income totals. A long-run counterpart to this archetypal example is the disappearance of home-baked bread, which clearly contributes an upward bias to the most recent estimates in the historical national income accounts. Even statistically, "home-style" bread cannot be mistaken for home-baked bread.

The issue of netness is much more difficult to settle. Economic welfare is identified with the collective basic wants of ultimate consumers. Therefore, except in a completely closed, Malthusian system, consumption is taken to be final; it is not identified with or made a prerequisite of the next day's consumption. This imposes a considerable range of ambiguity upon the net product accounts, as it does upon the income tax return. The most important source of this ambiguity, historically, is the definition of government product. Some of the expenditure of the public sector is clearly identifiable as final product—public medical care and the preservation of a few green places in our cities, for example. But there are vast expenditures that cannot be so neatly identified: how should we allocate the cost of roads between Sunday driving and long-distance freight trucking? Insofar as national product statistics count government outlays as final spending, we should keep in mind the upward bias imposed upon the welfare index. In general, it should be clearly remembered that the increasing complexity of industrial production and the resulting decline in net product relative to gross activity are aspects of economic growth that simply do not appear in the net product accounts.

In order that we may aggregate changing bundles of

physical goods and services to get an index of output, it is necessary to apply a meaningful system of weights. Prices provide a meaningful system, but a system unavoidably laden with distortions or ambiguities. Mechanically, the physical quantities of each year, say, are weighted by prices of the given year and then summed to get a national product dollar total. Then, since prices have changed, it is necessary to deflate the dollar totals by an index of price change in order to get the dollar series into comparable units. We are then in a position to ask, for any pair of years: Would the bundle of goods produced in the later year have been available in the earlier year? The apparent simplicity of the question, however, should not be allowed to mask the essential ambiguity (rather than bias) of the answer. The price weights were introduced to deal with the fact that a bill of goods does not simply grow or decline, retaining its percentage composition, from year to year; the proportions change. But not only does the composition of goods and services change; the system of relative prices changes, and changes, furthermore, in a manner that is closely connected to the fact of economic growth. Goods that were scarce and highly priced at the start of industrialization tend to fall in price relative to the initially abundant goods at whose expense production proportions have changed. Therefore, a series valued at end-of-period prices will give the heaviest weights to the goods whose output has increased least and the least weight to those goods which have multiplied most; growth will appear to have been less rapid than it would have been if measured with the prices of the earliest period. Neither approach is "wrong"; it is wrong only to ignore the distinction or to use early weights for one series and later weights for another, related series. Quite apart from this index-number problem, there is another involved in the choice of weights employed in the construction of the price index itself. If the index of physical volume obtained by deflation is to be consistent with itself, then the deflator applied to each year should be based on the physical weights pertaining to that year. It is not clear how much distortion is included from this source in the series presented here.

Three additional, more difficult problems of welfare estimation appear when we look closely into the valuation procedure. First, a distortion arises from the fact that price data tend to underreport new products and that they cannot take account of quality changes. The second problem arises from the difficulty of pricing capital goods and government services. Almost certainly the prices used for these products, reflecting costs in far from perfect markets, do not reflect with any accuracy their marginal utilities. Capital formation is valued at the discounted worth of expected future yields as seen by the entrepreneur or manager making the investment decision, not by the owners or beneficiaries of the acquired capital. Similarly, it is virtually impossible to say what is the relationship between the cost to the government—which is the net product accounting value placed on government services— and their marginal utility to citizens. Pork barrel or no, the voting process cannot be viewed as being a market mechanism that reflects preferences in prices.

The third problem of consistent valuation is inherent in the fact of changing income distributions: How can a single index of national income account for the gains and losses that arise from changing relative income positions? Schumpeter pointed out (though not without opposition) that the great relative price declines since industrialization began have occurred for the consumer goods that figure most in the budgets of the lower income groups. This observation alone should force us to raise questions about the adequacy of the valuation and aggregation procedures of the national income accounts, which cannot take cognizance of the distributions that underlie the various totals.

Welfare theorists, having shown first that we can say virtually nothing that is unequivocal about aggregate welfare in the light of distribution changes, have lately given us ground for belief that some of our judgments about the totals may be plausible. This is especially the case if the outputs of most or all goods have increased when the income totals rose and, second, if the elasticity of substitution among different consumption bundles is high. Much the same result is achieved if it can be reasonably assumed that there are not striking class-bound differences of taste. Finally, we can (and will in the present discussion) examine the degree of inequality explicitly. Armed with sufficient *sang-froid* to believe in the declining marginal utility of income at given aggregate levels, we can accept the fact that increasing equality of income shares may leave us uncertain about the exact size of welfare changes and still not have to give up the evidence on the direction of the change.

In any event, armed with these caveats, we can proceed to use the national income statistics to measure long-term economic growth. The spelling-out of the shortcomings of the aggregate series was intended to be salutary rather than carping; there will not be any attempt to display the biases as they occur in the history.

To sum up, then, this digression should stand as a forewarning that the scope of social accounting procedure underreports the products of home and farm at the beginning of the history and also that modern developments, such as the necessity to drive considerable distances to work in order to have some grass to cut when away from work, may represent real costs of factory production. It is more difficult to say in what sense we are forearmed against the error inherent in the pricing of capital goods: How shall we balance the myopia of savers against the optimism of corporate managers? Finally, we shall concentrate wherever it is necessary on the changing composition of the net product and the shape of the increasingly egalitarian income distribution, avoiding as much as possible the dangers of reading indexes as if they measured real quantities. To follow the opposite course to its extreme, that is, to eschew net product measurements and to try to study economic growth at best by means of biography and at worst by antiquarian anecdotage, is to risk abdicating from economics altogether. This chapter will contain a small share of anecdotal history, but the argument depends ultimately upon the timing of income growth.

III. Evidence

If we take the multiplication of conveniences as our criterion, then the growth of net national product provides a quantitative summary of the transformation of the economy. For roughly half the period of United States national history, that is, from 1869 to the present, the data on net product are continuous and, within the limits of the concept, comprehensive. For the first half, from 1780 to the Civil War decade, the data are patchy and incomplete and, where available, suspect, at best. What does this evidence show?

For the early period, before 1869, the only continuous national income estimates in constant prices are in the series compiled by Robert F. Martin.[5] (The estimates, unfortunately, are probably not much better than crude impressions dignified by a show of numerical exactness. Reconstructions of his procedures by Simon Kuznets and by William Parker and Franklee Whartenby make it impossible to accept their exaggerated concreteness.[6]) Martin's figures show an eightfold growth of real net income (in prices of 1926), from $1.1 billion in 1799 to $9 billion in 1869. But real income per capita increased from $216 in 1799 to only $273 in 1869, a percentage change of barely 10 per cent over a period of seventy years. For the first three decades, from 1799 to 1829, he shows a decline of 24 per cent in the income-per-head series, and it was not until 1849 that the rise was sufficient to carry past the initial-year level.

It will be argued in this chapter that the decade of the forties was the first upsurge in the process of industrialization

in the American system. In a recent statement by Raymond
Goldsmith before the Joint Economic Committee, 1839 or
some date "not very long before 1839" was offered as the break
in the trend of growth of real net product per capita. Since
that year, he estimates, real income per head has grown at
an annual rate of 1⅝ per cent. It would require evidence of
implausibly low living standards in the eighteenth century to
support the argument that incomes were rising at a rate of
even 1 per cent for sustained periods before 1839. Goldsmith's guess for the average rate of growth from the mid-
eighteenth century to 1839 is not above ½ per cent per year.[7]
It is hardly credible that there was a real worsening of living
standards over the first third of the century, as Martin has
stated. The impressionistic contemporary accounts of Harriet
Martineau and Alexis de Tocqueville give no evidence that
the country was going through a decline in living standards;
much less do they speak of any changes in distribution unfavorable to the mass of the nation.[8] On the other side, however, Professor Schumpeter characterized this period, to 1840,
as the downswing of a long Kondratieff cycle, a period of
absorption and derivative development rather than of strong,
sustained growth.[9] There were two severe commercial crises,
both of which may have been primarily speculative and
financial in origin but which had strong disruptive effects,
especially upon the young industrial sectors. From 1815 to
1820 there was a flood of textiles from England, sufficient to
push almost all the New England mills to the point of catas-
trophe (with the notable exception of the Boston Manufacturing Company) and to drive down prices and employment in
every manufacturing center.[10] In 1837, enterprise, and especially new industry, ground to a halt again, braked this time
by the aftermath of overenthusiastic acceptance of every
credit facility offered by English merchants and by the internal
drain on funds that resulted from political solutions to the
serious surplus problem and other monetary strains. There is
some indication, then, that the first third of the century was

a sluggish period in which the level of aggregate income may not have grown much faster than the population that produced it. The growth of population, 223 per cent from the turn of the century to 1839, is of course evidence of growth, but it hardly compares with the signs of development in the next forty years.

There are current dollar output and employment statistics in the decennial census, starting in 1810, plus some scattered figures on wage rates. We shall now turn to the real wage evidence.[11] In the first decades of the nineteenth century, money wages rose only briefly, during the war years, and then fell back sharply under the impact of depression, until 1820. Similarly, wholesale prices and consumer prices reached peaks in 1814 and then, by 1821, fell to the lowest level reached since the turn of the century. Whatever real wage gains had been made by 1810 appear to have been wiped out by 1820. Wage rates then held steady or rose slightly until the panic of 1837, but prices continued an almost unbroken fall until 1834. In the early forties, money wages gained, if at all, only weakly, but prices continued their fall after the sharp rise (twenty-seven index points in two years) of the pre-1837 boom. (Recall that it is during this decade that Martin's per capita income series finally turns upward sufficiently to carry incomes beyond the turn-of-the-century level. His real per capita income estimate increases further from $235 to $296 from 1849 to 1859.) During the fifties, farm wages rose everywhere, but especially in the South, where cotton, sugar, and tobacco all recovered smartly. Even the mild New England farm-wage increase is worth reporting, since it stands in contrast to the decidedly minor industrial wage gains recorded in the textile centers. Hansen's real-wage index falls sharply from 1849 to 1858. (There is a Ricardian quality to this wage and price behavior which we shall discuss later.) The movement of wages in the Civil War decade was remarkably mixed, by region and by occupation, but rates appear to have gone up by as much as 50 or 70 per cent over-all. Prices, of course, kept up a similar pace and, in the South especially, more than balanced the wage change. The Civil War inflation is especially severe in Martin's figures, sufficient indeed to wipe out in the course of the decade all the gain of the previous decade. This is refuted by every available real-wage estimate. In W. I. King's series of per capita national income and in Lebergott's independent wage data a fairly similar real level appears at the beginning and end of the decade. Wesley Mitchell, having computed a real decline in wages from 1860 to 1865 (although he suspected that it might have been exaggerated by the data), wonders at the fact that "few complaints were heard from them [the great mass of wage earners] of unusual privations." By 1870, real wages had more than regained the lost ground in his series.[12]

The figures on wage rates are, of course, not the same as an income series. But, since we have some contemporary testimony that there was not a redistribution unfavorable to the working class, the relatively minor gains in wage rates would seem to indicate that there was at best only a minor gain in the per capita total income series over the period. There were two serious setbacks before the relatively mild depression of 1857. The revival after the second decline (1837–43) seems to be a significant upturn and to mark the end of the long period of relative stagnation.

In spite of the extreme paucity of good data for the period, it may be useful to consider a suggestive theoretical view of the beginning of the century. In Schumpeterian terms, especially as extended by the work of the Swedish historian Erik Dahmén, the otherwise surprisingly low rate of per capita income growth would be typical of a period of industrial preparation.[13] From that point of view, the first three decades of this history appear to have been a period in which structural tensions and disparities among the rates of development in different industries make a kind of breathing spell. This pause—an "incomplete development block"—was broken, initially and tentatively, by the canals and then, in the forties, by the great surge of industrial change set off by railroad expansion. Eastern industrial progress had been carried forward almost to the limit that water power, however efficient, could permit; its further progress, to be based largely upon steam power, waited for the supply of cheap coal. The availability of coal, in turn, waited upon the great transportation innovations of the fourth and fifth decades of the century. Similarly, the now-classic Schumpeterian description of conflict between the "new" and the "old" seems to fit the two major crises of the period. In each decline, but especially in the first, the panic came on the heels of an aggressive period of dumping by English merchants; after each, but especially after the second, the panic was followed by a period of rapid technological change and capital development. Finally, the conflict between Chestnut Street in Philadelphia and Wall Street in New York characterized the financial confusions and tensions from the last years of the Second Bank of the United States to the downturn of 1837.[14] These lags and structural imbalances add some preliminary support to the impression given by admittedly imperfect statistical evidence. Later, in Section V, we shall examine the structural changes in detail.

For the period since 1869, we are the beneficiaries of Professor Kuznets' massive researches on the net national product.[15] From the decade 1869–78 to the recent five years 1950–54, his data indicate a rise in net national product, at 1929 prices, from $9.5 billion to $142.7 billion (annual averages), that is, an average rate of change of more than 4 per cent per year. During the same period, population rose from 44.6 million persons to 157.5 million, an increase of about 350 per cent. Real per capita product, therefore, increased more than four times, from $213 to $906 (in 1929 prices), an annual rate of change of 2 per cent. But the range about these averages is extremely wide, and the short-run details are therefore more interesting for the history of United States economic growth than is the single long-run index of change.[16]

There were two periods of accelerated growth during the last part of the nineteenth century. The first and more dramatic surge took place in the two decades after the Civil War. Recall that this was a period generally characterized by the severe panic of 1873 and the long depression to 1879 and by the outcries of Greenback and silver agitation. From the minor contraction in 1869–70 to the uncertain peak in 1881–83, the average annual rate of growth was approximately 9 per cent. (The span, starting and ending at opposite phases of the business cycle, imparts some upward bias to the rate.) The remarkable aspect of the seventies is the continued growth in output, while the fall of prices and the level of unemployment dominated the commercial sense of the period. Average real net product in the decade 1874–83 increased by almost 46 per cent over the average for 1869–78. The national product in 1929 prices rose from $7 billion in 1869 to $14 billion in 1879; by 1884 it had passed $18 billion.

The second burst of development came as the economy recovered from the financial crisis of 1893. By the turn of the century another upsurge was under way, less rapid than the first but clearly different fom any of the cyclical recoveries in the intervening period and more rapid than anything we have experienced since that time. The rate of growth between the decade averages for 1889–98 and 1899–1908 was almost 6 per cent per year. From 1894 to 1903, national product grew from $22 billion to $37.7 billion, in 1929 prices. The per capita increase was 5 per cent per year in the first spurt and 3 per cent per year in the second; in between, it fell as low as 0.9 per cent in the late eighties and early nineties. These, then, were the second and third breakthroughs in the process of industrialization, periods of advance and structural change in which net product moved ahead much more rapidly than did population.[17]

The rate of growth fell off sharply at the end of the first decade of this century and began to recover, though somewhat uncertainly, in the years of the World War. The spectacular rise in the twenties and the aftermath, in which income fell by enough to give a negative rate of change for the interval between 1924–33 and 1929–38, are sufficiently close to us in time to make detailed consideration here unnecessary. Quite apart from the experience of the Great Depression, there is some indication that the rate of growth has been declining since the post–Civil War decades of the nineteenth century. Professor Kuznets' data show a decline in the percentage change per decade in both national product and national product per capita since 1869. In the interval from the end of the Civil War to the eve of the World War, the average decadal rate of growth in the two indices was 56 per cent and 27.5 per cent, respectively. Between the periods 1894–1903 and 1950–54, the decade averages were 33.8 per cent and 16.4 per cent. But these long averages tell us very little, after all. It is extremely difficult to say now whether or not the depression years will continue to dominate the recent statistical picture for very long. The long postwar boom has not been sufficient to overcome the impression of secular decline in the growth rate.[18]

We shall concentrate upon an attempt to explain hisrorically the three great surges of industrial growth during the nineteenth century. Finally, we shall compare the structural changes in those periods of accelerated development with the structural changes of the more recent years.

IV. A Theoretical Model of Income Change

What we have found, then, is a long period of sustained growth, punctuated by three sharp drives upward. During the process of industrialization, the output series showed sudden discontinuities in the early forties, the seventies, and the late nineties. It is not entirely clear that the break identified here in the seventies is really distinct from the sustained push that began in the forties. However, since the Civil War

decade did constitute a complete disruption and reorganization in the economy, it will be worthwhile, at least initially,
to study the two periods separately.

What we find in statistics, as in other forms of experience,
is likely to be just what we are looking for. With data as
rough and ready as that which we have here, especially for
the first half-century, the way we ask the questions may well
determine the answers we get. Inevitably, we approach evidence with some expectations; historical research should
begin, therefore, with a rigorous statement of preconceptions
—in more sophisticated terms, a model. In much of our literature the preconceptions about variations in growth rates are
obvious in the terminology. Nineteenth-century economists
spoke of panics and crises. Few people in the thirties, however, wrote about the "panic of 1929"; by then the profession
had learned that it was studying cycles. Since World War II
we have changed our focus once again. We are concerned
with the problems of development and sustained growth; we
tend to look for "breakthroughs," "takeoffs," and "big pushes."

This chapter was conceived as an attempt to explain
historically the evolution of American living standards. The
research was guided by the expectation that major variations
in the rate of growth of national income could be explained
by changes in the structure of the economy. *Structure* in this
context refers to the technological and organizational relationships that determine how the system will respond to variations from outside itself, to population change, perhaps, or to
the assumption of new responsibilities by the government.
In more rigorous terms, the structure discussed here is the
given part of a theory of income generation—that is, the fixed
terms that define the relationship between income and the
outside, or exogenous, variables. If we think in terms of
formal relationships, the structure may be defined by the
numerical values of the constants in the familiar multiplier-
accelerator equations (i.e., the parameters).

In multiplier-accelerator models of income growth there is a two-way relationship between investment and income. Increases in the production of goods and services can be achieved only with appropriate increases in the stock of capital equipment, given "the" capital-output ratio. Therefore, income changes will determine (in part) the required level of investment. On the other hand, investment in excess of intended saving will, via the multiplier process, cause further, magnified increases in the level of income. Within this capital-adjustment process, autonomous investment—that is, investment not simply called for by the growth of income— and other long-term exogenous developments, such as population growth and technological change, can set off and, if they are at all continuous, possibly maintain the growth of income. Now, in this context, structural changes will be looked upon as once-over developments that affect the way in which the economy's capital-adjustment process responds to the autonomous shocks or long-run developments. Following Professor Duesenberry,[19] the most important changes, indicating in what way each one will affect the income growth rates, are listed.

1. Increases in the propensity to consume (once the industrial growth process has begun and the system has advanced beyond near-zero saving ratios) or decreases in the lag between income and consumption will cause the rate of growth to rise. In the United States the initial relatively high degree of equality of income shares and later improvements in the payments mechanism were among the possibilities that operated in this direction.

2. A rise in the dividend pay-out ratio, and *a fortiori*, any development that causes a reduction in the use of retained earnings (that is, an increase in borrowed funds) for investment will *ceteris paribus* cause the growth rate to increase.

3. A change in the rate of return will have a favorable effect on the marginal efficiency of capital; if it does not arise

from a decrease in competition and limits on the entry of new firms, the change is almost certain to be fully favorable to more rapid growth of investment.

4. Improvements in techniques in the investment-funds markets, which were crucial through much of the nineteenth-century history, will cause both capital and income to respond more rapidly to outside changes.

5. Technological changes that increase the capital intensity of the economy will obviously heighten the response of the accelerator mechanism; to the extent that the innovations are financed by borrowing—and this is the Schumpeterian argument—the effect will be in the direction of even greater buoyancy. The nineteenth-century history of this economy is punctuated by a series of developments, within industries and among industries, that increased the capital intensity of the productive process.

6. It is simple enough to state that government expenditure will have a buoyant effect, just as an increase in private enterprise would, and that an increase in effective tax rates will act as a drag on the economy. But there is more to the impact of government activity, of course, and it will be necessary to watch for changes in debt position and in the management of the debt if we are to understand how the government impinged upon the growth process in the difficult surplus periods of the last quarter of the century.

Technological change has appeared in this list several times. Had we decided to discuss nineteenth-century income growth in terms of the technical relationships between physical inputs and outputs—the production function—the direct effect of technological improvement upon the efficiency of resource use would have been the central part of the story. Instead, by concentrating upon the level of income-generating activity, we are able to bring in productivity change largely in terms of the rate of return and the incentive to greater investment (see footnote 60).

These are the major structural changes that affect the way in which the dynamic multiplier-accelerator interaction responds to outside shocks. Some of these changes, in addition to altering the parameters or givens in the model, are themselves put into effect as outside shocks; technological change, since it cannot usually be realized without a burst of investment, is precisely of this nature. The income history of the United States in the nineteenth century will be explained in this chapter in terms of the structural changes just outlined. We shall be able to refer directly to the values of the constants only rarely, for example, the capital-output ratio or the debt-income ratio. For the most part, we shall simply try to identify such changes as shifts in industrial composition, the appearance and development of new industries, and organization and technological innovations, on the one hand, with the major increases in the growth rate during the period of industrialization, on the other.

The point of all this is to argue that the surges of income growth that we are going to examine are something more than recurrent, short-run discontinuities in the rate of increase of national output. If there were not more than that involved, we should simply be arguing circularly (and trivially) that a change in the pace of activity "caused" an acceleration in the income growth rate. For example, the fact that we were building railroads at a certain time, since railroads tend to be large and expensive undertakings, would stand as an obvious reason for a spurt of activity. But this study is aimed rather at posing the question: How did the railroads change the structure of responses of the economy so that there were as a result new values in the income-determining relationships? The railroads, to continue with this example, provided a powerful injection of autonomous investment, of course. But more was involved; the railroad caused revolutionary changes in the scale, the techniques, and the focus of American agriculture. (American nineteenth-century income growth was achieved in a primarily agricultural economy, remember.) Railroad expansion around the Civil War changed the technological and capital-market bases, among others, and thereby raised the level of activity and development permanently. It should be clear that not every cyclical upswing has this effect and that cyclical declines have not generally set the economy down from its new plateaus. (Only once, from 1929 to 1933, did it appear that the productive system had retrogressed. And then, on one side of the stagnationist controversy of the late thirties, it was thought that we might have settled down to a chronically low level of activity. But the pressure of growth after World War II, although not completely reversing the evidence of long-run retardation, dispelled, at least for the time being, the fear of long-run stagnation.)

This complicated description of the income growth process is not introduced on the chance that we might find the numerical values for the parameters in the income relationships and in that way describe the conditions necessary to generate a steady-growth path (although it would be an an exciting and tempting possibility). Rather it is of interest in the setting of this study because of the suggestions that it makes toward combining structural change and dynamic processes. A dynamic process, like the simple multiplier-accelerator relationship just described, contains a law of change; given appropriate initial conditions and parameters in the behavior relationships, it will, once started, generate by itself a path of growth (or decline, or fluctuation). An alternative to this is a static—or, better, a comparative static —production model in which the variation in the rate of production (not the rate of growth) is explained by variation in the underlying basic data. There is no logical reason why these must be alternatives.[20] A fruitful procedure for historical explanation would seem to be to use a simple dynamic theory in which we can examine the changing numerical values of the income relationships much as if we had a whole set of comparative static equilibrium situations under scrutiny. The law of change in a dynamic process may itself change, of course; some of this will be expressed in changing parameters. When such changes do take place, or when the system is subject to sharp external shocks, there will be once-for-all variations in the rate of growth. The identification of such structural changes is the goal of this history.

The use of a single theory of the growth process, however general, imposes a logical strain when it is applied over a period as long as the nineteenth century. If we are tracing the stages in the metamorphosis of the American economy to full-fledged industrialism, then it may seem that one relatively simple closed model, although it might be useful in explaining one stage of development, could not possibly be appropriate for an earlier or later stage. The only answer to this seems to be that we are not so much interested in the stages of a metamorphosis—it is at least questionable that this is a plausible description of the history of the American economy—as in the way new commodities and technological or organizational innovations change the structure of relationships and, thereby, the rate of growth. Innovations and changes in the composition of industry will, by affecting capital intensity, credit creation, and connections among other parameters in the system, change the growth path.

The multiplier-accelerator process described above is not the only model "true" for the period we are examining, nor is it asserted that this model is equally true at all times. Rather, we have looked for a description of growth sufficiently general so that structural changes could be traced to their income-growth outcomes without having to scrap and replace the theory at every step of industrial development. If we find that the changes we observe would be expected to have brought about the variations in growth that did indeed take place, then we shall have an explanation for the historical growth path of income in the period since 1800.

V. The Early Period of Accelerated Growth

With this approach in mind, what is to be explained? We have said repeatedly "the rate of growth of income." But we have seen, too, that, while the rate of growth was sustained for quite long periods, there have been relatively short spurts of rapid increase surrounded, if not by stagnation, at least by stretches of more sluggish movement. We shall ask, then, what caused the first period of accelerated development after the depression of 1837 and the two great advances, in the seventies and at the turn of the century.

It would not do, here, to follow the recent analyses of economic development in their emphasis upon backwardness and the initial push or "takeoff."[21] The United States at the opening of the nineteenth century may have been growing slowly, in preindustrial fashion, but it would be difficult to find good evidence of stagnation, much more so for backwardness. Instead, we shall concentrate first upon the conditions behind the surge in the rate of growth that followed the rise out of the crisis of 1837, observing that the United States, as a latecomer vis-à-vis British industrialization, gained much from British technology.

The American economy before 1840 appears to have grown not significantly faster than the population, that is, at a decade rate of growth of income that declined from 36 per cent in 1800–1810 to 33 per cent in 1830–40. Industrial development was slow, but there were some changes in the composition of production during this period, which opened the way for a great spurt in the pace of income growth. The share of the total gainfully occupied population that was employed in agriculture fell from 72.8 at the turn of the century to 68.6 in 1839; the drop in the share of agricultural income in Martin's national income series was very sharp over the first decade (from 39.5 to 34.0) and then appears to have settled down at about 34.6 per cent through 1839.[22]

Between 1810 and 1830 the production of pig iron and castings in this country rose from 54,000 tons to 192,000 and, by 1840, to 287,000; the making of bar and other wrought iron rose from 25,000 to 113,000 and then to 197,000. The weight of imported, unmanufactured iron and steel rose from 15,000 tons in 1827 to over 100,000 in 1839, and manufactured iron and steel imports (hardware and cutlery) appear to have fallen between those two dates. The increase in the output of manufactures between 1810 and 1840 was on the order of 200 per cent. This, then, is a crude indication of the pace of industrialization before the decade that we are counting as the initial upsurge.[23]

Section III attempted to demonstrate that there was a significant upturn out of the crisis of 1837–43. We can now look for the change in composition or concentration that the Gerschenkron or Rostow analyses would lead us to expect and then go on to consider the structural changes in more detail. In every real measure of industrial composition, there was a sharp change between the decades before and after the depression. The percentage of gainfully employed in agriculture, which had been going down by not more than two points in any previous decade, dropped by five points in the forties and again in the fifties.[24] In the decade ending in 1849 manufacturing output (value added) grew at a rate of 152 per cent and in the overlapping decade (to 1854) 133 per cent; in the same periods agriculture grew at rates of 26 per cent and 39 per cent, respectively. The shares in value of total commodity output moved in comparable fashion: agriculture, from 72 per cent in 1839 to 56 per cent in 1859; manufactures, from 17 per cent in 1839 to 32 per cent twenty years later.[25]

The expansion of primary metal manufactures and heavy industry is an important part of industrialization. But the production of iron and steel in the forties was dominated by tariff changes; between 1840 and 1847 annual output increased by more than 200 per cent. Then, under the influence of the tariff of 1846, importation increased and production

declined by about 100,000 tons annually. Ezra Seaman estimated, however, that the annual consumption of iron and
hardware increased from less than 400,000 tons to about 1
million tons between 1840 and 1850. Finally, between 1850
and 1860 domestic manufactures of iron and steel increased
by 40 per cent, and the fabrication of steam engines and
agricultural implements increased by 66 per cent and 159
per cent, respectively.[26]

In these statistics, fragmentary and of widely varying
credibility, there seems to be an unmistakable and consistent
picture of an economy changing its direction. The pace of
industrialization did not leap up from zero; what did happen
was a marked acceleration in the trend toward manufacturing
and construction. Within the manufacturing sector, the trend
turned toward the heavy industries. The increase in the rate
of investment, measured in terms of fixed capital per worker
ratios, was greater between 1849 and 1859 than in any comparable period in the century: from $50.60 to $69.60. Output
of fixed capital increased by approximately 90 per cent over
the decade of the fifties. This is the evidence. What can be
said about the causes?[27]

The Changes in Institutional Structure

The most important institutional changes in the upsurge
and during the preceding period of preparation were directed
toward making credit more cheaply and efficiently available
for the growing manufacturing and railway industries. However unfortunate the destruction of the Second Bank of the
United States may have been from the point of view of the
long-run development of central banking in this country,
it did have a beneficial impact in shifting the locus of the
money market from the mercantile business community in
Philadelphia to the more aggressive manufacturing centers in
New York and Boston. Loanable funds continued to be
scarce, and low interest rates were almost unavailable.
Long term credit, especially, was in extremely short supply.

But by 1850 the growth in intermediary banking institutions —savings banks and insurance companies, primarily in the East, and the wildcats and new state banks in the South and West—had been sufficient to make the accumulation of capital, even by small investors, much more feasible than it had been.

The investment history of the Massachusetts Hospital Life Insurance Company is very interesting in this respect. Before 1830 the company's investments were concentrated in western Massachusetts farm mortgages, rarely for a term longer than one year. About 1830, and especially after 1837, securities and business loans became more important in the portfolio, and the locus shifted to the neighborhood of Boston and to the textile industry. In the forties, when textile selling agents would not generally lend for more than six months, and commercial banks for only three or four, the savings banks and the Massachusetts Hospital Life were practically the only sources of funds at terms of a year or more. This evidence may be taken as having more than anecdotal significance, considering the expansion of savings bank capital in the late forties and the fifties and the singular importance of the Massachusetts Hospital Life in the textile capital market.

The first savings banks appeared in New York in 1817. By 1846 the New York institutions held deposits of $112 million; a decade later, in the single year 1857, there was a growth of $25 million more. The Massachusetts savings banks grew in number from thirty-one in 1839 to eighty-six in 1859; deposits increased from $5.6 million to $39.4 million. There was a similar growth in insurance companies; in New York, insurance capital increased from $16 million in 1827 to $75 million in 1860. Another important change took place in the emerging role of the note broker over this period. Having been a suspect "money-shaver" in 1819, by 1837 he was dealing among the banks and in 1857 began to deal in paper on his own account very much in the manner of the commercial paper house. In the same year, the newly formed New York Clearing House made a tentative effort toward dealing with the crisis by extending clearing-house certificates for the first time.[28]

Throughout the prewar period, of course, the dependence upon foreign funds continued, especially in the financing of railway construction. But the changes in domestic banking that were taking place made a real difference in the form and availability of finance in the drive of the forties and fifties. A strong indication of this change is given in Lance Davis' study of the pattern of textile finance before 1860. Equity capital was the most important form over the whole period, although it declined from 1827 to 1860 while loans increased in significance. Although retained earnings obviously can become important only with advancing age of the corporations, they declined in weight over historical time (for given ages). Another measure of the change is the cost of capital; in New York average interest rates on prime commercial paper declined from 10.14 for the decade ending in 1840 to 8.4 in the following decade. The decline in Boston was from 8.68 to 7.68.[29] But the *availability* of credit and especially of long-term loans was even more important for capital accumulation than were interest costs in this period, And, in this respect, two special participants in the capital markets are significant: the Western wildcat banks and the state governments. The wildcats, by providing currency and credit for agriculture and local industry in the West, and the governments, by financing internal improvements, provided for long-term credit needs that could not have been met from the East without a serious strain on the supply of funds and a subsequent rise in the interest rates to industrial borrowers.

Two more direct influences upon the supply of capital remain to be discussed, the government budget position and the most important source of funds for investment, the inflow of capital from London. In the thirties, largely under pressure of the fiscal surplus, the federal government took an increasing share of the responsibility for road construction and internal improvements. Jackson's opposition and the fears for state sovereignty that prompted it are written in the Maysville veto. The fact remains, however, that from 1831 to 1835 federal expenditures for roads and canals almost doubled the amount spent in the preceding five years. The Jackson administration spent over $25 million on public works, more than double the total for internal improvements by all previous administrations. But it was the *state* governments that played an active promotional if not entrepreneurial role during this period. To a large extent, the venture capital for transportation improvements came from the public treasury or at least was made more available on the basis of public credit. States, without using their tax power to service the loans, picked up the weak notes and securities of private companies and issued in turn the apparently stronger debt instruments of the government. One of the most important indirect effects of this state backing was to increase the willingness of foreign capitalists—British, primarily, but also in the French and Low Country markets—to invest in American transportation and land development. The direct assumption of responsibility by the states, coupled with strong supports for property rights, made investment in the new country much more attractive than could otherwise have been the case.

In the 1840's, seven federal budgets contained a deficit. Under free banking and the Independent Treasury, persistent surpluses caused a deflationary flow of currency into government vaults; the deficits, however poorly managed, at least had the advantage that they did not reduce circulation and cause a tightening of credit as the undistributed surplus did. It is especially significant, therefore, that in 1850 the federal budget moved up to a surplus position and continued so for eight years and that in 1850, 1853, and 1854 the net United States commodity trade and specie balance was negative and relatively high. The previous heavy inflow of capital occurred in the thirties, of course, and reached peaks of $61 million in 1836 and $41 million in 1839.[30] This observation is not intended as an assertion of causal connection between the federal surplus and the negative balances in the early fifties. Rather it is intended to show that from the middle thirties until the middle fifties growth was accompanied by either a government deficit or net capital imports. British capital was far more important in providing the initial funds for the spurt of investment and in maintaining the pace until the panic of 1857, but an undistributed surplus—rather than the actual deficit—might have caused a real drag on accumulation in the 1840's. Before leaving this discussion of the capital-market developments, it may be useful to warn the reader against the dangers of looking at these events from a rigid Keynesian position. Keep in mind that the fiscal consequences of a surplus obtained by high tariffs on imports are different from a surplus achieved by taxation; there is much less deflationary pressure. Indeed, to the extent that income was redistributed to the disadvantage of the working class, and by virtue of the protection afforded the textile industry, the tariff may have had a stimulating effect on capital accumulation in some sectors of the economy.

All these developments must have had the effect of increasing the availability of credit in the period under review and therefore of increasing the ratio of borrowing to income. Such changes increase the rate of investment, reduce the level of business saving relative to the demand for funds, and shorten the lags between changes in income and changes in investment demand. Indeed, after 1850 there appears to have been a sharp increase in the ratio of primary securities to income and a corresponding reduction in the ratio of money supply to primary securities.[31] It was not until the second half of the century that the banking system began to approach maturity, and even then the period of adolescence was singularly chaotic. But through the episode from 1830 to 1860, the capital-market changes were sufficiently bunched and sufficiently in the right direction to have made possible the financing of a large investment block. In this respect, it is interesting to note during how much of this development the central government, far from taking over the functions of the banking system, struggled fitfully and unsuccessfully to stay out of the money market, in sharp contrast to the Italian and Russian experiences described by Professor Gerschenkron.[32]

Public Policy and the Structure of Enterprise

There was much more in the government's role in the early American environment than the invention of substitutes for a mature banking system, however. The shifts, alterations, and adaptations in the state's part in the growth process constitute a series of structural changes of the first rank of importance. The United States is often said to have become what it is economically because the government did not interfere in business affairs. Is there a kernel of truth in that assertion, or more? In the first half of the nineteenth century the federal government probably was less directly involved in private business affairs than were most European governments. There was no substantial feudal class whose interests were to be defended. There were few established, generally accepted traditions or legacies of form that inhibited pragmatic adaptation and experimentation with legal institutions. (Another chapter in this book discusses the peculiar institution of the antebellum South, in which a feudal structure operated within an effective interregional capital market.) There can be no doubt, finally, that American legal traditions, as they developed after the Revolution, were most solicitous of property rights.

Freedom from established patterns, however, conferred an opportunity to experiment with more as well as less government involvement in private enterprise. There were few restraints imposed by custom, and the potentialities in this freedom were well recognized by many interested parties. The Federalists made the exploitation of these potentialities for business and economic development a central objective in their programs. Even the Jeffersonian opposition, while proclaiming resistance to industrialization and preference for agriculture as a way of life, rarely failed to support policies conducive to the new manufactures.

The most uniquely American experiments in government relationships to business in this early period involved the role of the corporate enterprise as an institution for organizing economic activity and accumulating equity risk-capital. True, the American legal attitudes toward the corporation have deep roots in Anglo-Saxon law. But the departures and innovations, and especially the reliance on the private corporation for organizing economic activity, require examination as among the most important structural changes in our history.

Until about 1830 the growth objective must have been less important in the policy toward incorporation than was the desire to regulate business enterprise. The privilege of incorporation was granted primarily to companies engaged in public service enterprises—banks and utilities. In the first decade of the century 82 per cent of new incorporations were in those two sectors, in the thirties the proportion was down to 58 per cent, and by the sixties it was down to one-third of the total.[33] The view has been advanced, partly on the basis of this evidence, that the corporation had few or no economic advantages and that regulation was the prime, if not indeed the only, public policy objective in the early period of incorporation. The case has been well stated by the Handlins:

> The attributes of peculiar economic efficacy, of limited liability, and of perpetual freedom from state interference were thus not present at the birth of the American business corporation. Divested of these characteristics, the form assumes a new significance. At its origin in Massachusetts the corporation was conceived as an agency of government, endowed with public attributes, exclusive privileges, and political power, and designed to serve a social function for the state. Turnpikes, not trade, banks, not land speculation, were its

province because the community, not the enterprising capitalists, marked out its sphere of activity.[34]

We are not going to argue that the social function in this sense was not central to the *origins* of incorporation in its American setting. But the crucial issue in the Handlins' interpretation is its rejection of the corporation, at least in the early United States, as a more efficient form for organizing economic activity. Without that advantage, the important characteristic of the corporation would lie in the act of chartering, which gave governments an opportunity to impose restrictions on business activities. Chartering (until the enactment of general incorporation laws) usually required formal legislative hearings, which were reasonably good forums for evaluating the legitimacy of an enterprise's objectives. Their *ad hoc* character, moreover, provided an opportunity to impose restrictions as might be deemed necessary. In this limited sense, regulation was certainly a central part of government policy in the period before 1850. But regulation is not incompatible with promotion of business enterprise, and the distinction between regulation and promotion has not been simple or obvious. There is no unequivocal reason why one institution could not serve as a means both of regulating and of promoting business activity—and the corporation would seem to have served both ends well.

Two basic advantages have usually been attributed to the corporation as a means of facilitating economic growth. First, the corporation serves to reduce and diversify risk-taking in capitalistic ventures. Second, and partly as a consequence, the corporation simplifies the task of accumulating private capital in large amounts. But it should be kept in mind that the first characteristic could have been established for other legal institutions. In fact, limitation on the liability of investors to those assets actually invested in the enterprise, exempting all other assets from claims against the corporation, was established for other organizational forms, such as special classes of partnerships. However, there are other ways in which the corporation reduces and diversifies risk—most notably, by introducing a minimal sort of parliamentary procedure and, with that, a system of checks and balances in the organization of business affairs. As with limited liability, this might have been achieved under some other form of business organization. But the relevant point is that the corporation is that form in Anglo-Saxon law which most effectively acquired both limited liability and rules of procedure for protecting the interests of many investor-participants. Moreover, these favorable effects were not limited to domestic capital sources. The flexibility of the corporate form combined with a strongly evident adherence to the received tradition of legal protection of private property to increase American access to foreign capital markets.

The main purpose of this digression, however, is to argue for a somewhat broader view of the economic significance of the policy toward incorporation in the early part of the century. It is generally recognized that whether large capital accumulations are advantageous or not will depend initially upon cost characteristics of an enterprise. It is not so well understood, however, that the initial desirability of large capital accumulations will also depend upon the nature of demand for a product or service. A cost advantage accrues to those possessing large capital blocks when there are significant economies of scale to be realized. Relevant illustrative cases are enterprises that require substantial capital simply to begin operations, such as turnpikes, water systems, and railroads.

Upon closer inspection, however, initial capital requirements seldom prove to be as large, in an absolute sense, as first suspected. For example, narrow rather than wide roads can be built; light rather than heavy track can be laid; small rather than large-diameter pipe can be used; fewer bridges can be built. The important point is not how much initial capital is needed but rather how much capital is needed to support an *efficient* level of operation. A new enterprise might face a long-run cost curve of the general shape of that shown in Figure 1. Strictly speaking, no initial investment

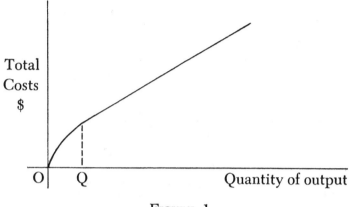

FIGURE 1

would be required, because the intercept with the cost axis (the vertical axis) is at zero. But even in this case a good deal of capital may be required to reach the efficient (low marginal cost) level of operations, corresponding to output levels equal to or greater than OQ. Under such circumstances, it would pay to start operations on a large scale as long as the market is large enough to absorb the efficient level of output at a compensatory price.

Market size depends, of course, upon demand conditions. Developmental possibilities depend primarily on the slope of the demand curve. If the demand curve is steeply pitched, the chances for development are greatly increased; it will be less necessary, under such conditions, to achieve immediate economies of scale. Development in that case will usually require far less original capital than if the demand curve were more nearly horizontal. The demand curves in Figure 2 illustrate this contrast. Demand curve D_1 has a steep slope. If it is possible to segregate the customers at the upper end of such a function from those at the lower end, the firm can enter into profitable production at relatively high prices and low levels of output. A common method of achieving this

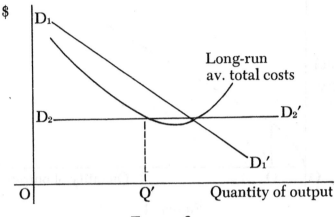

FIGURE 2

with a new product is to divide the market in time; the firm might begin on a small scale and still make a profit. Furthermore, the first sales might acquaint a larger group of potential consumers with the product, so the whole curve might shift to the right. The firm could then "plow back" its initial profits to expand operations, cutting prices as necessary to sell all the increased output.[35] With the horizontal demand curve D_2, there is no equivalent possibility of using price discrimination as a tool to finance development. Under such conditions it is necessary to build a plant sufficient to produce output OQ' if profits are to be made. Other things being equal, then, initial capital requirements will be correspondingly greater in the second case.

Can we use this theoretical excursion to illuminate the government policy toward enterprise in the nineteenth century? First, observe that public policy made demand curves like D_2 more likely in utilities, transportation, and banking than in manufactures. Rate regulation, especially, introduces a horizontal portion on the demand function at the maximum rate level. The upper limit placed on interest charges by usury laws has a similar effect. By extension, any tilt in the demand curve indicates the existence of some degree of monopoly position. In the United States, public demands to limit monopoly pricing powers have generally been greatest for utility services, "natural" monopolies whose privileged position is least likely to be eliminated by later entrants into the industry. In manufacturing and trade, on the other hand, monopoly is less natural, and governments have been correspondingly less ready to interfere with the market mechanism.

As a consequence, then, the need for a corporate charter as a means of raising a large block of capital is likely to be greatest in those situations in which rate regulation is to be expected. The use of the corporate charter to regulate economic activity creates its own demand for charters as an aid in raising capital. The regulatory aspect and the economic advantages of the corporate charter are intertwined in the market.

The potentialities for promoting private capital accumulation and entrepreneurial activity seem to have been recognized at an early stage in our national history. The strict English precedents controlling the grant of corporate charters began to be modified in America in the colonial period. While technically subject to the requirement that "letters patent" were to be obtained from the Crown, the colonies adopted the privilege of incorporation by delegated authority, exercised under proprietary patent or royal commission or instruction. The adaptation was obvious: Colonial legislatures began to grant privileges of incorporation. The net result was that obtaining a corporate charter became a substantially simpler process in America than in England even before independence was achieved.[36]

Democratic aversions to any apparent or real forms of

special privilege and the desire to promote economic development made state legislatures even less exacting after independence was achieved. The culmination was the emergence of the general incorporation law, which changed the whole legal basis of the act of organizing a corporation from one of privilege to one of right. With general incorporation, the obtaining of special permission, even legislative, was no longer necessary. A corporate charter could be obtained for almost any lawful purpose by meeting a modicum of formal conditions. Government regulation of the corporation was, in short, severely reduced.

The first general incorporation act is usually considered to be the New York statute of 1811. It permitted the general incorporation of certain kinds of manufacturing firms with less than $100,000 of subscribed capital. A Connecticut law, enacted in 1837, greatly extended the scope of unrestricted incorporation and would be considered by some authorities to be a better example of a truly general incorporation act. At any rate, the practice spread quickly so that by 1860 general charters were not uncommon and by 1875 special charters were essentially unimportant.[37]

The importance of this development can hardly be overstated. Whenever large amounts of capital were required for efficient output levels, the corporation had substantial advantages over most other available institutional forms as a method of organizing the business enterprise. Further, the development of general incorporation laws meant that the regulatory, as contrasted with the promotional, aspect of government participation in business affairs declined almost to nonexistence over the middle decades of the century. This was more than laissez faire. Combined with the direct encouragement given to banking and internal improvements by state and local governments, these prewar innovations implemented the capital flows from Europe and promoted the early development of a singularly effective (if sometimes unstable) market in equity capital in this country.

Changes in the Structure of Production

The second set of structural changes to be considered are much more familiar. They are technological rather than institutional innovations and operate directly upon the degree of capital intensity and the productive relationships. It has been pointed out by Victor Clark that the depression of 1837 was accompanied by changes in business conditions so great that we would be justified in making that year the dividing line between two industrial eras.[38] There are really two kinds of change involved here: (1) changes in the nature and intensity of capital use in the manufacturing sectors, especially in textiles and primary metals, and (2) epochal expansions in transportation and, derived from this, in agricultural development.

In the manufacture of textiles all the major technical difficulties holding back the introduction of steam power and the use of large-scale productive units had been cleared away by the thirties. By the 1840's, Clark reported, New England industries began to outgow the available water power. The first technological change to make larger units possible came in hydraulic-turbine and water-wheel design. Then, in the period between 1840 and 1850, the Massachusetts mills became the scene of a conflict between steam and water power. Widespread utilization of the new steam-based methods waited another decade, however, until coal became cheaply available to New England. Between 1850 and 1860, the mechanical improvements were so extensive that the Lowell mills were said to have been stripped down to shells and practically reconstructed in the course of the decade. In primary metal production, between 1830 and 1850, a number of major innovations were introduced, either taken from British technology or developed here as a result of the increased supply of mineral fuels. The basic change, perhaps, was the introduction of coke between 1837 and 1840, which, together with the use of anthracite, made a new era in iron technology. These changes made possible the use of hot blasts, with a saving of 40 per cent in fuel costs. Finally, in consequence of the adoption of the new fuels and the hot blast, there came increased furnace capacity, a much wider use of puddling and refining, and great economies in labor requirements.[39]

These innovations appear to have increased the capital-labor ratio in New England cotton manufacture by roughly one-half between 1840 and 1850 and to have increased the capital-output ratio by one-third.[40] For all mining and manufacturing, the rate of growth of value added was greater in the decade ending in 1849 than was the rate of growth of manufactured producers' durables over the same period, but the growth rate of total commodity output was much lower. In the following decade, producers' fixed capital increased much more rapidly than either total or manufactured output.[41]

Within a multiplier-accelerator model, technological changes that increase capital intensity will increase the rate of growth both of investment and of income. The first increase occurs because greater capital intensity requires more investment; the second is the result of the multiplier effect upon income. The technical changes in textiles and in iron and steel production, both of which had high capital coefficients relative to all other mining and manufacturing, meant an increase in the rate of growth in these sectors beyond the average for the economy and therefore an increase in the volume of investment and in the degree of capital intensity. (Almost two-thirds of the very high capital coefficient for agriculture consisted of the value of land in 1850. While agricultural expansion may have a strong effect in absorbing savings, it does not have a comparable impact upon the investment goods industries.) Finally, to the extent that iron and steel required large, relatively indivisible units, expansion in that sector took place to a large extent ahead of demand, thereby boosting further the impact of the multiplier.

It may be even more illuminating to consider the effect of these changes in the disaggregate setting of input-output analysis. Industries are not linked in simple sequences—from primary to intermediate to final. There is, rather, a complex set of interrelationships such that virtually all the sectors might be called "intermediate." The significance of this interdependence lies in the process by which structural changes reverberate through the economy; for example, changes in the cost of fuel made possible by the railroads affect the cost of primary metals, which, in turn, affect capital costs throughout the economy (including the price of railway equipment and therefore the cost of delivered fuel). The changes in textile methods increased the demand for steam engines and other producers' hardware, thereby increasing pressures upon the iron and steel and metal fabricating sectors and making more likely the achievement of further economies of scale in those primary sectors. The technical advances in iron and steel production, in turn, had even more important reverberative effects. The primary metals flow directly or indirectly into literally all other commodity-producing sectors in the economy. Therefore, a productivity increase in iron or steel becomes a productivity increase, in the sense of reducing (marginal) capital costs at given capital-output ratios, everywhere in the system. In addition, of course, the lower costs of the primary metals may provoke the use of more capital-intensive methods elsewhere.

There are, within these relationships, certain flows that are especially strategic. Savings in those industries whose outputs flow primarily to other producing sections rather than directly to the ultimate consumers will exert a heavier, wider impact on the technical structure than would comparable direct savings in the "consumer goods" industries. The manufacturers of fabricated structural metal and textile-mill products, which we have been discussing, are among the first four industries in a complete list of forty-five ranged according to the proportion of the industry's total gross output in 1947 that went forth as interindustry inputs (including capital formation).[42] The primary manufacturing sectors were (and are) in an extremely strategic position in the chain of innovation; the technical breakthrough and the cost savings introduced in those industries were especially important in closing the developmental block of the thirties and therefore in releasing a Schumpeterian wave of innovation. The changes in textile production had another expansive effect in that they made American cheap cotton goods competitive in world markets from the 1830's on. To sum up; by virtue of their very high capital intensity, relative to mining and manufacturing as a whole, and their position in the input-output relationships of the economy, the technical changes in textiles and in primary metals had strong reverberative impact throughout the economy. In addition, of course, the rapid growth in these sectors, following upon the reduction in their costs, increased the average capital intensity of the whole system and thereby the rate of growth of aggregate capital and of income.

The classical explanations of growth in this period are correct, of course, in their emphasis upon the railroads. First, as a capital-intensive, heavy-borrowing sector, railroad construction (1) increased the rate of growth of capital directly and (2) provided a strong offset to business savings elsewhere in the economy. Second, in so far as they were built to the West ahead of demand, the railroad exerted an even stronger upward pressure upon the aggregate investment schedule. These are double-barreled effects similar to the impact of technical change in the textile and primary metals industries. In addition to the effects of capital intensity, however, the railroads, by lowering transport costs and pushing ahead of population into the West, changed the geographical focus and the nature of operations of the agricultural sector. First, the railroads held off the Ricardian effect mentioned earlier; by reducing shipping costs for the staple crops, the railroads made it still more advantageous for farming to move out of the low-yield eastern sectors into the rich Northwest (now Middle West) region. In addition, by increasing agricultural productivity and reducing labor requirements on the farm, the population shift was, in effect, releasing farm labor for industrial employment in the manufacturing centers. Agricultural employment increased, of course, and immigrant Irish and German workers reduced the pressures in the industrial labor markets. But the point is that the flow of domestic and immigrant labor directly into nonagricultural occupations would not have been possible without major improvements in agricultural productivity.

It is impossible to separate the effects of the London cereal market from the effects of domestic supply and demand upon American agricultural prices. However, it is a sign of improved yields that agricultural prices should have declined more rapidly than construction prices in the face of the new demand pressures arising from immigration into the Eastern industrial centers during the late forties. The price decline was achieved in spite of the rising export of foodstuffs to England in the late years of the decade. The sharp rise that did occur in the middle fifties can be attributed as much to the Crimean War and the poor French and British harvests as to any Ricardian pressures on food prices in a rapid industrialization.[43] There has been much attention lavished upon the effect of railroads in creating national markets for Eastern manufactures by reducing transport costs. It seems clear, however, that what the railroads carried back from the West—for the manufacturing centers as well as for export—was more essential to industrialization than the manufactured goods that they carried out.

The squeeze upon manufacturers' profits that was predicted by Ricardo was made inoperable in the United States of the forties and fifties by the opening of new, fertile agricultural areas. But this is an exceedingly negative point of departure. First, agricultural produce—cotton, primarily, and cereals—formed the basis of the high trade balances in 1840, 1843, and especially, 1846 and 1847. Second, the opening of new food-producing regions imposed a strong autonomous investment push within the multiplier-accelerator process. Considerable investment was required for urban service centers, ahead of demand, not balanced by previous savings, and with strong local multiplier effects. This increase in western incomes, spent on goods that could be exported interregionally (in contrast to the services of marketing facilities that could not), increased the induced investment pressures in the East, which in turn made new jobs, absorbed more immigration, and made necessary the further development of food production in the new Northwest.[44]

Granting the implications of this analysis, what was the timing of the impetus to capital formation? In the twenties and early thirties, the canals initiated the period of transport innovation. In 1841 there was the first peak in railroad mileage added, which was followed by a sharp decline to 1843 and 1844. From that time until the war, and especially between 1849 and the peak in 1856, the increase in railway mileage was continuously and increasingly above the trend of growth for the period 1831–1910.[45] The population shift to the marginal (in the geographical, not the productivity, sense) areas occurred a decade earlier, in the forties; for the territory added to the census enumeration after 1830, the population increase in the forties was 677,000, and in the fifties, 2.4 million.[46] It seems clear, in the light of this analysis and this timing, that the railroads, however powerful they were in absorbing capital and promoting further mechanical innovation elsewhere in the system, may have had their most powerful effect in accelerating the tremendous innovation embodied in the shift of population and the industrialization of agriculture. As a measure of the change in the structure of farming, note that the share of agricultural equipment in the total of manufactured producers' durables doubled between 1839 and 1859 and that farm improvements grew at a rate of 45.4 per cent between 1849 and 1859.[47] These agricultural innovations and the shift in population that supported them were an indispensable part of the industrialization of the American economy.

Beginning in the decade of the thirties and accelerating in the two decades following, a series of structural changes in the sources of capital, the new textile manufacturing sector, and the basic metal industries combined to raise the growth of capital at given capital-output ratios and to increase the capital intensity of the economy, directly and indirectly. The development of railroads absorbed capital, increased the borrowing-income ratio for the system, and was essential for the opening of the fuel- and food-producing regions. The timing and concentration of these changes and the probable direction of their impact upon the parameters and exogenous variables in the multiplier-accelerator process provide both evidence and explanation for a surge of income growth in the American economy in the period of recovery after the depression of 1837.

VI. The Post–Civil War Period

When we pass the Civil War and enter the decade of the seventies, the way in which the war interrupted the press of developments that had been under way since the early forties becomes clear. In the South, activity was disrupted entirely, but, in the North, development and growth were in many ways spurred in the war years. Whether the data simply average these effects, masking the northern industrialization, or whether the war did indeed set back the pace of development is a moot question. There was a remarkably slight depression beginning late in 1865. Then, after the low point in 1867, a railroad boom began which carried business through a brief contraction in 1870 to the precipitous break of 1873. But in spite of the panic and the severe decline in prices, per capita real income grew over the decade. Again, a railroad boom carried the drive, beginning in 1877, well before the turn in overall activity in 1879. By the time it turned down in the early eighties, the spurt had raised the net output level at an annual rate higher than any experienced before or since. It is debatable whether this period is really distinguishable, in the sense of structural change, from the surge that characterized the two decades before the war. For example, Schumpeter considered the war to have been only an interruption in the upswing of the second, the *bourgeois,* Kondratieff long wave. In his chronology, the peak was reached in the seventies, and from then until the turn of the century the system absorbed and adjusted to the great changes of the railroad era.[48] We shall follow the calendar suggested earlier in examining the pace of change over the forty-year period after the war.

Schumpeter argued that the disruptions of the war were swamped by the rising tide of railroad expansion that began or continued immediately after the end of fighting. What were they? Destruction was limited entirely to the South, and it was also in the defeated region that the great social upheaval and inflation occurred. In fact, it is not difficult to make a strong argument for the hypothesis that the North conducted its war finance on a good Keynesian basis and that it was mismanagement *after* the war that created the intolerable strains in the money market. But in the South the breaking of normal capital flows and commercial relations intensified the tremendous organizational uncertainties and the difficulties of getting the large-scale, speculative cotton agriculture under way again. The result, a generation later, was that the South had settled into the role of a colonial economy, backward in every economic sense of the word.[49] But there were other strains and imbalances outside the South. The pressure of rapid debt reduction and the general maladministration of the revenue surplus added to the confusion over monetary panaceas; these problems were not solved until the late nineties. However, the combination of war and tariff had fostered the manufacturing sector and brought about a greater independence of England than had been achieved in the whole first half-century. Industry emerged from the war in a highly liquid state, and we shall find that the impact of deflation in the time of prosperity fell largely upon the unfortunate farmers. The basic financial confusion helped nobody, but the regressive fiscal policy worked to the advantage of the saving classes in a period of strong demand for investment funds. With this background, we can summarize some of the important magnitudes of the postwar development and study the structural changes that might have caused it.

As was mentioned earlier, there were two periods of rapid growth, separated by almost two decades of relatively sluggish, absorptive activity. The first strong push began about 1867, stopped short in 1873, and then continued from 1877 to 1881 or 1882. The difference in rate of growth of income between the postwar boom and the low point in the early nineties was on the order of 3:1 for net national product (measured in decade averages) and about 7:1 for net product per capita. The drive starting in the late nineties was little more than half as rapid as the earlier one in the aggregates and much less than half as rapid in per capita terms.[50]

Let us try now to relate these developments in the rate of growth to changes in the underlying structure of the economy. The change in industrial shares simply continued the trend that had started in the prewar burst of industrialization. Agriculture's value added, although it grew very rapidly in the late seventies, slowed down drastically in the late eighties. In terms of employment, the farm share of gainfully occupied barely declined in the seventies and then fell sharply in the next decade. The rate of growth of value added in mining and manufacturing rose through the seventies and eighties, while farm value added grew at a rate of 15.3 per cent in the war decade, 51.1 per cent in the next, and then slowed down to a rate of 24.6 per cent in the eighties. There was no great change in the ratio of farm value added per worker to the average for the whole commodity-producing sector in 1869–79, and it is probably safe to conclude that agricultural productivity increased about as rapidly as productivity in the rest of the producing industries. In the eighties, however, the rate of growth of value added became negligible in agriculture, while in mining and manufactures the rate of increase was 2½ times what it had been earlier.[51]

It is difficult to see any concentration upon capital formation as opposed to consumers' goods in the first postwar
boom. Rather, the figures on aggregate capital intensity increase fairly steadily to the end of the century. The share of
gross capital formation in gross national product (GNP) was
22.5 per cent from 1869 to 1878, less than one percentage
point greater than it was in the succeeding decade. The
share of capital formation in the seventies was almost two
points less than the proportion in the nineties. There was,
then, a fairly steady increase in the proportion of income
that flowed into savings over the period. In marginal terms,
that is, in the relative *changes* in investment and net product,
there is an upward trend that reached its peak in the increase
between the decades 1879–88 and 1884–93. Finally, capital
intensity, measured by the ratio of reproducible capital to annual net product, increased from 2.83 in 1879 to 3.36 in 1899.
As remarked earlier, increasing capital intensity causes the
growth rate to increase in multiplier-accelerator income
models. It is difficult to say what was the increase in capital
ratios between the war and postwar decades, but the increase
to the end of the century must have given added impetus to
the second surge in the growth rate. Within Kuznets' capital-
formation totals, the share of construction grew markedly between 1869–78 and 1884–93, while the share of producers'
durables declined at first and then increased sharply in the
first decade of the present century. This change supports
Schumpeter's suggestion that the first part of this surge of
industrialization was propelled by the railway expansion and
the second part by technical change in the manufacturing
sectors. These observations can now be used as a vantage
point from which to consider the specific effects of growing
industries on the rate of increase of income.[52]

The postwar railroad boom started in 1867 and reached
its peak in 1872. By then, the total value of road and equipment was over $8 billion, and the gross capital expenditure
for the year $604 million. Expenditures turned down for the

rest of the decade but were still sufficient to account for over 20 per cent of the total gross capital formation. The proportion fell to 15.6 per cent in the next decade and then fell to half of that until the twenties, when of course it declined even more.[53] Between 1868 and 1871 the rate of growth of railway mileage averaged 12 per cent annually, not comparable to the 22 per cent around 1850 but not to be approached again except for the two years 1880–81.[54] The numerical effect of this capital growth on the national average is obvious, and the reverberative impact has been discussed with respect to the earlier boom.

Two other aspects of railway development should be added to the discussion at this point: (1) the lead of railway building over population inflows in the postwar boom and (2) the manner in which the roads were financed. Whereas before the Civil War railroad construction lagged behind immigration and behind the movement of population into the West, after the war the railroads led both these series. Part of the explanation for the change lies in the labor requirements and the dependence upon immigrant manpower for construction in the fifties. Part of it lies in the speculative, promotional, colonizing aspect of much of the western railway development in the later period.[55]

Even more important than the effect that railroad building ahead of demand had upon the investment-output ratio were the effects arising out of the financing practices of the railway companies. More than any other form of investment in the nineteenth century, although it was to be matched later by the utilities, railway expansion required tremendous creation of credit, at first by state governments, then by English banks and individuals, and finally, as the major stock traded in the financial exchanges. The danger of this speculation is evident in the crisis of 1857 and more drastically, after the Northern Pacific failure, in the crisis of 1873. In the light of the capital intensity of railroad expansion, the high propensity to borrow, and the tendency to build ahead of demand, the impact of railroad investment upon the parameters of the multiplier-accelerator relationships in the postwar decade cannot be reasonably questioned.

The capital-intensive public utilities and street railways gave the second great impetus to capital formation, well after the first upsurge. In 1877, the telephone was introduced; in 1882, electric light and power; in 1887, the electric street railway. In each case, the expansion was rapid, and together they were sufficient to make the recovery after the depression of 1893 carry on to become the upswing of the third Kondratieff. Whatever the importance of electric power in manufacturing, which had become significant in cotton mills after 1882, Schumpeter dismissed this use of electricity as signifying little compared with the development of the electric tram. The role of capital intensity in these sectors in raising the level of capital formation in the nineties hardly bears repeating. What is less well recognized, however, is the strength of an organizational innovation that accompanied the street railway and raised all the parameters dependent upon the availability of credit: the holding company. In subsequent periods the holding company (and other forms of combination and monopoly introduced about this time) might, by increasing profits and retained earnings and by increasing barriers to entry, reduce the rate of growth of investment and therefore of income. But at this point in the development of the industry, given the nature of the utility and the state of the capital markets, it is unlikely that the monopoly elements of the holding company counted for more in a depressing sense than did its usefulness in facilitating borrowing and the absorption of investable funds. The net short-run effect must have been positive.

Within manufacturing, the scarcity of labor, which persisted despite the waves of immigration, was met by a series of innovations that, without exception, involved increased capital intensity. The capital-output ratio increased by 10 per cent in each of the two decades following 1874–83, and the capital-labor ratio (limited to reproducible capital) rose from $2,320 per member of the labor force in 1879 to $2,770 in 1889, $3,560 at the end of the century, and $4,170 in 1909 (all in 1929 prices and without adjustment for the reduction in hours). The result was an increase in value added per worker in mining and manufacturing of 18.4 per cent in the decade 1869–79, 46 per cent in the following decade, and 9.3 per cent in the last decade of the century (all in prices of 1879). The value of output of fixed capital grew increasingly from the end of the Civil War to the decade of the nineties, when it declined. Where and when did these changes arise? Schumpeter lists the sources for us: efficient coking in the prosperity before 1873; use of petroleum for lighting at the end of the war and the development of petroleum for other purposes later in the period; manufactured gas and natural gas, especially in the late seventies and eighties; farm implements, the output of which rose four times between 1860 and 1890; the Singer sewing machine and the McKay shoe-sewing machine, especially after 1860; textile improvements, which had started early and continued through the period. Iron mining did not change technically, but between 1870 and 1890 there was a shift from the eastern states to the ore fields of the Central West and South, which was sufficient (with some foreign imports) to bring the price down to one-third over the two decades. The Bessemer process and other technological changes in milling were increasingly adopted up to the late eighties. Finally, the iron and steel industry may stand as an example of the development of another of the great institutional innovations before the end of the century: the vertical combination.[56]

Manufacturing and mining have the lowest capital-output ratio among the major groups in the economy, so the producers' goods innovations, simply as a source of investment activity and increased capital intensity for the system, might not have been sufficient to carry the two periods of increasing growth rates without the expansion of railroads and utilities and the shift in population. What is unquestionable, however, is the effect of the improvements in the producers' goods sector in reducing the costs and prices of manufactured goods and thereby expanding markets and releasing innovation elsewhere in the system. The labor savings have been mentioned already; literally without exception the cost of materials declined as a proportion of the value of product in the manufacturing industries between 1880 and 1890. In the following period, as agricultural prices and minerals prices rose, the cost-of-materials ratios increased slightly; but in only one case, the nonferrous metals, was the change sufficient to wipe off the technical gains of the previous decade.[57]

The development of capital in agriculture is an essential part of this story. We have already discussed the role of the investment created by the shift of population into the undeveloped western north central region. Without a great deal of mechanization, however, the shift to more fertile areas would not have been sufficient to release workers to industry and to keep down the prices of food products in the face of the demand pressures of industrialization and immigration in the last third of the century. Actually, agricultural prices came down over the period in almost exactly the same degree as all commodity prices. Manufactured goods and mine products had a greater price decline than the average for the whole system, and construction prices came down hardly at all, actually rising in the last two decades. The two decades between 1859 and 1879, and especially the ten years after the Civil War, were the period of greatest increase in farm improvements and introduction of capital equipment. This timing, in addition to its importance in preventing the Ricardian pressures from inhibiting the growth of industry, is extremely important for subsequent farm history because of its coincidence with the period of peak farm prices. Farmers are both encouraged and enabled to make capital purchases in periods of high agricultural prices; the mortgage burden is usually felt later—in this case, in the long deflation that came after the war decade of the sixties.[58]

Finally, it is necessary to consider the changes in the organizational structure of industry and in the capital markets that accompanied and reinforced the changes in technology and composition that we have outlined. Recall that, in Schumpeterian terms, the importance of capitalist enterprise is primary; without entrepreneurial innovation, inventions count for nothing. Furthermore, he argued, entrepreneurship requires a governmental atmosphere of laissez faire, if not open support. In the analysis of Professor Gerschenkron, the development of entrepreneurial abilities and the complicity (in some cases the innovational drive) of the government are both essential first steps, if not prerequisites, of the initial spurts of growth. In the United States, the acquisitive instincts reached full flower in the nineteenth century, and the last third of the century carried the development of Social Darwinism to its extreme. For twenty years after the Civil War, the government—either through an honest conviction that unfettered competition promised the greatest social advance or through outright corruption during such scandals as the Gold Corner panic of 1869 or the Crédit Mobilier affair three years later—maintained a remarkable "anything goes" atmosphere in the business community. The first reform administration, Grover Cleveland's, succeeded in withdrawing government operations from the underworld. But he failed to deal effectively with the surplus problem and with the silver forces and the protectionists. The century ended with the Dingley tariff, the rescue operations of J. P. Morgan, and the final victory of the sound-money forces and the gold standard. Schumpeter called the second Kondratieff, whose upswing contains the first and the beginning of the second surge we have described, the *bourgeois* Kondratieff. The third Kondratieff wave, which began with the spurt of income growth at the end of the century, he called the *neo-*

mercantilist. Whether or not we agree that mercantilism, in the sense that focuses economic policy on the needs of the state, characterized the first quarter of this century, it must be agreed that Theodore Roosevelt and Woodrow Wilson represent a rebirth of government after the familiar history of social irresponsibility in the last third of the nineteenth century. The laissez faire posture of that period is all the more remarkable when it is contrasted with the role of the government in financing and promoting railroads and disposing of public lands before, and to some extent in, the years immediately following the Civil War.

If the state was guilty of few crimes of commission— that is, of outright interference with entrepreneurial activity —it must nevertheless answer for its omissions in the monetary sector. In the persistent, misguided effort to stay out of the money market, to abide by the letter and the spirit of the Independent Treasury legislation, the government added to the confusion and missed the opportunity to contribute to maturity in the capital markets. This is not to say that change did not take place but simply to argue that what changes came about were almost all made *in spite of* the Treasury. The monetary sector adapted sufficiently to the needs of industry so that in the course of the last third of the century the ratio of money to income rose from 0.18 to 0.45. (The ratio in 1955 was 0.59). That the ratio of primary securities to national income rose from 1.23 in 1860 to 2.13 in 1870 to 3.24 in 1900 is of more interest as an indication of the availability of credit and the extent to which expansion was financed by borrowing (as opposed to retained earnings).

During the last decade of the century, three innovations in the securities markets changed the nature of industrial financing. The first was the introduction of "trust" certificates and industrial preferred stock, which were traded at the stockholder level. The second, coincidental with the merger promotions, was the expansion of the market for new securities to include direct public sale. The next step, the Morgan stage, was the growth of underwriting at the turn of the century.

The economy approached industrial maturity in this period with the shaky assistance of a hectic but slowly maturing financial community. The seasonal concentration of funds in New York and the willingness of the banks to employ short-term funds for long-term uses were the most dangerous elements of immaturity, apart from the fundamental inadequacy of the national banking system's "control." Between 1850 and 1900 the assets of financial intermediaries—the banking system, including savings and insurance institutions, investment companies, and government financial institutions—rose from $75 per head of population to $494 (in dollars of 1929). This development facilitated the growth of income, of course. But the booms and speculative bursts that unregulated banking fostered also contributed to the severity of the letdowns after each burst of real investment.[59] That is another story.

To recapitulate, the two bursts of income growth in the last third of the nineteenth century appear to have been closely associated with two major structural changes. One was a wave of railway building that constituted per se a tremendous demand for capital. In addition, railroad development released a chain of other innovations, economies of scale, and reorganizations that closed a development block and changed the nature of American industry. Second, by the end of the century, two new capital-intensive industries had appeared, electric utilities and street railways, and a set of institutional changes in the scale of enterprise and the organization of the capital markets made possible another spurt of growth. In the period since then, income has grown at a declining rate until the most recent war and postwar era. Capital-output ratios have been declining, and the capital-labor ratios have similarly been falling, until the burst of investment made necessary by the war. The increase in leisure, which does not figure in the net national product index, has continued and may be accelerating. It is extremely difficult to distinguish the results of technological change, in the sense of shifts in the production function, from the results of the increased use of capital. However, an experiment with aggregate production functions by Professor Solow attributes seven-eighths of the doubling of output per man-hour to technical change since 1909.[60] These developments should probably stand as the characteristic features of the rate of growth in the last half-century.

VII. The Distribution of Income

The final part of this history relates to the distribution of income, which has been conspicuous by its absence from several parts of the previous discussion. The degree of inequality is at once cause and effect in the complicated interrelations of economic growth. Changes in capital intensity, the withdrawal from agriculture, the pressure of obsolescence in nineteenth-century technological change—all these elements of the growth process would seem likely to make for rapidly changing income shares. On the other side of the model, the inequality of incomes is a major determinant of the size of the market for consumers' goods as well as the supply of capital.

To the extent that a large part of the population has a margin above subsistence, the market for manufactured goods and, especially in more recent years, for consumer durables will be expanding more rapidly than output as a whole. To the extent that the profit rate is maintained and that concentrations of capital are possible, the incentive and the availability of capital accumulations will be ensured. There is a *simpliste* view of the last point that should be guarded against; Marx has already pointed out for us the absurdity of the fairy tale of good and frugal capitalists who save and save until they wake up rich.[61] The important part of the process is the investment of the funds in productive capacity and, particularly, in innovations sufficiently labor- and resource-saving to keep the rate of return from falling under the pressure of growing capital stocks.

For the early period we have few benchmarks from which to measure the trend of inequality. At the end of the eighteenth century it was observed that "although the wage of common labor is much higher here [than in Great Britain], yet that of the artificer is not."[62] This relatively narrow spread between skilled and unskilled wages was laid, correctly, it would seem, to the agricultural demand for labor. Under this pressure the narrow differential for skill was maintained without much change until after the Civil War, with the following few exceptions. The common-labor rate fell relative to the skilled groups (and to farm labor) under the impact of immigration in the immediate prewar period. The rate for female labor in the new textile mills rose much more rapidly than other wages, at least over the first two-thirds of the century. The war and the emancipation had little effect on the regional differentials for skilled workers but did, of course, have a vast effect upon skill differentials and farm wages within the South. In sum, laborers' wages appear to have increased more rapidly than skilled wages before the Civil War and then to have fallen behind, with the exception of the late seventies, when manufacturing labor suffered more than did agricultural.[63]

For the wage share in total net product, we have even less information. From 1839 to 1849, wage rates and value added per worker (both in constant dollars) were rising. Since wage rates appear to have been going up more rapidly, this would indicate an increasing share of value added being paid out in wages. In the next ten years, real wages fell, but value added per worker increased; the wage share, within the limits of this crude approximation, probably fell between 1849 and 1859. Now, we know that the capital-labor ratio was rising throughout this period and that there was some decline in the rate of return (as measured by interest rates on prime commercial paper). If this is acceptable evidence, then the innovations, which were clearly not capital-saving, were not sufficiently labor-saving to prevent the apparent decline in the rate of return. Given the pressure of immigration in the decade of the fifties, relatively more labor-saving innovation would have plunged wage rates more sharply down.

An excellent series of wage-shares estimates for the period from 1849 to 1910 by Professor Edward C. Budd indicates a rise in the wage share in private income from 37.6 per cent in 1849–50 to a peak in 1889–90 (49.7 per cent), after which there was a decline to 46.1 per cent at the turn of the century and then a rise to 47.8 per cent ten years later. Had there been no change in the proportion of hired to self-employed, the wage share would have risen less; similarly, had there been no shift out of agriculture, there would have been less gain by the wage-earning group. To round out the institutional developments, upon which Professor Budd largely relies for his explanation of the change, it should be remarked that a great part of the increase of wage share in agriculture took place in the period from 1860 to 1870 as a result of the emancipation of the slave-labor force and the consequent swelling of the hired-labor ranks. In that decade and in the eighties, most of the change took place. In the earlier increase in wage share, most of the gains were caused, within the institutional explanation offered, by improvements within non-farm industry; the decline in the weight of the farm sector contributed about one-quarter of the gain. In the second major change, the decline in the agricultural proportion in total employment was the main factor, with the share increase within industry providing a little less than two-fifths. Over all, the fall in the wage share in agriculture and the declining importance of agriculture in total employment, combined with the slight rise within industry, together account for the increase of about 9.5 percentage points over the seven decades to 1910. The gain was concentrated in industry in the decade of the eighties; the most significant fluctuation occurred again within industry in the nineties, when the wage share dropped by almost five points.[64]

What can we infer about the trend in inequality of incomes, first from the evidence on the fluctuations in the wage share in industry and, second, from the decline in the agricultural proportion of net product? The over-all effect would seem to be in the direction of increasing inequality. This is important, first, because of the direct relationship between inequality and savings and, in addition, because the high mean income and the mass of the distribution concentrated above the margin of subsistence increased the market for mass-produced consumer goods and, especially, for consumer durables. We have, again, some impressionistic reports. James Bryce, in 1891, observed that sixty years before he wrote there had been "no great fortunes in America, few large fortunes, no poverty." At the end of the eighties, he went on, "there is some poverty (though only in a few places can it be called pauperism), many large fortunes, and a greater number of gigantic fortunes than in any other country in the world." He expected the growth of fortunes and of inequality to continue, probably even to increase, on the grounds of native boldness and the scale of American industrial operations.[65]

It seems clear that Bryce was right in the decades immediately following but that he was wrong in his prediction over the long run; the degree of inequality has decreased since he wrote *The American Commonwealth*. But he would certainly have found support in more recent studies of the period between the Civil War and the nineties. Professor Kuznets has argued that inequality probably increased in that period. Partly, this is an inference from (1) the degree of unemployment at the end of the century, (2) the increased spread between agricultural and nonagricultural incomes, and (3) the trend toward industrial concentration after 1870, which by concentrating capital gains and asset holdings would have been sufficient to overcome the decline in the property income share over the period.[66] Over the last quarter of the century there was a rise in the ratio of savings to income and in the share of net capital formation in national income; there must, of course, be an intimate connection between these facts and the trend in inequality. It should be added, also, that the rise in aggregate real-income levels, which we have been accustomed to discuss as one result of the rate of capital formation, is itself a cause of the rise in the rate of savings. Marginal productivity has little to add to this story. The increase in capital stock should have reduced the rate of return on capital, but this is turned about by the strength of innovation, the relative labor-saving impact of the technological changes of the period, and the flood of immigration, which swelled both the labor force and the demand for housing.

All this discussion has been in terms of pretax incomes. What role did the government play in the shape of the distribution? With the exception of pensions to veterans, there was very little redistributive expenditure in the period before or after the Civil War. But more important than any expenditure program was the policy of cheap land sales and land grants, which may be characterized by the Distribution Act of 1836, the Preemption Act of 1841, and the triumphant Morrill Act of 1862. Interest payments and the military departments dominated the budget expenditures; public works were small, averaging about 7 per cent of expenditures in the postwar decades and rarely rising above 10 per cent. Aside from the pensions, the only redistributive expenditures, in the social-security sense, would be the payments for aid to Indians. (If interest payments are counted among the redistributive elements, rather than as factor payment for the use of capital, then it should be noted that they would have had a strongly regressive effect.) The budgetary impact, therefore, would be highly regressive, arising as it did from a tax system composed largely of regressive excises and protective tariffs. In 1861 a 3 per cent tax on incomes above $800 was passed by Congress, and in 1864 it was made progressive with rates ranging between 5 and 10 per cent over the income range from $600 to $5,000 and above. After the war, taxes were reduced with enthusiasm, and in 1867 the exemption was raised and the rate reduced to a flat 5 per cent. In 1870, western congressmen extracted a two-year extension in exchange for a compromise reduction, but the end was in sight, and, two years later, the tax was repealed. In 1894 western and southern agrarians and the urban industrial labor force achieved an income-tax clause in the Wilson-Gorman tariff bill. The constitutionality of the tax was denied in the *Pollack v. Farmers' Loan and Trust Company* case the following year, and the second income tax died, having yielded a grand total of $77,000 in revenue.

Under Theodore Roosevelt, as part of what was called earlier the beginning of neomercantilism, expenditures for social services, primarily in disaster relief and public health, plus the conservation and agricultural development programs, set in motion the use of federal expenditures for income redistribution. This is not to assert that redistribution was the intention of these services, as might be the case with unemployment relief or direct farm aid, but rather to indicate that the change in the nature of federal expenditures at this time did have the effect of changing the distribution of incomes. In the same direction, the Payne-Aldrich bill brought forth a renewal of the debate on progressive taxation. Finally, the compromise act contained a corporation "excise" (really an income) tax and was followed by the income tax amendment. In 1913 the progressive income tax became a permanent part of the federal revenue law. Before World War I, it is highly unlikely that the impact of government finance upon income shares in the economy was ever neutral, much less progressive. With the beginning of new government responsibility in the administration of Theodore Roosevelt and the change in relative importance of the income tax and the excises, the federal budget began, increasingly, to redistribute income in the direction of greater equality. That trend has not been reversed.

In sum, what was the relationship between income inequality and the surges of rapid development that we have been observing? In the first period, the wage share gained initially and then fell, in industry, in the decade of the fifties. It is likely that income inequality increased over the whole period. After the Civil War, the wage share increased into the decade of the eighties, but there appears also to have been a rise in the number of large fortunes. Certainly, in the spurt that got under way in the nineties, there was a decline in the wage share in national income and a decline in the equality of personal income shares. The decline in the rate of return that one might expect to result from the tremendous increase in capital stock was held back by a sufficient rate of labor-saving innovation. The periods of increasing inequality occurred at times favorable to increases in saving out of income and, therefore, for capital accumulation and more rapidly rising investment and income growth rates. That the mean income level was relatively high, compared with England and the European industrial nations over the period, made for a large and stable market for manufactured goods and directed and accelerated much of the initial industrial development of the American economy.

To the extent that the great mass of the American nation approached riches and/or gaiety over the course of industrialization in the nineteenth century, the approach was accomplished not by a redistribution of income shares in their favor but rather by a continuous sharing in the gains of productivity upon which the growth of income rode. Real wages rose almost continuously, falling back only once, in the depression of the seventies, and losing ground significantly (but briefly) only after 1890, at the height of the third industrial and organizational spurt. The equality which struck European visitors was remarkably high in comparison with the European experience. The movements of the wage share worked toward increased equality; the declining fortunes and importance of the farm sector probably tended to increase the spread, the gap between highest and lowest incomes. Rapid technological change maintained the rate of return on capital and the institutional developments in the direction of industrial concentration maintained the position of the largest wealth-holders. Over all, it is likely that the period of industrialization that we have been studying witnessed some increase in inequality. It is likely, finally, that "the approach to delicacy" over the period more than balanced any loss of relative position, even for the least skilled and the least well-situated in the mass of the nation.

VIII. Conclusion

This chapter has attempted to explain the growth of national income in the nineteenth century by applying a simple capital-adjustment theory of growth to the three accelerations that marked the period. There are several assumptions implicit in this procedure; the most important follow. First, it has been assumed that industrialization took place in the United States in a series of clearly defined forward surges—specifically, in the period between the depression of 1837 and the Civil War, the decade and a half following the end of the war, and the decade centered on the turn of the century. Second, it has been assumed that the changing values in a multiplier-accelerator model could be used to explain the changes in the rate of growth of the economy. Third, it has been assumed that structural changes that increase directly or facilitate the rate of accumulation of capital will provide the driving force behind the surges of income development. It was observed that, in each of the rapid-growth periods, there was a change in the composition of activity that increased the importance of industries which, because of their position in the network of interdependence of production, were especially powerful in creating chains of demand for manufacturers and closing structural blocks elsewhere in the system. The major of these technical breakthroughs were, in the first two cases, carried forward by the railroad development and, in the last case, by institutional developments in the capital markets. Agriculture, in most respects the losing sector, maintained or supported the pace of industrial development by a series of technological improvements and geographical relocations that released the growing labor force for industry and made possible the feeding of the growing urban work force at steadily declining prices.

While the first quickening of growth, in the forties and fifties, may be labeled the industrial revolution by virtue of its precedence, it makes more sense to speak of a continuing revolution. In the first upward surge there was a great shift from consumers' to producers' goods in the composition of output; the economy lost its essentially commercial focus, turning toward industry. After the Civil War, on the second railroad wave, the nature of agriculture changed, and a series of reverberations back from the heavy-goods needs of the railroad opened the way for innovations in heavy industry and, in turn, in the sectors dependent on metals for equipment and materials. In this period and until the late nineties, the interruptions to growth were bred in the extremely unstable capital market, an area of structural tension. By contrast to European experience, especially among the imitators of English industrialization, the government contributed largely by taking a stiff laissez faire posture toward the more extravagant promotional behavior of the last third of the century, by imposing a series of protective tariffs, and by maintaining a generous policy with respect to the disposal of the public lands. The tariffs, by adding to the fiscal surplus, may have caused more harm than good.

There had been a revolution by the end of the century, a bourgeois revolution whose dimensions it would take the Karl Marx of the *Communist Manifesto* properly to celebrate.

The greatest "approach to delicacy" in history had been achieved. In the period that followed, the rate of income growth declined, and in the neomercantilist revival the state moved in to close some of the structural gaps and tensions that were part of the legacy of industrialization.

NOTES TO CHAPTER 4

1. Samuel Johnson, *Journey to the Western Islands of Scotland* (New York, 1924), p. 20.

2. Phyllis Deane, "The Implications of Early National Income Estimates for the Measurement of Long-Term Economic Growth in the United Kingdom," *Economic Development and Cultural Change*, IV, No. 1 (1955); U.S. Bureau of Labor Statistics, *History of Wages in the United States from Colonial Times to 1928*, Bulletin 604, 1934, pp. 12, 24.

3. See Joseph A. Schumpeter, *The Theory of Economic Development* (Cambridge, Mass., 1934). Some more recent explanations that depend upon changing conditions of production are those by Alexander Gerschenkron, "Economic Backwardness in Historical Perspective," in Bert F. Hoselitz (ed.), *Progress of Underdeveloped Areas* (Chicago, 1952); and "Notes on the Rate of Industrial Growth in Italy, 1881–1913," *Journal of Economic History*, December, 1955; Walt W. Rostow "The Take-off into Self-sustained Growth," *Economic Journal*, LXVI, No. 261 (March, 1956), 25–48; and James S. Duesenberry, *Business Cycles and Economic Growth* (New York, 1958). A convenient summary of Professor Kuznets' long-term estimates is "Long-Term Changes in the National Income of the United States of America since 1870," *Income and Wealth*, Series II: *Income and Wealth of the United States—Trends and Structure* (Cambridge, England, 1952), pp. 29–220.

4. The following references consider in detail one or more aspects of the major problems discussed below: Simon Kuznets, "Quantitative Aspects of the Economic Growth of Nations: Levels and Variability of Rates of Growth," *Economic Development and Cultural Change*, V, No. 1 (1954), 40–48; J. R. Hicks, "The Valuation of the Social Income," *Economica*, n.s., VII (1940), 105–24; Alexander Gerschenkron, "Problems in Measuring Long Term Growth in Income and Wealth," *Journal of the American Statistical Association*, LII (1957), 450; Paul A. Samuelson, "Evaluation of Real National Income," *Oxford Economic Papers*, n.s., II (January, 1950) 1–29; Moses Abramovitz, "The Welfare Interpretation of Secular Trends in National Income and Product," *The Allocation of Economic Resources* (Stanford, 1959), pp. 1–22.

5. Robert F. Martin, "National Income in the United States, 1799–1938," *National Industrial Conference Board Studies*, No. 241 (New York, 1939).

6. Simon Kuznets, *Trends and Structures, op. cit.*, pp. 221–41; William N. Parker and Franklee Whartenby, "The Growth of Output before 1840," *Trends in the American Economy in the Nineteenth Century* ("Studies in Income and Wealth," Vol. XXIV), pp. 191–216.

7. *Employment, Growth, and Price Levels, Hearings before the Joint Economic Committee*, 82d Con., 1st sess., statement of Raymond W. Goldsmith, in Part 2: "Historical and Comparative Rates of Production, Productivity and Prices," 1959, pp. 243, 278.

8. Harriet Martineau, *Society in America* (New York, 1837), II, 53–63; Alexis de Tocqueville, *Democracy in America* (New York, 1954), I, 48–56.

9. Joseph A. Schumpeter, *op. cit.*, p. 289.

10. Victor Clark, *History of Manufactures in the United States*, (1607–1860), (New York: Carnegie Institute of Washington, 1929), I, 381; George Sweet Gibb, *The Saco-Lowell Shops—Textile Machinery Building in New England, 1813–1949* (Cambridge, Mass. 1950), pp. 26–29.

11. Martin, *op. cit.*, pp. 9–12; Stanley Lebergott, "Wage Trends, 1800–1900," *Trends in the American Economy in the Nineteenth Century* ("Studies in Income and Wealth," Vol. XXIV), pp. 449–99; Robert G. Layer, "Earnings of Cotton Mill Operatives, 1825–1914" (Cambridge, Mass.: Committee on Research in Economic History, Inc., 1955); U.S. Bureau of Labor Statistics, *op. cit.*; Alvin H. Hansen, "Factors Affecting the Trend of Real Wages," *American Economic Review*, XV, No. 1 (March, 1925), 27–42.

12. Willford I. King, *The Wealth and Income of the People of the United States* (New York, 1915); Wesley C. Mitchell, *A History of the Greenbacks* (Chicago, 1903), pp. 349–51; *Employment, Growth, and Price Levels*, *loc. cit.*, statements by Ethel D. Hoover and George R. Taylor, Table 1, p. 395; Table 2, p. 397.

13. See Alexander Gerschenkron's review of Erik Dahmén, "Entrepreneurial Activity in Swedish Industry in the Period 1919–1939," *Review of Economics and Statistics*, XXXIX, No. 4 (November, 1957), 471–76.

14. An interesting interpretation of the last days of the Second Bank has been suggested to us by Paul David: that the conflict was between export-oriented banking (the Philadelphia bank with its southern and western interests) and import-oriented banking in New York and Boston.

15. Kuznets, *Trends and Structure, op. cit.*

16. Kuznets, "Quantitative Aspects," *op. cit.*, Tables 1 and 2 and Appendix, Table 14, pp. 14, 10, 13, 82–85.

17. Kuznets, "Long-Term Changes," *op. cit.*, Tables 3 and 4, pp. 50, 55.

18. Kuznets, "Quantitative Aspects," *op. cit.*; Moses Abramovitz, "Resource and Output Trends in the United States since 1870," *American Economic Review*, XLVI, No. 2 (May, 1956), 5–23.

19. James S. Duesenberry, *Business Cycles and Economic Growth* (New York, 1958), esp. chaps. 9 and 10.

20. Wassily Leontief, *Studies in the Structure of the American Economy* (New York, 1953), pp. 20–22.

21. Gerschenkron, "Economic Backwardness," *loc. cit.*; Walt W. Rostow, *op. cit.*, pp. 43–47.

22. Kuznets, "Long-Term Changes," *op. cit.*, Appendix, Table 51.

23. Ezra C. Seaman, *Essays on the Progress of Nations in Civilization, Productive Industry, Wealth and Population* (New York, 1852), pp. 157–58; Timothy Pitkin, *A Statistical View of the Commerce of the United States of America* (new and enl. ed.; New Haven, 1835), pp. 295–96.

24. U.S. Department of Commerce, *Historical Statistics of the United States, 1789–1945*, Series L 1–14, 1949, pp. 231–32.

25. Robert E. Gallman, "Commodity Output in the United States, 1839–1899," *Trends in the American Economy in the Nineteenth Century*, Table 4.

26. Seaman, *loc. cit.*

27. Gallman, *op. cit.*, Table 11; "Commodity Output in the United States, 1839–1899," Conference on Research in Income and Wealth, September 4–5, 1957, National Bureau of Economic Research, Inc., New York, Table 18. (Mimeographed.)

28. Gerald T. White, *A History of the Massachusetts Hospital Life Insurance Company* (Cambridge, Mass., 1955), chaps. iii and iv; Margaret G. Myers, *The New York Money Market* (New York, 1931), pp. 41, 318 ff.

29. Lance E. Davis, "Sources of Industrial Finance: The American Textile Industry, a Case Study," *Explorations in Entrepreneurial History*, IX, No. 4 (1957), 198–203; Alfred H. Conrad and John R. Meyer, "The Economics of Slavery in the Ante Bellum South," *Journal of Political Economy*, LXVI, No. 2 (April, 1958), 102, Table 3. Computed from data taken from the following: Federal Reserve Bank of New York, *Monthly Review*, March 1, 1921, p. 3; A. O. Greef, *The Commercial Paper House in the United States* (Cambridge, Mass., 1938); Joseph G. Martin, *One Hundred Years' History of the Boston Stock and Money Markets* (Boston, 1898), pp. 52–53.

30. U.S. Department of Commerce, *Historical Statistics*, 1949, Series M, 42–55, pp. 244–45. See Paul Studentski and Herman E. Krooss, *Financial History of the United States* (New York, 1952), p. 101.

31. John G. Gurley and E. S. Shaw, "The Growth of Debt and Money in the United States, 1800–1950: A Suggested Interpretation," *Review of Economics and Statistics*, XXXIX, No. 3 (August, 1957), 250–62.

32. Gerschenkron, "Reflections on the Concept of 'Prerequisites' of Modern Industrialization," *L'Industria*, II (1957), 375–83.

33. G. H. Evans, *Business Incorporations in the United States, 1800–1943* (New York, 1948), p. 20. In the sixties, it is important to note, the sample represents only four out of thirty-three states.

34. Oscar and Mary Handlin, "Origins of the American Business Corporation," *Journal of Economic History*, 1945. Reprinted in F. C. Lane and J. C. Riemersma (eds.), *Enterprise and Secular Change* (Homewood, Ill., 1953), p. 123.

35. This is essentially Schumpeter's description of the way a monopoly is exploited by a market innovator.

36. See J. S. Davis, *Essays in the Early History of American Corporations* (Cambridge, Mass.: Harvard University Press, 1917), chap. i.

37. For a concise summary of these developments see Evans, *op. cit.*, pp. 10–12. Recall the limitations of the sample: in 1875 and later, special-charter corporations continued to be important in a number of southern states.

38. Victor Clark, *op. cit.*, p. 381.

39. *Ibid.*, pp. 410–12, 434.

40. Computed from data in George Tucker, *Progress of the United States in Population and Wealth in Fifty Years* (New York, 1843), chap. 19; J. D. B. DeBow, *Compendium of the Seventh Census* (1850), U.S. Census Office (1854), Table CXCVI, p. 180.

41. Gallman, *op. cit.*

42. The ranking of industries by proportions of intermediate flows was computed at the Harvard Economic Research Project by Mrs. Virginia McK. Nail. The basic reference on input-output is, of course, Wassily W. Leontief, *The Structure of the American Economy* (2d ed., enl.; New York, 1951). See also Hollis B. Chenery and Tsunehiko Watanabe, "International Comparisons of the Structure of Production," *Econometrica*, October, 1958, pp. 487–521; and Goran Ohlin, "Balanced Economic Growth in History," *American Economic Review*, XLIX, No. 2 (May, 1959), 348.

43. Walter B. Smith and Arthur H. Cole, *Fluctuations in American Business, 1790–1860* (Cambridge, Mass., 1935), pp. 37–43.

44. Douglass C. North, "The United States Balance of Payments, 1790–1860," *Trends in the American Economy in the Nineteenth Century*, pp. 573–627.

45. Melville J. Ulmer, "Trends and Cycles in Capital Formation by United States Railroads, 1870–1950," *Studies in Capital Formation and Financing* (National Bureau of Economic Research, Occasional Paper 43) (New York, 1954).

46. U.S. Bureau of the Census, *A Century of Population Growth, 1790–1900* (1909), Table 9, p. 55.

47. Gallman, *op. cit.*

48. Joseph A. Schumpeter, *Business Cycles* (1st ed.; New York, 1939), I, 383–97.

49. C. Vann Woodward, "Origins of the New South, 1877–1913," *A History of the South* (Baton Rouge, 1951), Vol. IX, chap. 9.

50. Kuznets, "Long-Term Changes," *op. cit.*, Tables 3 and 4, pp. 50, 55.

51. Gallman, *op. cit.*

52. Kuznets, "Long-Term Changes," *op. cit.*, Tables 12, 34, 39, 41.

53. Ulmer, *op. cit.*

54. *Ibid.*, Table A-1, pp. 60–61.

55. Brinley Thomas, *Migration and Economic Growth* (Cambridge, 1954), pp. 83–122.

56. Schumpeter, *op. cit.*, pp. 303–18, 383–97; Kuznets, "Long-Term Changes," *op. cit.*, Table 11, p. 78; Gallman, *op. cit.*

57. U.S. Census Office, *Abstract of the Twelfth Census of the United States, 1900* (1902), Table 156, p. 324.

58. Gallman, *op. cit.*; Alvin S. Tostlebe, "The Growth of Physical Capital in Agriculture, 1870–1950," *Studies in Capital Formation and Financing* (National Bureau of Economic Research, Occasional Paper 44) (New York, 1954).

59. Gurley and Shaw, *op. cit.*, Tables 3 and 6, pp. 256, 258; Raymond W. Goldsmith, *Financial Intermediaries in the American Economy since 1900* (Princeton, N. J.; National Bureau of Economic Research, Inc., 1958), Tables 8 and 9, pp. 62–63, 65–66. See T. R. Navin and M. V. Sears, "The Rise of Market for Industrial Securities, 1887–1902," *Business History Review*, Vol. XXXIX, No. 2 (June, 1955).

60. Robert M. Solow, "Technological Change and the Aggregate Production Function," *Review of Economics and Statistics*, XXXIX, No. 3 (August, 1957), 312–20. See also Solomon Fabricant, *Basic Facts on*

Productivity Change (National Bureau of Economic Research, Occasional Paper 63, 1958), pp. 319–27.

61. Schumpeter, *History of Economic Analysis* (New York, 1954), pp. 573–74.

62. U.S. Bureau of Labor Statistics, *op. cit.*, p. 12, quoting from a manuscript letter of George Cabot, September 6, 1791, in Hamilton Papers, Library of Congress.

64. Edward Budd, "United States Factor Shares, 1850–1910," *Trends in the American Economy in the Nineteenth Century.* See also, Albert Rees, "Patterns of Wages, Prices and Productivity," in *Wages, Prices, Profits and Productivity,* American Assembly, 1959, Tables 4 and 7.

65. James Bryce, *The American Commonwealth* (2d ed.; London, 1891), II, 616–720.

66. Kuznets, "Proportion of Capital Formation to National Product," *American Economic Review,* XLII, No. 2 (May, 1952), 522–23; Clarence D. Long, *Labor Force under Changing Income and Employment* (Princeton, N. J., 1958), Table C-1, p. 345.

5

An Input-Output Approach

to Evaluating British Industrial Production

in the Late Nineteenth Century

I. INTRODUCTION

The rate of growth of British industrial production clearly slowed down in the last quarter of the nineteenth century. The relative decline is frequently explained as a result of the loss by the United Kingdom[1] of its overseas market for industrial goods. Such an explanation has great intuitive appeal, since the slowdown in the growth of production was accompanied by a significant drop in the rate of expansion of British export markets—explicitly, from a figure of 4.5 per cent per year in the 1840–60 period to one of 1.5 in the period from 1900 to 1913.

Despite the emphatic character of this downturn in the export market, however, it has been argued that it is insufficient to explain the decline in industrial expansion. The point is at least superficially convincing: the difference between actual exports in the last quarter of the nineteenth century and an extrapolated bill of goods based on an assumption of continued export growth is not sufficient to account for all the output lost by the reduced growth. The flaw in this argument, of course, is its failure to take account of the indirect as well as direct effects of export decline. Consequently, the primary focus of this study is upon just this problem—measuring the indirect as well as direct effects of a fall in exports. The principal analytical tool for achieving the objective is an input-output table for the British economy at the turn of the present century. To anticipate, the principal conclusion will be that if British exports had continued to grow in the last quarter of the century as they had in the third, English industrial output would have more than maintained the rapid pace of the earlier years.

Of course, while the model can indicate the possible empirical validity of this one counterfactual hypothesis, it will not, in and of itself, disprove other explanations. Consideration is therefore given to the alternative, specifically internal (or endogenous) explanations of the reduced growth, and indication is given why, in general, they seem to be of less substance.

Finally, accepting—at least temporarily—the primacy of the export factor, a variety of possible underlying causes or explanations of the change in the export market are investigated. A particular effort is made to avoid the common tendency toward exclusive explanations that are not related to other hypotheses or possibilities. In short, a more eclectic approach is adopted in the hope of obtaining a few fresh insights into understanding this first great "stagnation" of a modern, industrial economy.

II. The Input-Output Model and the Empirical Results

Under almost any set of realistic assumptions, increments of industrial exports should increase the value of total production by more than their own value. Such a statement embodies nothing more than the simplest application of multiplier theory to foreign trade.[2] For present purposes, this means that the indirect as well as direct effects of the late-nineteenth-century export decline must be somehow evaluated if any claim of completeness is to be advanced for the empirical measures of the impact of that decline.

About the best means now known for obtaining such measurements is the Leontief input-output table. The author has constructed such a table for the British economy of 1907, as shown in Table 7. The particular year 1907 was chosen because it marked the English government's first censuses of production in industry, agriculture, and fishing.[3] The crucial assumption underlying use of the input-output table in this fashion is that the so-called technical coefficients would not have been materially altered if English economic development had taken the far different course implied by continued export growth. This is a rather difficult assumption to justify on a priori grounds and is obviously an area for further research. However, the impression gained from hasty comparisons of the 1907 table with more recent tables for the English and United States economies is that the table would not have been drastically modified by a different pattern of growth, primarily because of the high degree of aggregation that is involved. In other words, the majority of changes apparently embody shifts within rather than between these broad industrial categories.

In constructing the table, it was assumed that production, as reported in the censuses, represented sales—an assumption that would be accurate within the range of inventory change. Transportation and merchandising costs were charged to the buyer rather than the seller and included in the charges to the undistributed sector; in fact, independent estimation indicates that these elements comprise about 62 per cent of the undistributed total. The direction of a sale was identified primarily, although not always, by the character of the product, for example, iron ore production by mines was listed, except for exports, as a sale to Iron, Steel, and Engineering, construction of new buildings as a sale to the Capital sector, etc. Export and Import values were taken from the *Annual State-*

TABLE 1

	Agric.	Chem.	Clay, Etc.	Cloth	Fisheries	Food, Etc.	Gas & Elec.	Iron, Steel, Etc.	Mines & Quarries
Agriculture....	15.915	.....	0.231	....	......	30.600	......	....	....
Chem. & Allied	9.359	18.973	....	1.831	......	2.270	0.086	0.530	0.150
Clay, Stone, Bldg. & Contracting..	....	......	10.046	....	......	....	2.300	....	....
Clothing.....	......	......	....	5.778	......	....	......	....	....
Fisheries.....	......	......	......	....	......	2.000	......	....	....
Food, Drink & Tobacco....	3.515	0.370	1.000	....	......	38.200	......	....	....
Gas & Elec. Utility Serv..	....	2.626	0.147	0.975	......	0.441	0.296	2.042	0.056
Iron, Steel, Engr. & Shipbldg....	1.387	1.181	10.572	0.534	0.051	0.026	2.977	110.299	0.409
Mines & Quarries....	......	2.673	9.315	0.790	0.120	2.500	10.690	10.745	15.959
Misc. Trades...	....	......	....	....	......	....	......	....	....
Other Metal (e.g., Copper, Zinc, Lead)..	....	1.039	5.317	....	......	....	......	11.112	....
Paper & Printing.....	....	......	....	....	......	1.009	0.010	....	....
Textiles......	2.415	0.078	....	20.600	0.405	0.607	......	7.217	1.255
Timber........	0.471	0.666	8.875	....	......	2.844	......	2.130	4.520
Leather, Canvas & Rubber...	0.200	0.040	....	8.548	0.060	0.239	......	3.638	0.033
Undistributed..	16.187	11.229	2.716	7.753	0.060	72.483	4.294	56.727	7.132
Wages, Rents, Profits, Taxes, etc..........	176.553	21.557	74.139	47.673	11.082	89.514	22.875	153.389	119.531
Gross Domestic Outlay......	226.000	60.432	122.358	94.483	11.778	242.733	43.528	357.839	144.977
Imports...............	....	14.600	20.591	14.500	......	62.500	......	17.704	3.049
Gross Outlay...	226.000	75.032	142.949	108.983	11.778	305.233	43.528	375.533	148.026
Net Outlay....	210.085	56.059	132.903	103.205	11.778	267.033	43.232	265.334	132.067

* Columns in this table represent purchases; rows represent sales.

ment of the Trade of the United Kingdom, which lists these figures at free-on-board prices. This meant that the exports included transportation and merchandising costs between plant and port, which had to be deducted to keep export sales by an industry consistent with internal sales. The Government sector includes only tax-financed services and were estimated from the Imperial and Local Government revenue and expenditure returns as reported in the *Statistical Abstract for the United Kingdom.* Nontax-financed government activities were reported under the relevant industrial heading, for example, government shipbuilding was included in the Engineering, Iron & Steel sector. Capital and Household expenditures were also taken from the *Census of Production,* with

INPUT-OUTPUT TABLE FOR THE UNITED KINGDOM IN 1907*

Misc.	Other Metals	Paper & Printing	Textiles	Timber	Leather, Etc.	Undist.	Capital	Government	Households	Exports
0.002	.....	.....	2.390	0.900	5.104	10.663	.....	16.741	139.054	4.400
.....	1.428	0.632	1.707	.....	0.096	6.434	.....	0.522	9.145	21.869
.....	.....	.....	.....	.....	.....	9.380	107.948	.....	7.509	5.766
.....	.....	.....	.....	0.048	.....	1.562	.....	0.324	88.905	12.366
.....	.....	.....	.....	.....	.....	1.018	.....	.....	8.000	0.700
.....	.....	0.800	1.000	.....	0.200	17.525	.....	0.097	223.029	19.500
0.013	0.828	0.387	1.181	0.213	0.019	4.383	.....	8.000	21.321	0.600
.....	0.089	.....	0.060	.....	0.385	11.593	117.990	5.095	18.383	94.502
0.033	2.189	1.070	4.800	0.350	0.315	14.277	.....	3.000	30.750	38.450
0.761	.....	.....	.....	.....	.....	0.072	1.138	.....	4.348	1.969
.....	11.553	.....	.....	.....	.....	0.466	.....	4.195	10.410	49.373
.....	.....	17.306	.....	.....	.....	20.183	.....	0.113	19.380	3.307
.....	0.210	0.527	120.808	1.337	.....	11.280	.....	0.225	40.570	129.177
.....	0.015	.....	.....	5.798	.....	2.545	2.084	.....	18.205	2.305
.....	0.020	0.041	1.930	.....	5.909	2.462	.....	.....	3.724	8.084
2.216	33.912	2.745	7.817	10.200	0.682	33.715	23.050	24.343	317.109	169.530
4.443	11.893	33.650	93.703	21.444	8.618	514.877	.....	141.286	322.480	140.000
7.468	62.137	57.158	235.396	40.290	21.328	762.125	252.210	203.941	1282.322	.....
0.820	31.328	4.150	100.949	6.100	13.600	41.775	3.322	2.000	216.678	91.942
8.288	93.465	61.308	336.345	46.390	34.928	803.900	255.532	205.941	1499.000	795.842
7.527	81.912	44.002	215.537	40.592	29.019	770.185	255.532	64.655	1176.520	703.900

the usual distinction between consumer durables and other capital goods being made so that consumer durables are listed under the Household sector. Finally, estimates of returns on foreign investments were taken from Paish's 1909 work. A more detailed description of sources and methods is presented in Appendix A at the end of this chapter.

The estimates undeniably contain errors. These errors, however, are probably not important enough to greatly modify the results, since the whole character of the application, particularly its static time dimension, is such as to make the final consequences of any errors minimal.[4] The estimates could be most readily improved by incorporating a railroad sector, thereby substantially reducing the undistributed component.

More detailed information on profits, wages, and rents would also be helpful so that this category could be broken down as finely as the equivalent column components of Capital, Government, and Household. The only knowledge necessary for reading the table is to note that the columns represent purchases while the rows indicate sales.

To estimate what the level of industrial output might have been in the United Kingdom in 1907 if the rate of export growth had been maintained, the export bill of goods can be computed that would have resulted if the 1854–72 growth had continued to 1907. The particular years 1854 and 1872 were chosen in a crude effort to eliminate the major effects of the business cycle; 1854 and 1872 were, like 1907, years of high level activity.[5] The hypothetical export bill for 1907, computed on this assumption of continued high-level growth, is shown in Table 2 along with 1907's actual exports; a comparison of the actual to the hypothetical gives a crude measure of a sector's failure or success in maintaining its world market position. Thus textiles, mining, chemicals, and engineering were particular trouble spots. The decline in textiles is not unexpected in light of the rise in the number of foreign looms, and, in the same way, the small ratios in chemicals and engineering could be explained by the growth of German, American, and other overseas competition.

The level of industrial activity that would have been generated if exports had maintained the 1854–72 rates of growth, everything else assumed unchanged, was found by replacing the actual exports with the theoretical exports. In an input-output analysis several different choices of the final bill of goods are possible. In general, the choice should be closely related to what is believed to be autonomous or predetermined in the economic system. For instance, if one chose to put all domestic capital expenditures, household consumption, exports, and government consumption expenditures into the final bill of goods, the tacit assumption has been made that these expenditure decisions are either lagged functions of previous levels of activity or determined by noneconomic or random influences.[6] Obviously, they might just as easily have been considered as determined by the current level and composition of activity. The choice is so arbitrary that a thorough analysis

TABLE 2

A COMPARISON OF ACTUAL AND HYPOTHETICAL 1907
EXPORTS BY SECTORS

	Hypothetical*	Actual*
Agriculture.........................	0.559	4.400
Chemical and Allied Trades...........	52.741	21.869
Clay, Stone, Building & Contracting...	4.120	5.766
Clothing Trades....................	26.677	12.366
Fisheries..........................	6.500	0.700
Food, Drink & Tobacco Trades.......	5.680	19.500
Gas & Electric Utility Services........	1.770	0.600
Iron, Steel, Engineering & Shipbuilding.	204.514	94.502
Mining & Quarrying.................	118.921	38.450
Miscellaneous Trades...............	0.012	1.969
Other Metals......................	46.118†	49.373†
Paper & Printing Trades............	2.658	3.307
Textiles...........................	492.739	129.177
Timber & Woodworking.............	0.156	2.305
Leather, Canvas & Rubber Trades.....	8.933	8.084
Undistributed*‡...................	372.461	169.530
Wages, Rents, Profits, Taxes, Interest, etc.*‡...................	311.977	142.000
Total........................	1656.536	703.900

*At plant values in 1907 prices.
†Inclusive of 33.303 in bullion shipments.
‡Estimated as changed in proportion to the changes in the other exports (on the basis that these sectors represent service inputs into the foreign-trade sector generally).

would necessitate computation under a wide range of assumptions about the composition of the final bill of goods; four different "final bills" that seemed of particular interest for the present analysis are shown in Table 3.

In the present instance, it is not evident just which division between determined and predetermined is conceptually superior. However, the focus is on the measurement of long-run responses, which points toward the inclusion of a maximum number of sectors in the closed part of the system. By contrast, if measuring just the short-run, say one-year, response of capital outlay to a change in exports, incorporation of all the indirect effects might not be wanted, since not all these responses would be realized in one year's time. On the other hand, several sectors, particularly Capital, Government, and Household, embody a great deal of autonomous outlay, which implies that use of strictly linear, homogeneous functions for extrapolation of the effect of export change on these industries could result in an overestimate of gross output.

Shown in Table 4 is a summary of gross-value outputs computed under the four different assumptions about the final bill of goods reported in Table 3. Also shown are the actual gross outputs for 1907. The final outputs computed on the basis of retaining all actual exports except Textiles is intended as a test of the impact of new textile competition; similarly, use of the actual export bill of goods except Engineering and Chemicals is aimed at gauging new competition in these fields. The last of the hypothesized final bills includes government, capital, and household expenditures as well as the hypothetical exports for each sector. The intent was to use this estimate to gauge the extent to which inclusion of exogenous factors in the closed part of the system, when including only

TABLE 3

HYPOTHETICAL FINAL BILLS OF GOODS

	All Hyp. Exports	Actual Exports except Textiles	Actual Exports except Chem. & Eng.	Actual Gov't, Capital & Consumption with All Hyp. Exports
Agriculture	0.559	4.400	4.400	156.354
Chemical & Allied Trades	52.741	21.869	52.741	62.408
Clay, Stone, Building & Contracting	4.120	5.766	5.766	119.577
Clothing Trades	26.677	12.366	12.366	115.906
Fisheries	6.500	0.700	0.700	14.500
Food, Drink & Tobacco Trades	5.680	19.500	19.500	228.806
Gas & Electric Utility Services	1.770	0.600	0.600	31.091
Iron, Steel, Engineering & Shipbuilding	204.514	94.502	204.514	345.982
Mining & Quarrying	118.921	38.450	38.450	152.671
Miscellaneous Trades	0.012	1.969	1.969	5.498
Other Metals	46.118	49.373	49.373	60.723
Paper & Printing Trades	2.658	3.307	3.307	22.151
Textiles	492.739	492.739	129.177	533.534
Timber & Woodworking	0.156	2.305	2.305	20.445
Leather, Canvas & Rubber Trades	8.933	8.084	8.084	12.657
Undistributed*	372.461	296.793	218.844	736.963
Wages, Rents, Profits, Taxes, Interest, etc.	311.977	248.597	183.306	....
Totals	1656.536	1301.320	935.402	2619.266

*Estimated as in proportion to the change between actual and hypothetical for all other sectors.

TABLE 4

A COMPARISON OF GROSS DOMESTIC OUTPUT UNDER DIFFERENT
ASSUMPTIONS ABOUT THE FINAL BILL OF GOODS*

	Actual	With All Hyp. Exports	Actual Exports except Textiles	Actual Exports except Eng. & Chem.	Actual Gov't, Capital & Consumption with All Hyp. Exports
Agriculture	226.002	673.158	514.246	404.796	260.051
Chemicals	60.432	165.017	106.456	120.931	149.154
Clay, Stone, etc.	122.358	364.019	276.240	219.382	149.394
Clothing	94.482	282.014	205.023	164.193	126.087
Fisheries	11.778	39.904	25.953	20.679	18.698
Food, Drink & Tobacco	242.733	697.624	539.203	428.746	319.116
Gas & Electric Utility	43.528	130.700	97.118	78.327	58.622
Iron, Steel, etc.	357.829	981.978	658.210	696.368	561.627
Mines & Quarries	144.977	433.883	270.345	225.214	292.407
Miscellaneous	7.468	17.102	14.804	12.094	6.245
Other Metals	62.137	107.632	90.048	83.660	108.022
Paper & Printing	57.158	158.730	121.558	97.514	78.298
Textiles	235.396	821.161	747.252	311.182	1231.598
Timber	40.290	114.358	87.730	71.397	53.041
Leather, Canvas, etc.	21.328	52.482	40.198	32.851	61.640
Undistributed	762.435	2119.020	1605.877	1286.774	1174.374
Wages, Rents, etc.	1738.473	5394.764	4056.170	3200.359	....
Total	4228.804	12553.545	9456.431	7454.467	4648.375
Industrial Activity Component	1511.588	4376.115	3293.577	2472.927	3254.066
Corresponding Industrial Growth Rate, %	1.75 to 2.0	5.06	3.81	2.86	3.76

(Actual 1854–1872 Industrial Growth Rate = 3.05)

*In millions of pounds sterling.

exports in the final bill, might have biased the gross output estimates.

The aggregative figures beneath the totals in Table 4 measure the industrial activity component present in the totals; that is, these aggregates represent the sum of everything except Agriculture, Fisheries, Utilities, Wages, etc., and the substantial non-industrial component of Undistributed. To obtain hypothetical industrial growth percentages corresponding to these totals, Hoffmann's index of British industrial production (including construction) was marked upward by the ratio of the hypothetical to the £1,511,585 actual total. These new or hypothetical annual growth rates for industrial production can be contrasted with the actual rates also derived from the Hoffmann index. The actual growth rate from 1854 to 1872 was (on a compounded basis) 3.05 per cent, and from 1872 to 1907 it was 1.75 or 2 per cent. The corresponding derived rates for 1872 to 1907 were 5.06, 3.8, 2.86, and 3.76 per cent. Since all but one of these figures is substantially greater than the 3.05 per cent actually realized in the 1854–72 period, the results tend to support the hypothesis that if the rate of growth in industrial exports had been maintained, the United Kingdom could have sustained its former high-level advance in industrial production. On the other hand, it is also reasonably apparent that Engineering and Chemical competition, even taken together, were not sufficient to account for the decline in manufacturing growth.

III. ALTERNATIVE ENDOGENOUS EXPLANATIONS OF THE BRITISH DECLINE

The input-output results, while substantiating the plausibility of retarded exports as an explanation of the late-nineteenth-century stagnation in the United Kingdom, hardly constitute a proof that export decline was *the* explanation. Sufficient expansion of any component of the final bill of goods could have produced similar results.

However, several external or a priori considerations originally suggested the export explanation. There was the rapid growth of nationalistic tendencies and protectionism which increased international competition in heavy industry and textiles; also, a decrease occurred in the late nineteenth century in overseas lending by the British. These are but a few of the many bits of evidence suggestive of the retarded export hypothesis. Further support derives from the fact that the level of British imports continued to increase throughout the last quarter of the nineteenth century at somewhere near previous rapid rates. This at least tends to eliminate any explanation that exports dropped because internal difficulties cut British foreign purchases and thus restricted the ability of other countries to buy from the British.

Still, the slower economic growth of Britain in the fourth quarter of the nineteenth century also has been plausibly explained in terms of strictly internal difficulties or failures. The rejection or minimization of these "internal" hypotheses, an act implicit in the earlier choice of final goods, therefore must be justified, at least tentatively. For the most part, the internal explanations rely on either an absolute limitation on an important factor of production or the necessity of using increasingly inferior factors. Under either assumed hypothesis, decreasing returns become operative—in the one case, because of the traditional reasons associated with the presence of a fixed factor in a given, fixed production process; in the other, because of the successive substitution of less and less efficient productive combinations.

Internal explanations of the stagnation are well illustrated by those hypotheses that place the blame on the depletion of English natural resources. In the usual formulation, British resources are pictured as being so limited and of such increasingly inferior quality as effectively to preclude maintenance of a high rate of industrial growth. A major objection to this argument is the possibility of importing the necessary raw materials or inputs, especially in light of the rapid advances in transportation technology made in the late nineteenth century. One particular resource or factor of production, however, namely labor, may have been somewhat less internationally mobile. Unfortunately for this explanation, English population grew by only 0.63 per cent annually in the rapid growth period from 1854 to 1872, while a 1.41 rate was maintained between 1872 and 1907.[7] It could be argued, of course, that even these one-sided figures are inconclusive, since total population is not necessarily or directly related to the potential laboring force. Stricter factory laws regulating child and female labor and overtime hours could cut potentially available working hours even though over-all population grew; conversely, available labor hours need not be related too closely to available units of labor productivity if shorter hours result in increased productivity per hour. When these countervailing tendencies are balanced, it would seem a relatively safe conjecture that a shortage of labor imposed no serious stringencies on British production possibilities between 1875 and 1900.[8] It would be interesting, however, to segregate the wage component from the aggregated figure for wages, taxes, interest, etc., in the input-output table and, with the aid of average annual sector wages, determine the labor input necessary to produce the 1907 hypothetical bill of goods. Such a labor requirement could then be compared with that actually available at the time.

Another "internal" explanation that has enjoyed popularity stresses a demise in the entrepreneurial vigor of British businessmen and industrialists. The implication is sometimes made that a really dynamic entrepreneurial group could have maintained industrial growth in the face of any and all difficulties. For obvious reasons, such a hypothesis is relatively difficult to test by any quantitative methods, requiring a reliance on more subjective and qualitative assessments of the situation. About the only immediate promising quantitative approach would appear to be one that measured the relative evaluations placed upon leisure by business managerial groups under differing economic and social conditions. For now, it will suffice to point out that a negative as well as a positive case can be constructed.[9]

In general, it would seem a reasonably safe presumption that the United Kingdom did not exhaust its available supplies of entrepreneurship, labor, or raw materials—particularly the latter two. At least no apparent shortages of these factors developed that were sufficiently stringent to limit absolutely British industrial growth after 1870. However, the United Kingdom's competitive position in the world market could have been weakened by *relative* shortages even when absolute limits were inoperative.

IV. ALTERNATIVE EXPLANATIONS OF THE BRITISH EXPORT DECLINE

The many explanations advanced for the late-nineteenth-century decline in the growth of English exports can be placed in two broad categories. One set of hypotheses looks to a retardation in the world rate of growth in exports and inquires into reasons for this global decline. The second stresses a deterioration of England's competitive position in the world market, which resulted in her capturing a smaller than proportionate share of world growth in exports.

Quantitative evaluation of the relative importance of these two possibilities is rather difficult because of the scarcity of world trade statistics for the period before 1870. What is definitely known is that British manufactured exports[10] grew at about a 4.8 per cent rate in the 1854–72 period and then slowed to an approximate 2.1 per cent average growth rate in the years from 1876 to 1910. World trade in this latter period, on the other hand, grew at a 2.55 per cent rate, which indicates that British exports were not growing as rapidly as those of some competitors.[11] Furthermore, even though data are lacking, there are good historical reasons for believing that this relationship between English and world export growth in the last quarter reversed the relationship existing earlier, that is, the general impression is that the British expanded their exports faster than others in the earlier years of the nineteenth century. Strictly speaking, however, the only permissible inferences with the limited statistics are that the rate of growth in the United Kingdom's exports did decline and that the British failed, but only slightly, to keep pace with the rest of the world after 1876.

If world export growth did dwindle in the last quarter of the nineteenth century, at least four explanations for such a decline seem worth investigation. The simplest and most popular explanation places the blame on the growth of nationalism, autarchy, and tariff barriers during the period after 1870; Germany's rather complete abandonment of free trade in the 1870's and 1880's is, of course, a favorite symbol of such changes. A second explanation, advanced by Keynes (9), is that increasing industrialization had narrowed the range of international comparative advantages, thus making it increasingly attractive to supply one's own needs rather than resort to international sources of supply. A third alternative, proposed by Rostow (14), considers a cutback in Britain's overseas lending as the main factor contributing to the decline in overseas markets. Actually, what is important, barring tie-in arrangements that stipulate that loans must be used for purchases from the creditor country, is the world level of lending. Since the English share of world lending was undoubtedly quite large, Rostow is probably justified in identifying a decline in English overseas lending with a reduction in the world demand for exports. Final evaluation, however, would necessitate estimating the movements in world as well as English lending during the period.

A fourth explanation of the late-nineteenth-century decline in world export growth—one that has not received the emphasis that it appears to deserve—can be found in the circumstance that this was a period characterized by a general depression or recession in the world economy. Schumpeter (24) describes the last quarter of the nineteenth century as the trough between the second and third Kondratieffs, those historical waves of cumulative, long-term expansion commonly associated with the construction of the railroad and electric utility industries. Measuring the international extent of this trough or retardation is not very easily accomplished; it involves comparisons of different national monetary units in addition to the usual index-number difficulties associated with finding an appropriate or accurate measure of business activity. There is, moreover, a serious data problem, since good historical series are available for only a very few countries. About the best solution, although not a very good one, seems to lie in an inspection and summarization of the National Bureau of Economic Research's well-known compendium of business annals with its wide historical and international coverage. The results of such a compilation are shown in Table 5. One obvious defect in the procedure is the employment of a neutral weighting scheme, which implicitly places such diverse industrial structures as nineteenth-century England and Brazil on exactly the same footing. Unfortunately, the only alternatives immediately involve monetary-unit and index-number difficulties. Accordingly, any impressions gained from the figures of Table 5 are, at best, somewhat heuristic.

TABLE 5

HISTORICAL CHARACTER OF INTERNATIONAL BUSINESS
CONDITIONS AS REPORTED IN BUSINESS ANNALS

Period	Total Number of Nation-Years Reported*	Nation-Years of Prosperity	Nation-Years of Depression
1850's	37	18.5	9.5
1860's	43	20.0	11.0
1870's	50	10.0†	25.0
1880's	50	20.5	13.5
1890's: All	170	52.5	78.5
Big Five‡	50	17.0	20.5
1900's: All	170	56.5	55.0
Big Five	50	17.0	17.0
1850–72	95	45.5	25.0
1873–1907: All	391	130.5	148.5
Big Five	185	57.0	68.5

*A nation-year designates the experience of a reported nation for a given calendar year. Total nation-years exceed the total of the subsequent columns by the number of recession and revival years. The coverage was as follows:

Entire Period....United States, England, France
1853 on.........Germany
1867 on.........Austria
1890 on.........Russia, Sweden, Netherlands, Italy, Argentina, Brazil, Canada, S. Africa, Australia, India, Japan, China

†9.5 of which occur in the prosperity of 1870–73.
‡United States, England, Germany, France, and Austria.
Source: W. C. Mitchell, *Business Cycles: The Problem and Its Setting*, chap. iv, pp. 361–450.

Still, it is reasonably clear that after 1873 a distinct change occurred in the ratio of what Mitchell and Thorp (25) call prosperous and depressed periods. Explicitly, prosperous years outnumber the depressed by almost 2 to 1 in the 1850–72 period and conversely are outnumbered by about 1.2 to 1 in the years from 1873 to 1907. The seventies and nineties stand out, moreover, as particularly depressed decades; the beginning of the third Kondratieff, generally dated about

1898, results in slightly improved figures for the 1900's.[12] When such cyclical behavior is combined with an income determination theory of international trade (or if we consider the world economy as a distinct, homogeneous entity), the decline in export growth can be explained as an inevitable consequence of the worldwide deflation.

Such an explanation, moreover, can be readily integrated with hypotheses emphasizing the United Kingdom's inabilities to share fully in world export growth. For example, it would appear that Britain's export losses were accelerated in the last quarter of the nineteenth century by a shift in world demand away from those goods in which the English enjoyed their greatest comparative advantages. The United Kingdom was especially well equipped for meeting needs in the field of railroad iron. Many investigators have pointed out that this left the British peculiarly ill prepared for the technological shift to steel. When this technical factor is reinforced with the shift away from railroad construction, England's commitment in railroad iron may have become an even more serious disadvantage.

A decline in competitive position in world markets can be attributed, of course, to many other possible factors. For example, the British, as already pointed out, are often charged with possessing less entrepreneurial vigor and developing fewer facilities for technical education than their principal competitors. Explanations in terms of manpower and raw-material shortages also can be reintroduced. Further, Britain's best competitive possibilities may very well have undergone a pronounced shift during this period away from industrial production and toward the service industries. Specifically, there is some evidence that the United Kingdom's comparative advantage increasingly lay in such areas as international finance, shipping, insurance, etc. The importance of any service industry expansion should not be overstressed though. If substantial, a growth in service activities should show up in national income statistics—which it does not. In fact, the average rate of growth for national income in the period from 1870 to 1910 is slightly less than that for industrial production.

V. Summary

The decline in British export growth that occurred in the last quarter of the nineteenth century, once the indirect effects are included, is seemingly more than sufficient to account for the slower rate of British industrial growth in that period. Indeed, the decline in textile exports alone would suffice to explain the stagnation of the late nineteenth century.

On balance, the British decline seems best explained as a consequence more of external than of internal causes. Several reasons for the decline in export growth can be identified. The most important appear to lie in a broad synthesis of many complementary possibilities. Though exact statistics are lacking, there are good reasons for believing that the rate of growth in total world trade underwent a decline during the late nineteenth century and that this played a major role in creating the British difficulties. Many reasons for this can be advanced, but particular emphasis perhaps should be placed on the fact that the world economy was in a relatively depressed state throughout a large portion of the last quarter of the century.

There is also evidence that the United Kingdom failed to keep its relative position in world markets. Internal deficiencies of resources and entrepreneurial ability could have had an adverse effect upon the United Kingdom's competitive position; also, changes in the composition of world demand may have occurred that worked to Britain's disadvantage.

Of course, only a very thorough investigation, both qualitative and quantitative, could assign the proper weights to assess fully the relative importance of these hypotheses. The main contribution here has been to offer additional support for the hypothesis that the reduced rate of growth in exports was responsible for the slower industrial development of the last quarter of the nineteenth century in the United Kingdom and to indicate some directions along which further analysis might develop.

APPENDIX A

Sources and Methods

Nothing usually makes more dreary reading than a list of empirical methods and sources, but, unfortunately, nothing is more indispensable for accurate evaluation of results. For the sake of those whose patience may understandably give out, the arrangement of topics in this appendix is to start with the most essential points and proceed down the rank order.

1. The basic assumption used in construction of the input-output table was that the year's production represented sales. This was obviously false to the extent that there were either sales out of or additions to inventories. In the particular case of the year 1907 there was probably more accumulation than decumulation of inventories, so the coefficients might have been slightly overstated.

2. Transportation and merchandising costs were charged to the buyer rather than the seller. This meant, for example, that Mining's sales to Households are recorded in terms of the at-mine cost of the products purchased by households. The transportation and merchandising charges on these items will be in the box of Undistributed's sales to Households, since both the commercial and transportation services were included under Undistributed. The decision to handle such service

charges in this fashion was dictated by the form of the returns of the Census of Production (3), which listed output at plant values.

3. The direction of sales was identified primarily by the character of the products, for example, iron ore production by mines was listed as a sale to Iron, Steel, and Engineering, construction of new buildings as a sale to the Capital sector, etc. In the cases of homogeneous, multipurpose outputs, such as coal or electricity, other means necessarily had to be used. Fortunately, in such cases the Census of Production (3) usually asked for voluntary returns from the industries as to either their consumption of such goods or the general direction of their sale of such goods. For example, coal and electricity consumed by each industry were so returned, and the coal industry itself divided its output into anthracite, household, steam, and other coals. In the absence of such returns, the distribution of some other products was not so easy— for example, many textile products, which could be consumed either by households or by the clothing industry. In the case of such textiles the distribution was made by analogy with the Leontief table for the 1919 United States economy (10), that is, it was assumed that the ratio of consumption of textiles (both foreign and domestic) to total value of output by British clothing makers in 1907 was the same as that for American clothing manufacturers, with the residual going to households. Since the total material costs of the United Kingdom's clothing industry were known, this distribution could be checked against the over-all costs for possible absurdities, such as, say, excess of textile sales to clothing over total purchases by clothing. No such absurdity appeared. Similar methods were also necessary to distribute manufactured gas sales and some very minor components of the output of the rubber goods and timber industries. In most cases, however, the distribution could be made by quite straightforward methods based on the principal sources: The Census of Industrial Production (3), the Agricultural Output of Great Britain

(19), and Ireland (18). The agriculture compilations were for the year ending June 4, 1908, in Great Britain and the calendar year 1908 for Ireland. Again, because of the historical purposes for which the table is being used, this difficulty was deemed not too consequential.

4. Export values in the *Annual Statement of Trade of the United Kingdom*, and as reproduced in the *Statistical Abstract for the United Kingdom, 1895–1909* (17) were listed at free-on-board prices. This means that these values included transportation and merchandising costs between plant and port that had to be deducted to keep export sales by an industry consistent with internal sales (see par. 3 above). For exports of shipping and railroad rolling stock no adjustment was made, for fairly obvious reasons. In less obvious cases, the usual method of adjustment was to assume that the quantities of a product that were exported did not differ sharply in value per unit from those quantities retained for internal consumption. With this assumption and the fact that export quantities were known for most items because of a fairly extensive product breakdown of exports, at-plant values of exports were computed by multiplying the total value of a product's output by the ratio of the physical quantity exported to the total quantity produced. If this led to an occasional absurdity, such as a computed value exceeding the listed free-on-board value, the assumption of equivalence between the value per unit of the product retained for home consumption and that for export was dropped. In these few cases, a straight percentage markdown of 15 per cent for such costs was used. This was the estimated average allowance for these costs made by the Census of Production's (3, p. 29) investigators on the basis of a limited sample study. Deduction of these export values, product by product, from an industry's output was, incidentally, the first step taken in the distribution of an industry, since this had to be done before making the domestic division.

5. Imports were distributed in a manner quite analogous

to the home production, that is, direction of sales was identified by the character of the product. In this case the free-on-board values of the Board of Trade figures could be used without adjustment, since the additional transportation and merchandising costs would appear under Undistributed just as they would for any domestic purchase.

6. Gross outlay for the residual sector, Undistributed, was estimated by adding up the following items (all figures in millions of pounds sterling): (*a*) Railroad gross receipts of 121.549; (*b*) Tramway gross receipts of 11.849; (*c*) Census of Production's (3) estimate (p. 33) for professional, banking, and sundry unenumerated private services, such as cabbies, chimney sweeps, etc., of 400.000; (*d*) Census estimate of approximately 50.000 for restaurant and hotel services; (*e*) Census estimate of 50.000 of industrial production missed in the enumeration; (*f*) Census estimate of 18.500 in raw materials produced in unenumerated industries; (*g*) 120.000 for shipping services both private and domestic based on Census estimates (p. 32) and checked against Bowley's (2); and (*h*) government nonfree services, such as post offices, telephone, postal telegraph, and waterworks valued at 32.000 (Tramway, Railroad, Post Office, Telegraph and other such receipts were reported in the *Statistical Abstract for the United Kingdom* (17); for the handling of other government services see par. 7). Wages, interest, taxes, etc., for the Undistributed sector were taken as the difference between Household, Government, and Capital expenditures and the sources for financing these expenditures, that is, the total wage, interest, and tax payments by industry. Thus the undistributed sector's wages, interest, etc., were set at a level to equate total wages, profits, interest, taxes, etc., with the expenditures on capital consumption, and tax-financed government services. An independent estimate of the wages, interest, profits, and taxes of the principal components of the Undistributed sector (i.e., Railroads, Commerce, Shipping etc.) of 550.000 further substantiated the 614.887 residual estimate, which would be ex-

pected to be somewhat larger because it included all and not just the major components of the sector. Undistributed's sales to every sector were computed as a residual between the known total cost of materials for the sector and the identifiable purchases the sector made from all the other sectors except Undistributed, that is, purchases from total known from the censuses. Similarly, sales to Undistributed were a balancing item to equate total sales (including additions to inventories where these were known) to total output for each sector. The final balancing factor in the table was capital export, placed at about £60 million.

7. Government activities appear frequently in the table. Under the heading Government itself appear all tax-financed services, which were estimated from the Imperial and Local Government revenue and expenditure returns as reported in the *Statistical Abstract for the United Kingdom from 1895 to 1909* (17). Government building and construction activities were reported under the sector heading of Clay, Stone, Building, and Contracting, and were recorded as sales to the Capital sector. These estimates were derivable from the Census of Production at cost-of-output valuations as distinguished from private construction values, which differ in that a profit margin is included. Government armaments and warship construction were similarly handled under Iron, Steel, and Engineering. (Railroad construction by railroad companies was also under this heading and was valued at cost.) Gas and electric utilities under government management were lumped together with the similar private utilities in the relevant sector. Finally, as already reported in paragraph 6 above, nongas and electric utility services provided by the government at a fee were put under Undistributed. All these distinctions were required for reasons of homogeneity between and within certain columns and rows. For example, the distinction between tax- and revenue-financed services makes the three columns of Government, Capital, and Household expenditures equivalent to the Wages, Interest, Taxes, Profits, etc.,

row. Such homogeneity makes it possible to solve the system on a seventeen-by-seventeen as well as a sixteen-by-sixteen basis, thus permitting greater flexibility in defining the composition of the final bill of goods.

8. The Capital sector includes all types of domestic investment, except in inventories, made by the economy, for example, depreciation allowances and replacement expenditures, residential housing, bridges. The usual distinction was made between consumer durables and household investment, so vehicles, for instance, were considered as household consumption rather than as an addition to capital. Total capital expenditure was taken from the Census of Production (3) estimate (pp. 35–36).

9. Total household expenditure was also taken from the Census of Production (3) estimates (pp. 30–34), a figure which checks remarkably well with the independent estimate for 1907 made by Bowley (1, p. 171), the domestics' wages, and other such items paid by households to households. Additionally, household expenditures include £10.000 of food consumption by agricultural families; this same £10.000 was added to the total value output of Agriculture and treated as an addition to wages paid by this sector, since it constitutes a payment in kind to itself.

10. In figuring the value added by agriculture, the Census of Production people, for some unknown reason, charged all domestic production of fertilizers and animal foods to domestic agriculture's material costs. Since about 75 per cent of the total output of these products was exported, these value-added and cost-of-material estimates obviously had to be revised before inclusion in the table.

11. The estimate of returns on foreign capital investments were taken from Paish (13).

In summary, while many assumptions were necessary to complete the table, the estimates, on the whole, stood up well where they could be double checked by independent estimates or by the double-entry accounting nature of the table.

With more time and research resources, additional sources might be found to improve the estimates. Less aggregation could also be obtained with an additional investment of effort. In particular, the Food, Tobacco, and Liquor sector could be easily broken down into its constituent elements—a step that would give the table roughly the same sector composition as Leontief's 1919 table for the American economy.

APPENDIX B

A COMMENTARY ON W. G. HOFFMANN'S HISTORICAL INDICES of BRITISH INDUSTRIAL PRODUCTION

Virtually all recent quantitative studies of the British economy in the eighteenth and nineteenth centuries are heavily dependent on the monumental work of W. G. Hoffmann (20) as the source of estimates on the level and rate of economic growth in the United Kingdom during the period from 1700 to 1950. Because Hoffmann's statistics and theories on British economic growth play such an important role, it seems worthwhile to digress a bit on their characteristics.

The most important single difference between Hoffmann's measures of British industrial production and its many predecessors lies in the relative completeness of its industry coverage. This was achieved by what Hoffmann aptly calls "a fresh examination of all the sources" and, at a technical level, amounts to an ingenious use of many indirect measures of productive output, for example, imports, exports, excise taxes. By this method individual indices on forty-eight "selected industries" were developed for varying portions of the 200-year total time period studied.

In order for these "selected industries" to provide a measure of total industrial output, it is, of course, necessary to know (1) the relative importance of each of these industries and (2) the percentage that the group of "selected industries" constitute of total industrial output. Both bits of information are necessary if the final index of total output is to be constructed from properly weighted constituent components. Essentially, both problems are therefore identical: that of finding the correct weights.

Curiously, Hoffmann's solution to these identical problems is very different. In the case of the selected industries, he divides the entire sample period into seven subperiods and computes separate weights for each period.[13] For the five periods before 1890, these weights are based on value added and net value of output, which were determined by intensive investigation of available statistical material for a year near the middle of each period; after 1890, the censuses of production of 1907 and 1924 provide the necessary information. Thus, within the limits of the available material, each selected industry is roughly weighted according to its relative importance at a particular point in history, the weights varying over time with changes in the industrial composition of the economy. In translating this ultimate index of variations in the "selected industries" into a final over-all index, however, Hoffmann uses considerably less care. Specifically, he makes no adjustment for the changing importance of the "selected industries" as a percentage of the whole, although the necessary material for making such an adjustment was actually accumulated, apparently in the course of the investigations of the relative importance of the individual selected industries, since there is a one-to-one correspondence between the years for which this information is supplied and the years on which the index weights are based. As might be expected, because of both better industry coverage and increased industrialization, the percentage of selected industries as a percentage of total net output of manufactures rises steadily during the eighteenth century and the first three quarters of the nineteenth, reaching a peak in the 1880's and declining steadily thereafter. Hoffmann's neutrally weighted index of total industrial production is really only an index of the variations in the selected industries and, indeed, of the extent of year-to-year coverage within the selected group; as a consequence, it suffers defects as an index of total output, since output will be understated at the beginning and end of the period under study and overstated in the middle. For example, the annual rate of industrial expansion in the last quarter of the nineteenth century rises from an approximate 1.75 to a considerably more respectable figure of a little over 2.0 if the over-all index is recomputed on the basis of the actual reported weights rather than of the unitary weights. On the other hand, correction for this weighting factor only reinforces the validity of one of Hoffmann's main, and also slightly surprising, conclusions that the rate of growth of British industry is at its lowest in the eighteenth century, since all the biases of Hoffmann's methods tend to overestimate total growth in this period.

Rate of growth is, of course, itself a concept capable of many interpretations. Hoffmann chooses to use as his measure the slope (as determined by least squares) of a semilogarithmic plot of output against time.[14] This is a thoroughly satisfactory measure, but it is not completely advantageous for all purposes. For example, it can make quite a good deal of difference in the growth rate of a particular period if different beginning and end years are chosen; this will be particularly true if the redefinition of a period drastically alters the number of depression and prosperity years included in the period, since, in essence, the efficacy of the method is based on the assumption that such years are included in roughly the same proportions. The technique will be particularly sensitive to the inclusion or exclusion of extreme depression years—just as all least-squares results can be greatly modified by the presence of extreme elements in the sample. Thus, a much lower coefficient of expansion would be found if the period from 1900 to 1921 was analyzed instead of the period from 1900 to 1920. In addition, use of the semilogarithmic slope coefficient implies as strict, albeit quite different, mathematical stipulation of the properties of the growth curves as either the Gompertz or logistic curves, despite Hoffmann's contention to the contrary. Indeed, a scrutiny of the plotted series in the appendices strongly suggests that in most cases the logistic would provide a much better fit to material spanning the entire 250-year period. It therefore might be superior for making long-term comparisons of the industries.

For limited time spans, however, the simple linear semilogarithmic function used by Hoffmann is undoubtedly the superior alternative and Hoffmann's industry-by-industry comparison of the changes in these rates over time reveals many important regularities. First, the producer-goods industries characteristically expanded at a much faster rate than the consumer goods up until World War I, when the roles were reversed. The historically more rapid expansion of the producer-goods industries is, of course, just what one would expect in a time of general industrial expansion achieved primarily by the application of increasingly more capital intensive processes. The reversal in importance of the two categories after 1920 is not, moreover, as enigmatic in the light of recent information as Hoffmann found it to be in 1939, when his first German edition appeared, since there is increasing evidence that industrial processes may be becoming less capital intensive, perhaps because of the employment of less durable equipment or perhaps because of the realization of greater relative economies in the production of capital goods. Second, there was a reasonably pronounced tendency for English industries with large export markets to expand more rapidly than those dependent on home markets. Such a finding lends at least partial confirmation to the view that British industrial growth was closely conditioned by the availability of export markets. Third, after due allowances were made for changes in the export market, industries selling in home markets believed, a priori, to be characterized by inelastic demand curves (e.g., food, beverages, and other necessities) were found to grow in close correspondence with the population—a result that roughly confirms the hypothesis that demand was in fact inelastic in such instances. Fourth, very rapid industry expansions are often traceable to the development of new products that created new or additional demands unsatisfied by previously available products. Fifth, industry growth seemed to depend on the extent not only of overseas markets but also of internal or home markets, since industries serving a higher proportion of total British needs expanded with relative rapidity. Not all these findings are, of course, surprising. Still, it is comforting to have the results confirmed by such careful empirical work.

Hoffmann also contributes to the study of business cycles with the discovery of what he considers to be a "strong resemblance in the 'rhythmical fluctuations' or 'long waves' of the separate industries." Specifically, he finds that after removal of two ten-year geometric moving averages the various industries display long waves with an average duration of eighteen to twenty years.

Moving averages are, of course, very difficult to interpret, and Hoffmann's results constitute no exception. As a rule, moving averages are used as a method of removing regularly recurring cyclical phenomena and thereby exposing trend. If the period of the moving average is chosen to correspond to the period of the cycle, this will indeed be the result; in the present case, therefore, the ten-year moving average was picked in order to eliminate the conventional cyclical fluctuations—the so-called Juglars—which have recurred with a periodicity of approximately seven to ten years.

Removal of two ten-year moving averages, however, is equivalent to removing a nineteen-year moving average with successive terms weighted as 1, 2, 3, . . . 9, 10, 9, 8, . . . 2, 1. It is therefore somewhat surprising that, if there were really an approximate nineteen-year cycle in the original data, this method did not eliminate such periodicity. The question therefore arises: Why can one observe eighteen- to twenty-year cycles in the data when one has technically removed cycles of eighteen to twenty years' duration? This is not readily explained, since, if the original periodicity of the series was actually ten years, the first ten-year moving average would eliminate all fluctuations except random fluctuations; if there was no such random element, the second ten-year moving average would average constants and therefore be a constant itself. On the other hand, if the original series was completely random, taking a nineteen moving average with weights 1, 2, 3, . . . 9, 10, 9, 8 . . . 2, 1 would result in a series with an average periodicity of thirteen or fourteen years. The discrepancy between this behavior, based on the assumption of complete random normality, and that actually obtained by Hoffmann is almost undoubtedly due to the fact that Hoffmann's series are not completely random. Specifically, it would be expected that series that already have some auto-correlation present, as Hoffmann's series do, would display oscillatory movements with a periodicity somewhat greater than that predicated upon the complete randomness assumption. No one, apparently, has worked out exactly how the presence of a certain autocorrelated pattern will modify the results deduced under a random normality assumption. The obvious intuitive guess would be, however, that, with a periodicity of seven to ten years in the original series, removal of two ten-year moving averages would almost inevitably result in series with an average periodicity of between eighteen and twenty-two years.[15]

Hoffmann discerns three typical stages in the growth of British industries: a first stage in which the rate of growth is continually increasing, a second stage in which absolute growth continues but at an ever slower rate, and a third stage in which absolute growth is negative. Hoffmann judiciously qualifies the hypothesis as being inapplicable in certain instances but, at the same time, produces a convincing body of empirical evidence to suggest that the three stages have certainly been characteristic of most British development.

Indeed, the exceptions to the rule are themselves quite revealing, since all are readily explicable either in terms of special government intervention or, more often, as instances in which new or young industries have not yet moved out of the first stage of development, for example, tin, paper, hempen goods, and tobacco products. Furthermore, the list of industries that have apparently entered the final stage, that of absolute decline, also agrees with a list that might have been drawn up on the basis of other, less quantifiable, data about the behavior of the English economy. For example, most textiles, beverages and spirits, mining, and building and transport industries all fall into this latter category.

In interpreting these extremely interesting findings, Hoffmann displays what is, at one and the same time, both commendable and disappointing discretion. Specifically, he either fails to raise or does not fully answer such significant questions as the following: What is it that causes this pattern of growth? Is this growth pattern evidence, perhaps, of secular stagnation? Or, quite to the contrary, is it really evidence of the dynamism of capitalistic economies that leads to constant substitution of new and better services and products for older, inferior economic goods?

Hoffmann, at first glance, clearly seems to suggest answers in agreement more with the secular stagnation alternative than with the product development hypothesis. Explicitly, he attributes absolute declines in production to four main causes: "(1) technical causes; (2) fiscal measures; (3) loss of competitive power in the home market which may be affected by changes in commercial policy; and (4) loss of competitive power in overseas markets." He places particular stress on the last two and states that a primary reason for the loss of these home and overseas markets is the extremely rapid growth of competing industries overseas. Even in the case of technical causes, Hoffmann has in mind such instances as the early exhaustion of high-grade British ore deposits more than he does technical obsolescence.

However, Hoffmann clearly recognizes that these hypotheses relate only to the development of specific industries and may or may not be true for the economy as a whole. For one thing, new industries are always being added to the industrial spectrum. In addition, manufacturing is only one of several important components of gross national product, and the other branches of the economy might very well experience different growth patterns.

APPENDIX C

INDUSTRY COMPONENTS OF THE
SECTORS IN THE INPUT-OUTPUT TABLE

I. Chemical and Allied Trades

Chemicals, coal tar products, drugs, and perfumery trades
Seed-crushing trade
Oil and tallow trades (excluding seed-crushing)
Fertilizer, glue, sheep dip, and disinfectant trades
Soap and candle trades
Paint, color, and varnish trades
Explosives, ammunition, and fireworks
Match and firelighter trades

II. Clay, Stone, Building, and Contracting

Brick and fireclay trades
China and earthenware trades
Cement trade
Asbestos and boiler coverings trades
Glass, stone, roofing felts, and miscellaneous trades

Building and contracting trades
His Majesty's naval establishments at home
His Majesty's Office of Works and Public Buildings
The Board of Public Works (Ireland)
Waterworks construction activities
Local authorities (United Kingdom)
Canal, dock, harbor and similar companies
The National Phone Company's construction activities
Telegraph and telephone construction undertakings

III. Clothing Trades

Clothing, handkerchief, and millinery trades
Boot and shoe trades
Hat, bonnet, and cap trades
Glove trade
Umbrella and walking stick trades
Fancy fur trade
Hatter's fur trade
Artificial flower and ornamental feather trades
Laundry and cleaning and dyeing trades

IV. Food, Drink and Tobacco Trades

Grain-milling trade
Bread and biscuit trades
Cocoa, confectionery, and fruit-preserving trades
Bacon-curing trade
Preserved meat, poultry, and fish, pickle, sauce, and baking
    powder trades
Butter, cheese, and margarine trades
Fish-curing trade
Manufacture of farinaceous preparations and trade
Cattle, dog, and poultry trades
Ice trade
Sugar and glucose trades
Brewing and malting trades
Spirit distilling trade
Spirit compounding, rectifying, and methylating trades
Bottling trade
Aerated waters, cider, British-made wines, and vinegar
    trades
Tobacco trade
Naval Victualling Yards (home establishments)

V. Iron, Steel, Engineering, and Shipbuilding Trades

Iron and steel (smelting, rolling, and founding)
Tinplate trade
Wrought iron and steel tube trade
Wire trades
Anchor, chain, nail, bolt, screw, and rivet trades
Galvanized sheet, hardware, hollow-ware, tinned and
    japanned goods, and bedstead trades
Engineering trades (including electrical)
Shipbuilding and marine engineering trades:
    (*a*) Private firms
    (*b*) Government yards and lighthouse authorities
Cycle and motor trades
Cutlery trades
Tool and implement trades
Blacksmithing trades
Needle, pin, fishhook, and button trades
Lock and safe trades
Small-arms trades
Heating, lighting, ventilating, and sanitary engineering
    trades
Railway carriage and wagon trades
Tramway construction activities
Railways (construction, repair, and maintenance of Perma-
    nent Way, etc.)
Royal ordnance factories
Naval ordnance factories

VI. Mines and Quarries

Coal and ironstone mines
Coke works at collieries
Manufactured fuel trade
Oil shale mines
Oil shale works
Iron mines and iron quarries
Mines other than coal or iron
Salt mines, brine pits, and salt works
Slate quarries
Limestone quarries and lime kilns
Quarries other than iron, slate, and limestone

VII. Miscellaneous Trades

Scientific instruments, apparatus, and appliances trades
Ivory, bone, horn, picture frame, and fancy articles trades
Musical instruments trade
Billiards tables and sports requisites trades
Toys and games trades
Wig-making trades

NOTES TO CHAPTER 5

1. For stylistic convenience, the labels England, Britain, and the United Kingdom are used interchangeably when strict usage would approve only the latter. Similarly, unless otherwise noted, whenever reference is made to unspecified rates of growth in exports or the United Kingdom's internal economy, industrial exports and growth is meant.

2. Nonlinearities in the functions, while they might temper the intensity of the effects at different stages of the cycle or in history, would not negate the fundamental position that any adequate measure of the total effect of a rise in exports must take account of indirect as well as direct effects.

3. For a discussion of the sources and techniques used in constructing the table, the reader is referred to Appendix A. Scrutiny of the table itself, incidentally, provides an interesting picture of the internal composition of the United Kingdom's industrial activity in 1907, since the table rearranges and summarizes on one page many of the most interesting aspects of these censuses. A breakdown of the industry components of the sectors in the table is provided in Appendix C.

4. On this and related points about the error properties of Leontief inverses, the reader is referred to D. Evans (23).

5. The extrapolation was carried out on the basis that the growth was at a constant rate per year. Such an assumption was made only after plotting some of the more important exports on a semilogarithmic chart. A more adequate treatment, of course, would have checked all components. The effect of price variations was removed by using Imlah's (7) index of English export prices. As a result of the index-number problem, the improvement in the estimates might be made either by figuring the sector growth rates and projections entirely in physical terms or by getting separate price indices for each different category of export.

6. In matrix notation the system can be expressed as $(y) = (a)(x)$, where (y) is a column vector composed of elements y_i representing the contribution of industry i to the final bill of goods; (a) is a square matrix composed of elements a_{ij}, which is the ratio of the amount (in value terms) of industry j's output consumed in producing i's output to i's net value output; and (x) is a column vector of the net outputs of each industry. For a detailed description of the methods and techniques used, the reader is referred to Leontief (10) or to H. Smith's very concise summary (22).

7. These rates were computed on the basis of the mid-year estimates for intercensal years made by the Registrar-Generals for England and Wales, Scotland, and Ireland and reported in the *Statistical Abstract for the United Kingdom* (15, 16, and 17).

8. If we consider the possibility of an agricultural "reserve army"

of underemployed, the possibilities of a labor shortage are further lessened.

9. Rostow (14) presents quotes from the *Economist* for the period of the Great Depression of the seventies that paint a picture of reasonably vigorous adjustment to adversity on the part of English entrepreneurs.

10. Manufactured exports, of course, are not strictly analogous to industrial exports, since the latter also include primary products, exclusive of agriculture. The years from 1876–80 to 1906–10 have been used instead of the years from 1872 to 1907 used previously because the world figures are not available prior to 1876 and it was considered desirable to present the United Kingdom figures on the same and hence comparable basis.

11. This seems particularly justifiable when account is taken of the fact that an important component of the over-all average is the British performance itself.

12. As does the tendency toward a more "international cycle," which is exemplified by the close agreement between the "Big Five" and over-all data for the 1900's.

13. Each period is, in turn, related by the method of link relatives.

14. The reader is advised, incidentally, to read Hoffmann's discussion of these points on pages 58–67 before proceeding beyond page 29.

15. Even if the presence of twenty-year "long waves" is accepted as an established reality, one could seriously disagree with Hoffmann's explanation of the causes. In particular, it is doubtful whether the presence of such cycles can be realistically attributed to the fact that the average expected age of much industrial equipment may be approximately twenty years. This, of course, is nothing but the so-called "echo effect" variation on the acceleration principle.

References

(1) A. L. Bowley, *An Elementary Manual of Statistics*. London, 1910.

(2) A. L. Bowley, *England's Foreign Trade in the Nineteenth Century: Its Economic and Social Results*. London, 1905.

(3) *Census of Production*, 1907, His Majesty's Stationery Office, London, 1909, 1910, 1912 (in 6 parts).

(5) John S. Chipman, *The Theory of Inter-Sectoral Money Flows and Income Formation*. Baltimore, 1951.

(6) J. H. Clapham, *An Economic History of Modern Britain, Free Trade and Steel, 1850–1886*. Cambridge University Press, 1932.

(7) A. H. Imlah, "Real Values in British Foreign Trade," *Journal of Economic History*, November, 1948, pp. 133–52.

(8) League of Nations' Secretariat, *Industrialization and Foreign Trade*. 1945.

(9) J. M. Keynes, "National Self-Sufficiency," *Yale Review*, June, 1933, pp. 755–69.

(10) W. Leontief, *The Structure of the American Economy, 1919–1939*, New York, 1951.

(11) W. Leontief, S. Fabricant, I. Friend, T. Koopmans, O. Morgenstern, W. Jacobs, M. Hoffenberg, and R. Goldsmith, "Input-Output Analysis and Its Use in Peace and War Economics" (a round-table discussion). *American Economic Review*, May, 1949, pp. 211–40.

(12) W. A. Lewis, *Economic Survey, 1919–1939*. Philadelphia, 1950.

(13) G. Paish, "Great Britain's Capital Investment in Other Lands." *Journal of the Royal Statistical Society*, September, 1909, pp. 465–80.

(14) W. W. Rostow, *British Economy of the Nineteenth Century*. Oxford, 1948.

(15) *Statistical Abstract for the United Kingdom in Each of the Last Fifteen Years, 1849–1863*. London: Her Majesty's Stationery Office, 1864.

(16) *Statistical Abstract for the United Kingdom in Each of the Last Fifteen Years, 1859–1873*. London: Her Majesty's Stationery Office, 1874.

(17) *Statistical Abstract for the United Kingdom in Each of the Last Fifteen Years, 1895–1909*. London: His Majesty's Stationery Office, 1910.

(18) *The Agricultural Output of Ireland*. London: His Majesty's Stationery Office, 1909.

(19) *The Agricultural Output of Great Britain*. London: His Majesty's Stationery Office, 1909.

(20) W. Hoffmann, *Wachstum und Wachstumsformen der englischen Industriewirtschaft von 1700 bis zur Gegenwart*. Jena, 1940. English

ed., W. O. Henderson and W. H. Chaloner, trans., *British Industry, 1700–1950*. Oxford: Basil Blackwell, 1955.

(21) R. Ruggles, *An Introduction to National Income and Income Analysis*, chap. 6, pp. 126–54. New York, 1949.

(22) H. Smith, "Uses of Leontief's Open Input-Output Models," chap. 6 of *Activity Analysis of Production and Allocation* (T. C. Koopmans, ed.). New York, 1951.

(23) Duane Evans, "The Effect of Structural Matrix Errors on Inter-industry Relations Estimates," *Econometrica*, October, 1954, pp. 461–80.

(24) J. A. Schumpeter, *Business Cycles: A Theoretical and Statistical Analysis of the Capitalist Process*, chap. 7, pp. 303–448. New York, 1939.

(25) W. L. Thorp and W. C. Mitchell, *Business Annals*. New York, 1926.

THREE

THREE

6

A Polemical Postscript

on Economic Growth

The three economies that we have looked at in this volume present three different aspects of economic development. The antebellum South was in the peculiar, difficult situation of a feudal remnant emerging into a modern, industrial market structure. The United States in the second half of the nineteenth century, in the large-scale agriculture of the West and South almost as much as in the industrial North and East, had become the archetype of burgeoning industrialism. And, as the century entered its last quarter, Britain's industrial expansion hesitated and entered a long, hard winter of stagnation. It is our design in this postscript to distill some generalizations about economic growth from the historical analysis of the three preceding essays. We are allowing ourselves a few observations about the pertinence of the historical conclusions to present-day problems. But, obviously, the lessons of history are to be drawn only with extreme caution, and these polemics are advanced to stimulate as much as to attempt a settlement of the continuing discussions.

1. In the chapter on the profitability of antebellum slavery, we listed and attempted an answer to several arguments that have been traditionally used to explain why slavery must have been unprofitable. We demonstrated that plantation slavery was not inconsistent with an efficient organization of the capital market: slaves were transported over con-

siderable distances, from regions where their employment in agriculture was marginally unproductive to land that would yield richly in co-operation with labor, whether chattel or free. These yields, which provided satisfactory profits, increased southern income, and—insofar as income increases are both a measure of and a potential support for growth— we could say that slavery was not inconsistent with growth, in purely economic terms. Finally, inferring from the effectiveness of the interregional capital market and some evidence of the use of slave labor outside of staple agriculture, we argued that slavery was not inconsistent with economic diversification.

Since we offered these interpretations of the antebellum southern economy, it has been pointed out that we may have overlooked the *real* retardative effects of the slave system for economic development, as distinguished from its profitability. Apart from the social patterns or institutional restraints—the anti-industrial ideology of the planter class, the dangers of educating slaves, the pressures for seigneurial consumption displays—these retarding elements may have centered in the inability of southern agriculture to accumulate capital and the failure of slavery to support a sufficient home market. John Moes developed the first argument on the theme of the absorption of savings in human capital and for the purpose of consumption; he concluded that a growing stock of capitalized labor is inimical to growth, at least in a society that is dependent upon its own capital supply.[1] The second point was argued strongly in a paper by Eugene Genovese.[2] He maintained that the southern dependence upon exports, in contrast to the northern "home market," and the self-sufficient nature of the plantation economy, prevented the reorganization of agriculture, which was a precondition for industrialization. Without industrialization and urbanization, in turn, "extensive diversification of agriculture was unthinkable."

The theory underlying these arguments has a long and respectable, sometimes distinguished, history. Cassius Clay

raised the question of the insufficient home market a generation before the Civil War. The most recent proponents of
the theory of regional polarization include Gunnar Myrdal
and Raul Prebisch. Briefly, their argument rests upon the
thesis that unregulated trade between regions or nations will
increase, rather than decrease, international inequality. The
reasoning is three-pronged. First, the terms of trade must
turn against primary producers, because of the monopoly
power of the industrial region or nation and because of the
operation of "Engel's law"—that, as income increases, a declining portion will be spent on primary products. Second,
the impact of cyclical downturns in the advanced region will
be accelerated as they hit the primary, agricultural region.
The backward regions are, in effect, set up in each boom,
to fall the harder in each decline. Third, and most important
in the present context, the progressive part of the economy
will draw capital away from the underdeveloped (or developing) industrial centers, at the expense of the agricultural region.

It is argued—has been argued in less sophisticated terms
since the antebellum plantation era—that the peculiar institution of slavery aggravated each of these influences. Our
earlier position was simply that the position of slavery was
firm, at least in part, *because it paid.* However, a more criti-
cal conclusion about economic development is suggested in
the question: If it is granted that slavery paid for the planters,
does that necessarily mean that it paid for the South? Was
slavery inconsistent with development because the production
function with which it was associated and its social implications both led to the "wrong" income flows?

2. An effective consideration of that question seems to
us to be tied to the analysis in the two other papers on industrial growth. Leaving aside the development of institutional and structural preconditions (or of effective substitutes), the development of the United States in the middle

and later nineteenth century rested upon the multiplier effects of the movement into the new western agricultural regions, supported by the inflow of capital from the external
markets. The large-scale "factory" plantation in the South,
concentrating upon the single staple crop, was a natural response to increasing demand for cotton, just as the organization of large-scale cereal farming in the Northwest was
the response to the European demand for wheat a generation later.

In the antebellum United States, and especially before
1840, the major exogenous developmental factor was the income earned by the cotton-exporting region. Expansions in
the second and fourth decades of the century were signaled
by improvements in the terms of trade for cotton. By the
time of the third prewar boom, however, population movements from Europe to America and from the eastern seaboard
to the western plains had become the most important exogenous elements. No *external* price increase was needed
to start the boom. Rather, the movement of populations started
domestic prices rising before the prices of export goods.

In the postwar period, shifts in the world market for
wheat tended to stimulate the western agricultural region
in much the same way that exogenous shifts in the price of
cotton acted upon the antebellum southern cotton economy.
Between the crop years 1865 and 1867, the price of wheat
rose in the United Kingdom from 552.9 deflated pence per
quarter to 774.7.[3] After a sharp but brief decline in 1869,
prices recovered and stayed above 600 per quarter over most
of the period until 1882. Over the next twelve years the trend
was strongly downward. The price level hit bottom, at 406.5
in 1894, and then shot up to 681 by 1897. But the rise was
short-lived and from 1898 to World War I the index rose
above 500 only four times.

The pattern, then, is one of export price rise, followed
by an effort to increase the supply of agricultural exports.
As the rate of growth speeds up, merchandise and capital

imports increase, and the balance of trade turns unfavorable. This paradigm fits the experience before as well as after the Civil War, though the closeness of fit is more striking in the first—cotton—half of the century. Our reason for drawing these parallels is to emphasize the similarities between the export relationships and growth experience in the western wheat economy and in the southern cotton economy, and especially to emphasize the role of these staple agricultural exports in the economic development of the nation. The relationship of the primary agricultural sectors to the industrial-commercial Northeast was not significantly different in the two periods. What we are suggesting is that the real deterrent to economic development in the South may not have been the existence of the slave system so much as the fact that the cotton states were confronted with the usual problems that make industrialization difficult in any economy that is heavily based upon a single export crop.

In 1880 the proportion of the labor force engaged in non-agricultural industry in the West North Central states was 65 per cent of the United States industrial proportion. In 1840, the proportion in the South-Central cotton states had been 67 per cent of the United States ratio. With or without the fact of slavery, there was no more reason for the South to have turned its resources from staple agriculture to manufacturing before the Civil War than there was for the wheat states to have industrialized in the decades after the Civil War. What is most telling, however, is the decline in the relative rate of industrialization in the South after the war. By 1880, labor force industrialization in the southern Atlantic states had fallen to 34 per cent of the national rate, from 49 per cent in 1840; in the eastern South-Central region the decline was from 38 to 28 per cent of the national rate; and in the western South-Central region from 67 to 29 per cent.[4] It is this postwar decline in the South's position that needs explanation. We are suggesting that southern slavery may perhaps have been an extraneous third variable, correlated with but not causally linked to the region's failure to industrialize. The explanation may rather be found in a parallel to the industrial incapacity of other underdeveloped societies that are dependent upon single export crops—again, usually without any handicap of slavery, though often with a plantation structure.

3. Where slavery enters the postwar picture is through its income distributional effects. At the end of the chapter on the antebellum South it was argued that much of the postwar depression in southern cotton agriculture, especially in the seaboard and eastern sections, was attributable to the fact that these states lost their earnings from the sale of slaves—from slave breeding, in short. The abolition of the slave markets had eliminated the major device for reallocating earnings among the different parts of the southern economy, as well as having reduced the total of these earnings over and above labor costs. Far from having restricted the movement of capital, slavery and the interregional slave trade maintained flows of capital among areas of strikingly varied productivity. After Emancipation and the abolition of the slave trade, the reason for the income flows ceased, and, although population continued to flow into the new, western parts of the South, the eastern section lost its share of the regional income.

During the antebellum period the income inequality may have held back the development of a home market for manufactures in the South, as has been suggested. Slavery produced an income distribution so skewed that it was difficult to support the large mass markets necessary to the development of local consumer goods production. Seigneurial consumption was not likely to be a substitute for the broad market that could have made it profitable in the South to manufacture consumer goods more sophisticated than the most elemental of subsistence wares. Also, seigneurial display that rested upon consumer debt, whether that debt was held within the South or by northern financiers, was inconsistent with growth, as "productive" or at least producers' debt would not have been.

This inequality need not have restricted income *growth* in the presence of strong demand pressures in the world cotton markets. However, it is not simply the size but the distribution of income that is crucial for structural change, and it is in respect to the degree of inequality that slavery could have injured the South's early chances for industrialization. Under the burden of this inequality and the consequent inefficiency of manufacturing enterprise, southern industry could not proceed against northern competition. Parenthetically, it may be remarked that it was this dichotomy that formed the source of the regional tariff conflicts of the second half of the century.

Now, given industrial interdependence, should northern manufacturing development not have stimulated further postwar southern large-scale agricultural development? There was an interregional multiplier effect of this type implicit in the growth experience we described for the western cereal economy. In the North-South case, however, the old cotton states of the Southeast could not share in the income that flowed from southern interdependence with northern softgoods manufacturing. The regional inequality of income persisted, indeed worsened. Second, the personal distribution of income, rooted as it was in plantation agriculture, was not made much more equitable in the decades following Emancipation, so nothing happened in the South to increase the mass-consumption base. Finally, given the lack of skill, the color prejudice, and the possibilities of tenant or subsistence farming, underemployed and unskilled former slaves were discouraged from migrating to the North, which might have raised productivity levels in the South. On the contrary, incentives were strong for skilled and enterprising white (and Negro) southerners to emigrate, in spite of the extravagant claims of the "New South" after Reconstruction. Again, this problem has not been unknown in the "cereal states" of the West.

4. The relevant comparison for the South is twofold. On the one side, there is the comparison—and contrast—with western staple agriculture. Cotton, in the first half of the century, and wheat in the following decades, provided the impetus for regional income growth and for much of the national development. The contrast between the southern and the western experience, however, was set in the consumption base and the multiplier effects provided by the institutional and technological structure of northwestern wheat farming, which were absent in southern cotton culture. We spoke of the consequences of the southern income distribution in the previous section, in relation to the expenditure on consumer goods. The income and social structure also had pinching effects upon social capital, for example on the construction of schools and roads. Moreover, the production function—for the cotton economy, not simply for the slave culture—used less inanimate capital, and offered fewer pressures for local overhead investment, which might have led directly to local industrialization. More investment in overheads—in elevators and stockyards and railroads—was a necessity in the flour and meat economy to a greater extent than in the cotton textile process. In this sense, cotton is comparable to the plantation agriculture of the "dual" economies: the focus is outward. The appurtenances are channeled away from the domestic economy. The multiplier effects were emphasized in the chapter on income growth, above, but the important contrast was not drawn there between the *plantation* system (as opposed to slavery, simply) and the freehold farming of the West.

The second part of the twofold comparison, then, is with the plantation agriculture of such Asian economies as Ceylon or Indonesia. The production relationships of the plantation economy, rather than staple agriculture alone or the institution of slavery, seem to provide the explanation for the failures of such societies to get beyond the dual economy level toward balanced economic development. The pattern of demand for labor, the dual wage structure, and the concentration of land-holding and political power provide much of the explanation for regional and structural dualism: backward, primitive, staple export economies existing side by side with, while not sharing in the development of, technologically advanced, industrializing sectors.[5]

5. The last and in many respects the most difficult lesson to be drawn from the history of American slavery is that the dislodging of vested interests that rest upon legally constituted and economically viable institutions like slavery are likely to require dramatic confrontations. There was, in 1860, no reason for slavery in the South to fade away.[6] There is little evidence that the conditions for a next stage, in either the Marxian or the Rostovian chronology, were developing. Indeed, we have suggested earlier that Lincoln's pressure upon the South, based as it was on grounds of political morality, was essentially incompatible with the Marxist views of economic determinism.

6. Discussions of economic development, in general, should be released from the conventional context of rigidly discontinuous sets of relationships, especially as they relate to the sharp contrasts between agriculture, industrialization, and urbanization. By extension, the analysis of slavery and plantation agriculture, and their implications for growth, in particular, ought to be set in a structural context of fairly continuous gradations from subsistence agriculture, at one extreme, to large-scale, fully urbanized industrialization, at the other. There are good reasons to be skeptical of the mystique that sometimes surrounds discussions of agriculture's role in economic development—the invocation of sharply defined "preconditions," for example. It is quite possible to have a high rate of economic development and a high stand-

ard of living within an agricultural economy as well as an industrial economy; one need go no further than Denmark, Israel, and the American West to substantiate the point. The more important questions relate to the kinds of agriculture that can support growth and to the population density that can be sustained as development gains momentum.

The ability of staple agricultural activity to support a particular level of population can be affected both favorably and unfavorably by a given structural advance. The elimination of the slave market reduced the personnel requirements of the "old" Southeast and simultaneously made it more difficult to execute required migrations. In the immediate postwar period the Southeast found itself with only a slightly war-reduced population and a considerably narrowed agricultural base. Difficulties were to be expected.

7. The real moral of the British stagnation paper seems to be that the continued development and expansion of world markets is one of the most effective ways to guarantee the maintenance of a fairly high rate of economic and industrial growth in the more industrialized nations. It would appear to be very much in the interest of developed countries to establish the monetary and trade institutions required to maintain a high rate of growth in world trade, with particular emphasis being placed on the seemingly unquenchable needs of the newly developing countries for industrial goods. Of course, a really clever and competent, perhaps brilliant, set of British entrepreneurs might have been able to maintain the high rate of English economic development of the middle part of the nineteenth century on into the last quarter of the century, even in the face of a declining world trade position. But such brilliance is rarely available to any nation, and under any circumstances it is probably more effective to devise means to expand world trade demands for conventional goods. Indeed, the choice confronting developed industrial countries near the economic and technological frontier may be

between expanding or creating new markets for conventional goods or accelerating the rate of development of new goods or technologies themselves. Crudely put, the choice appears to be between the Marxian view on how capitalist countries maintain their rate of expansion and the Schumpeterian view of expansion and development via innovation and new technologies. But the history of the last century suggests that the possibilities for national policy are continuous and not a simple dichotomy. There is little evidence in either the United States or the British experience to support the assertion that industrial economies face an inevitable pressure to move along the path either of imperialism or of rapid capitalist decline.

NOTES TO CHAPTER 6

1. J. E. Moes, "The Absorption of Capital in Slave Labor in the Ante-Bellum South and Economic Growth," *American Journal of Economics and Sociology*, October, 1961, pp. 535–41.

2. E. D. Genovese, "The Significance of the Slave Plantation for Southern Economic Development," *Journal of Southern History*, 1962, pp. 422-37.

3. F. M. Fisher, *A Priori Information and Time Series Analysis* (Amsterdam, 1962), Table 4.2.1, pp. 66–67. The deflator used was the Sauerbeck-*Statist* index of the price of forty-five commodities.

4. R. A. Easterlin, "Interregional Differences in Per Capita Income, Population, and Total Income, 1840–1950," in *Trends . . .* , esp. pp. 81–88 and Appendix A. The South-Central cotton states consist of Alabama, Mississippi, Louisiana, and Arkansas. Texas was included in the western South-Central group in 1880.

5. Cf. R. E. Baldwin, "Patterns of Development in Newly Settled Regions," *The Manchester School of Economics and Social Studies*, May 1956, pp. 161–79.

6. Dr. Barry Supple has drawn our attention to a parallel situation in the "feudal reaction" of the thirteenth century in England. In that case, the manorial economy and the institution of dependent labor were clearly not incompatible with the development of a monetary economy. Indeed, as the lords extended their domains under the stimulus of rising agricultural prices, the increased demand for labor was satisfied by the successful extension of serfdom and the intensification of quasi-feudal obligations, just as the interregional slave trade in the antebellum South proved to be an effective mechanism for meeting the demand for field labor in the expanding cotton economy.

INDEX

INDEX

Index of Names

A

Abramovitz, Moses, 178n, 179n
Agricultural Output of Great
Britain, 219n
Agricultural Output of Ireland,
219n
Allan, William, 114n
American Anti-Slavery Society,
112n
American Colonization Society,
114n
Annual Statement of the Trade
of the United Kingdom,
185, 202
Ashton, T. S., 19

B

Baldwin, R. E., 234n
Bancroft, Frederic, 71, 85n,
112n
Barrow, R. H., 113n
Bayes, Thomas, 34
Berlin, Isaiah, 31
Beveridge, William H., 18
Board of Trade, 203
Bowley, A. L., 203, 205, 219n
Braithwaite, R. B., 14, 29n, 30n
Bryce, James, 171, 182n
Budd, Edward C., 170, 182n

C

Cabot, George, 182n
Cairnes, J. E., 43, 111n
Cash, W. J., 96, 112n
Census of Production, 186, 219n
Chaloner, W. H., 220n
Chenery, Hollis B., 181n
Chipman, John S., 219n
Clapham, J. H., 219n
Clark, Victor, 151, 179n, 180n
Clay, Cassius, 224
Cleveland, Grover, 165
Cole, Arthur H., 18, 181n
Collingwood, R. G., 6, 29n, 31,
33
Collins, W. H., 70, 71, 111n,
112n
Commissioner of Patents' Annual
Reports, 111n
Committee on Research in Eco-
nomic History, 179n
Croce, Benedetto, 6, 7, 12, 29n,
30n

D

Dahmén, Erik, 126, 179n
David, Paul, 179n
Davis, J. S., 180n